McGraw-Hill Education

MCAT

BEHAVIORAL AND SOCIAL SCIENCES & CRITICAL ANALYSIS

2015

McGraw-Hill Education
MCAT
Test Preparation Series

- Biomolecules
- Molecules, Cells, and Organs
- Systems of Tissues and Organs

- Physical Foundations of Biological Systems
- Chemical Foundations of Biological Systems

- Perception and Response
- Behavior
- Self and Others
- Social Structure
- Social Strata
- Critical Analysis and Reasoning Skills

- Practice Test 1
- Answers and Explanations
- Practice Test 2
- Answers and Explanations

McGraw-Hill Education

MCAT

BEHAVIORAL AND SOCIAL SCIENCES & CRITICAL ANALYSIS

2015

George J. Hademenos, PhD

Candice McCloskey Campbell, PhD

Shaun Murphree, PhD

Amy B. Wachholtz, PhD

Jennifer M. Warner, PhD

Kathy A. Zahler, MS

Thomas A. Evangelist, MA Contributor

New York Chicago San Francisco Athens London Madrid
Mexico City Milan New Delhi Singapore Sydney Toronto

1 2 3 4 5 6 7 8 9 10 RHR/RHR 1 0 9 8 7 6 5 4

ISBN 978-0-07-182561-0
MHID 0-07-182561-4

e-ISBN 978-0-07-182230-5
e-MHID 0-07-182230-5

Library of Congress Control Number 2014947045

Amy B. Wachholtz, PhD, would like to thank Christopher Ayala, MA, for assistance with fact checking and editing the behavioral and social sciences material in this volume.

This book is printed on acid-free paper.

Contents

Unit II Behavior

Unit III Self and Others

Unit IV Social Structure

PART 2 CRITICAL ANALYSIS AND REASONING SKILLS

About the Authors

George J. Hademenos, PhD, is a former Visiting Assistant Professor of Physics at the University of Dallas. He received his BS from Angelo State University, received his MS and PhD from the University of Texas at Dallas, and completed postdoctoral fellowships in nuclear medicine at the University of Massachusetts Medical Center and in radiological sciences/biomedical physics at UCLA Medical Center. His research interests have involved potential applications of physics to the biological and medical sciences, particularly with cerebrovascular diseases and stroke. He has published his work in journals such as *American Scientist, Physics Today, Neurosurgery,* and *Stroke.* In addition, he has written several books including *The Physics of Cerebrovascular Diseases: Biophysical Mechanisms of Development, Diagnosis and Therapy,* and *Schaum's Outline of Biology.* He currently teaches general and advanced physics courses.

Candice McCloskey Campbell, PhD, received her doctorate in organic chemistry from Georgia Tech in 1985. She has been teaching at the undergraduate level since 1987. She currently teaches at Georgia Perimeter College in Dunwoody, Georgia. Her professional work has been in synthetic organic chemistry and mechanistic organic chemistry. She has been active with the Two-Year College Chemistry Consortium to enhance the chemistry curriculum at the two-year college level.

Shaun Murphree, PhD, is Professor and Chair of Chemistry at Allegheny College in Meadville, Pennsylvania. He received a BA in chemistry from Colgate University (Hamilton, New York) and a PhD in organic chemistry from Emory University (Atlanta, Georgia), and he conducted post-doctoral study at Wesleyan University (Middletown, Connecticut). His current research interests include microwave-assisted organic synthesis (MAOS), synthetic methodology, and heterocyclic synthesis. In addition to the present work, he has coauthored a monograph on microwave chemistry, several chapters and reviews on heterocyclic synthesis, and numerous articles in both the synthetic chemistry and chemistry education literature.

Amy B. Wachholtz, PhD, MDiv, MS, is an Assistant Professor of Psychiatry at the University of Massachusetts Medical School and the Director of Health Psychology at UMass Memorial Medical Center. Dr. Wachholtz completed her BA in psychology at DePauw University. She graduated with a Master of Divinity degree from Boston

University, where she specialized in bioethics. She then continued her education to earn a Master's and PhD in clinical psychology from Bowling Green State University, where she had a dual specialization in behavioral medicine and psychology of religion. She completed internship through fellowship at Duke University Medical Center, where she focused on medical psychology. She has also completed a post-doctoral MS degree in psychopharmacology. Dr. Wachholtz has multiple funded research projects with her primary focus on (1) bio-psycho-social-spiritual model of chronic pain disorders and (2) the complexities of treating of comorbid pain and opioid addiction in both acute pain and chronic pain situations. She enjoys teaching students from a variety of health disciplines, both in the classroom and on the clinical floors of UMass Memorial Medical Center Hospitals.

Jennifer M. Warner, PhD, is the Director of the University Honors Program and a member of the faculty in the Department of Biological Sciences at the University of North Carolina at Charlotte. She received her BS in Biology from the University of North Carolina at Chapel Hill, her MS in Biology with a focus in microbiology from the University of North Carolina at Charlotte, and her PhD in Curriculum and Teaching from the University of North Carolina at Greensboro. Her current research interests revolve around variables that influence student success and retention in the sciences. She currently teaches a variety of courses including principles of biology, human biology, the nature of science, and pathogenic bacteriology.

Kathy A. Zahler, MS, is a widely published author and textbook writer. She has authored or coauthored numerous McGraw-Hill Education preparation guides for tests, including the GRE®, the Miller Analogies Test, the Test of Essential Academic Skills (TEAS®), and the Test Assessing Secondary Completion™ (TASC™).

How to Use the McGraw-Hill Education MCAT Preparation Series

Welcome to the McGraw-Hill Education MCAT Preparation series. You've made the decision to pursue a medical career, you've studied hard, you've taken and passed the most difficult science courses, and now you must succeed on this very tough exam. We're here to help you.

This series has been created by a dedicated team of scientists, teachers, and test-prep experts. Together, they have helped thousands of students to score high on all kinds of exams, from rigorous science tests to difficult essay-writing assignments. They have pooled their knowledge, experience, and test-taking expertise to make this the most effective self-study MCAT preparation program available.

The four books in this series contain a wealth of features to help you do your best. The four volumes are organized as follows:

MCAT Biological and Biochemical Foundations of Living Systems provides:

- **A general introduction to the MCAT,** including basic facts about the structure and format of the test and the kinds of questions you will encounter.
- **Important test-taking strategies** that can help you raise your score.
- **An in-depth review of all the topics tested in Part 1 of the exam: Biological and Biochemical Foundations of Living Systems.** This is the exam section that assesses your knowledge of foundational concepts in biology and biochemistry, and your understanding of how biological processes function both separately and together in living systems, including the human body.
- **Minitests modeled on Part 1 of the exam.** These practice exams are designed to simulate the actual MCAT in format and degree of difficulty. The questions ask you to use your scientific research and reasoning skills to solve problems demonstrating your mastery of the skills required for success in medical school.

MCAT Chemical and Physical Foundations of Biological Systems provides:

- **A general introduction to the MCAT,** including basic facts about the structure and format of the test and the kinds of questions you will encounter.
- **Important test-taking strategies** that can help you raise your score.
- **An in-depth review of all the topics tested in Part 2 of the exam: Chemical and Physical Foundations of Biological Systems.** This is the exam section that assesses your knowledge of foundational concepts in organic chemistry and physics, and your understanding of how chemical and physical processes function both separately and together in living systems, including the human body.
- **Minitests modeled on Part 2 of the exam.** These practice exams are designed to simulate the actual MCAT in format and degree of difficulty. The questions ask you to use your scientific research and reasoning skills to solve problems demonstrating your mastery of the skills required for success in medical school.

MCAT Behavioral and Social Sciences & Critical Analysis provides:

- **A general introduction to the MCAT,** including basic facts about the structure and format of the test and the kinds of questions you will encounter.
- **An in-depth review of all the topics tested in Parts 3 and 4 of the exam: Psychological, Social, and Biological Foundations of Behavior and Critical Analysis and Reasoning Skills.** Part 3 of the exam tests your knowledge of basic concepts in psychology and sociology that are important for understanding how behavioral and sociocultural factors affect health outcomes and the provision of health care. Part 4 of the exam tests your ability to analyze, evaluate, and apply information from reading passages in a wide range of social sciences and humanities areas.
- **Minitests modeled on Parts 3 and 4 of the exam.** These practice exams are designed to simulate the actual MCAT in format and degree of difficulty. The questions ask you to use your scientific research and reasoning skills to solve problems that demonstrate your mastery of the skills required for success in medical school.

MCAT 2 Full-Length Practice Tests provides:

- **A general introduction to the MCAT,** including basic facts about the structure and format of the test and the kinds of questions you will encounter.
- **Important test-taking strategies** that can help you raise your score.
- **Two full-length practice MCAT tests** designed to simulate the real exam in structure, format, and degree of difficulty. Of course, these practice tests can provide only an approximation of how well you will do on the actual MCAT. However, if you approach them as you would the real test, they should give you a very good idea of how well you are prepared.

- **Explanations for every question.** After you take each test, read carefully through these explanations, paying special attention to those you answered incorrectly or had to guess on. If necessary, go back and reread the corresponding subject review sections in the earlier volumes.

Different people have different ways of preparing for a test like the MCAT. You must find a preparation method that suits your schedule and your learning style. We have tried to make this series flexible enough for you to use in a way that works best for you, but to succeed on this extremely rigorous exam, there is no substitute for serious, intensive review and study. The more time and effort you devote to preparing, the better your chances of achieving your MCAT goals.

Introducing the MCAT

Read This Section to Learn About

- MCAT Basics
- The Computerized Test Format
- Where and When to Take the MCAT
- How to Register for the MCAT
- Taking the MCAT More Than Once
- Your MCAT Scores
- How Medical Schools Use MCAT Scores
- Reporting Scores to Medical Schools
- For Further Information
- The Format of the Test
- What Is Tested in the Science Sections
- What Is Tested in Critical Analysis and Reasoning Skills
- General Test-Taking Strategies

MCAT BASICS

The Medical College Admission Test (MCAT) is a standardized exam that is used to assess applicants to medical schools. The test is sponsored by the Association of American Medical Colleges (AAMC) in cooperation with its member schools. It is required as part of the admissions process by most US medical schools. The test is administered by Prometric, a private firm that is a leading provider of technology-based testing and assessment services.

The questions on the MCAT are basically designed to measure your problem-solving and critical-thinking skills. Two test sections assess your mastery of fundamental concepts in biology, biochemistry, general chemistry, organic chemistry, and physics. A third section tests your understanding of concepts in psychology, sociology, and biology that are important to understanding how behavioral and socio-cultural factors affect health outcomes and the provision of healthcare. For most questions in these sections, choosing the correct answer requires more than just a rote response; you must calculate a solution, interpret and evaluate given data, or apply a particular scientific principle to a given situation. You will need to demonstrate that you can reason scientifically and employ the principles of research methodology and statistics. There is also a fourth section that tests your ability to analyze, evaluate, and apply information from reading passages on topics in ethics, philosophy, cross-cultural studies, and population health.

According to the AAMC, the skills tested on the MCAT are those identified by medical professionals and educators as essential for success in medical school and in a career as a physician. The importance of the biological, biochemical, and physical sciences is self-evident. Psychological and sociological concepts are included, according to the AAMC, because "knowledge of the behavioral and social determinants of health and wellness [is] becoming more important in medical education," and "tomorrow's doctors need to know [these concepts] in order to serve a more diverse population and to understand the impact of behavior on health and wellness."

THE COMPUTERIZED TEST FORMAT

You will take the MCAT on a computer. You will view the questions on the computer screen and indicate your answers by clicking on on-screen answer ovals. As you work through the on-screen questions, you will be able to highlight relevant portions of the reading passages for easy reference. You will also be able to strike out answer choices that you know are incorrect. This will help you use the process of elimination to pick the correct answer. You will also be allowed to make notes on scratch paper (although all of your notes will be collected at the end of the test). Within each test section, you will be able to go back, review questions that you have already answered, and change your answer if you decide to do so. However, once you have finished a test section, you cannot go back to it and make any changes.

Don't be concerned if you are not a whiz with computers; the skills required are minimal, and in any case, on test day you will have the opportunity to access a computer tutorial that will show you exactly what you need to do.

WHERE AND WHEN TO TAKE THE MCAT

The MCAT is offered at approximately 275 sites in the United States (including the US territories of Puerto Rico and the Virgin Islands) and at 12 sites in Canada. All of these sites are testing labs operated by Prometric. The test is also offered at numerous locations outside North America, including sites in Europe, Great Britain, the Middle East, Africa, Asia, and Australia.

There are 22 test dates every year. Two of the dates are in January, and the rest are in the period from April through early September. Most test dates are weekdays, but a few are Saturdays. On some dates, the test is given only in the morning; on others, it is given only in the afternoon. On a few dates, the test is given in both morning and afternoon sessions.

It is a good idea to take the MCAT in the spring or summer of the year before the fall in which you plan to enroll in medical school. That way, you have enough time to submit your scores to meet the schools' application deadlines.

For up-to-date lists of testing sites and also for upcoming test dates, make sure to check the official MCAT website at www.aamc.org/mcat.

HOW TO REGISTER FOR THE MCAT

You can register for the MCAT online at www.aamc.org/mcat. Online registration for each test date begins six months prior to that date. Registration is available until two weeks before the test date. It's a good idea to register early, because seating at the testing centers may be limited and you want to make sure you get a seat at the center of your choice. When you register, you are charged a fee, which you can pay by credit card. If you wish to change your test date, you can do so online.

TAKING THE MCAT MORE THAN ONCE

If your MCAT score is lower than expected, you may want to take the test again. You can take the MCAT up to three times in the same year. However, the AAMC recommends retesting only if you have a good reason to think that you will do better the next time. For example, you might do better if, when you first took the test, you were ill, or you made mistakes in keying in your answers, or your academic background in one or more of the test subjects was inadequate.

If you are considering retesting, you should also find out how your chosen medical schools evaluate multiple scores. Some schools give equal weight to all MCAT scores; others average scores together, and still others look only at the highest scores. Check with admissions officers before making a decision.

YOUR MCAT SCORES

When you take the MCAT, your work on each of the four test sections first receives a "raw score." The raw score is calculated based on the number of questions you answer correctly. No points are deducted for questions answered incorrectly. Each raw score is then converted into a scaled score. Using scaled scores helps make test-takers' scores comparable from one version of the MCAT to another. For each of the four sections, scaled scores range from 1 (lowest) to 15 (highest).

Your score report will be mailed to you approximately 30 days after you take the MCAT. You will also be able to view your scores on the online MCAT Testing History (THx) System as soon as they become available. (For details on the THx system, see the MCAT website.) MCAT score reports also include percentile rankings that show how well you did in comparison to others who took the same test.

HOW MEDICAL SCHOOLS USE MCAT SCORES

Medical college admission committees emphasize that MCAT scores are only one of several criteria that they consider when evaluating applicants. When making their decisions, they also consider students' college and university grades, recommendations, interviews, and involvement and participation in extracurricular or health care–related activities that, in the opinion of the admission committee, illustrate maturity, motivation, dedication, and other positive personality traits that are of value to a physician. If the committee is unfamiliar with the college you attend, they may pay more attention than usual to your MCAT scores.

There is no hard-and-fast rule about what schools consider to be an acceptable MCAT score. A few schools accept a score as low as 4, but many require scores of 10 or higher. To get into a top-ranked school, you generally need scores of 12 or higher. A high score on the Writing Sample may compensate for any weaknesses in communication skills noted on the application or at an interview.

Note that many medical schools do not accept MCAT scores that are more than three years old.

REPORTING SCORES TO MEDICAL SCHOOLS

Your MCAT scores are automatically reported to the American Medical College Application Service (AMCAS), the nonprofit application processing service used by nearly all U.S. medical schools. When you use this service, you complete and submit a single application, rather than separate applications to each of your chosen schools. Your scores are submitted to your designated schools along with your application. There is a fee for using AMCAS. If you wish to submit your scores to other application services or to programs that do not participate in AMCAS, you can do so through the online MCAT Testing History (THx) System.

FOR FURTHER INFORMATION

For further information about the MCAT, visit the official MCAT website at

www.aamc.org/mcat

For questions about registering for the test, reporting and interpreting scores, and similar issues, you may also contact:

Association of American Medical Colleges
Medical College Admission Test
655 K Street, NW, Suite 100
Washington, DC 20001-2399

THE FORMAT OF THE TEST

The MCAT consists of four separately timed sections as outlined in the following chart.

MCAT: Format of the Test

Section	Number of Questions	Time Allowed (minutes)
1. Biological and Biochemical Foundations of Living Systems *Break: 10 minutes*	65	95
2. Chemical and Physical Foundations of Biological Systems *Break: 10 minutes*	65	95
3. Psychological, Social, and Biological Foundations of Behavior *Break: 10 minutes*	65	95
4. Critical Analysis and Reasoning Skills	60	90
Totals	**255**	**375 (= 6 hours, 15 minutes)**

WHAT IS TESTED IN THE SCIENCE SECTIONS

The natural sciences sections of the MCAT (Sections 1 and 2) test your mastery of the concepts and principles of biology, biochemistry, general chemistry, organic chemistry, and physics as they apply to living systems, including the human body.

The behavioral and social sciences section of the MCAT (Section 3) tests your understanding of the behavioral and sociocultural factors that play a role in health care.

These three sections have three main organizing principles:

1. **Foundational concepts:** what the AAMC calls the "big ideas" in the sciences that underlie the subjects taught in medical school
2. **Content categories:** the topics that support the foundational concepts
3. **Scientific inquiry and reasoning skills:** the skills needed to solve scientific problems

Foundational Concepts and Content Categories

According to the AAMS, the foundational concepts and categories for sections 1, 2, and 3 of the MCAT are as follows:

BIOLOGICAL AND BIOCHEMICAL FOUNDATIONS OF LIVING SYSTEMS

Foundational Concept 1: *Biomolecules have unique properties that determine how they contribute to the structure and function of cells and how they participate in the processes necessary to maintain life.*

Content categories:

- Structure and function of proteins and their constituent amino acids
- Transmission of genetic information from the gene to the protein
- Transmission of heritable information from generation to generation and the processes that increase genetic diversity
- Principles of bioenergetics and fuel molecule metabolism

Foundational Concept 2: *Highly organized assemblies of molecules, cells, and organs interact to carry out the functions of living organisms.*

Content categories:

- Assemblies of molecules, cells, and groups of cells within single cellular and multicellular organisms
- Structure, growth, physiology, and genetics of prokaryotes and viruses
- Processes of cell division, differentiation, and specialization

Foundational Concept 3: *Complex systems of tissues and organs sense the internal and external environments of multicellular organisms and, through integrated functioning, maintain a stable internal environment within an ever-changing external environment.*

Content categories:

- Structure and functions of the nervous and endocrine systems and ways in which these systems coordinate the organ systems
- Structure and integrative functions of the main organ systems

CHEMICAL AND PHYSICAL FOUNDATIONS OF BIOLOGICAL SYSTEMS

Foundational Concept 4: *Complex living organisms transport materials, sense their environment, process signals, and respond to changes using processes that can be understood in terms of physical principles.*

Content categories:

- ➤ Translational motion, forces, work, energy, and equilibrium in living systems
- ➤ Importance of fluids for the circulation of blood, gas movement, and gas exchange
- ➤ Electrochemistry and electrical circuits and their elements
- ➤ How light and sound interact with matter
- ➤ Atoms, nuclear decay, electronic structure, and atomic chemical behavior

Foundational Concept 5: *The principles that govern chemical interactions and reactions form the basis for a broader understanding of the molecular dynamics of living systems.*

Content categories:

- ➤ Unique nature of water and its solutions
- ➤ Nature of molecules and intermolecular interactions
- ➤ Separation and purification methods
- ➤ Structure, function, and reactivity of biologically-relevant molecules
- ➤ Principles of chemical thermodynamics and kinetics

PSYCHOLOGICAL, SOCIAL, AND BIOLOGICAL FOUNDATIONS OF BEHAVIOR

Foundational Concept 6: *Biological, psychological, and sociocultural factors influence the ways that individuals perceive, think about, and react to the world.*

Content categories:

- ➤ Sensing the environment
- ➤ Making sense of the environment
- ➤ Responding to the world

Foundational Concept 7: *Biological, psychological, and sociocultural factors influence behavior and behavior change.*

Content categories:

- ➤ Individual influences on behavior
- ➤ Social processes that influence human behavior
- ➤ Attitude and behavior change

Foundational Concept 8: *Psychological, sociocultural, and biological factors influence the way we think about ourselves and others, as well as how we interact with others.*

Content categories:

- Self-identity
- Social thinking
- Social interactions

Foundational Concept 9: *Cultural and social differences influence well-being.*

Content categories:

- Understanding social structure
- Demographic characteristics and processes

Foundational Concept 10: *Social stratification and access to resources influence well-being.*

Content category:

- Social inequality

Scientific Inquiry and Reasoning Skills

The scientific inquiry and reasoning skills that are tested on Sections 1, 2, and 3 of the MCAT are as follows:

- **Skill 1:** Knowledge of Scientific Concepts and Principles
- **Skill 2:** Scientific Reasoning and Evidence-Based Problem Solving
- **Skill 3:** Reasoning About the Design and Execution of Research
- **Skill 4:** Data-Based and Statistical Reasoning

To demonstrate mastery of **Skill 1: Knowledge of Scientific Concepts and Principles**, you need to be able to recall and apply basic scientific concepts and principles to solve problems in science. In many cases, you will need to analyze and interpret information presented in diagrams, charts, graphs, and formulas.

To demonstrate mastery of **Skill 2: Scientific Reasoning and Evidence-Based Problem Solving**, you need to be able to understand and use scientific theories, to propose hypotheses, and to analyze scientific models or research studies in order to identify assumptions, make predictions, and draw conclusions.

To demonstrate mastery of **Skill 3: Reasoning About the Design and Execution of Research**, you need to be able to identify appropriate research designs for investigating specified research questions, to critique and evaluate those designs, to predict results, and to recognize ethical issues involved in research.

To demonstrate mastery of **Skill 4: Data-Based and Statistical Reasoning,** you need to be able to interpret data or to describe or evaluate the results of a research study using statistical concepts.

WHAT IS TESTED IN CRITICAL ANALYSIS AND REASONING SKILLS

The Critical Analysis and Reasoning Skills section of the MCAT (Section 4) tests your ability to comprehend information in a reading passage, to analyze and evaluate arguments and supporting evidence, and to apply concepts and ideas to new situations. The passages in this section cover a wide range of topics in both the social sciences and the humanities. You may encounter readings in philosophy, ethics, cultural studies, and similar topics. All the information you need to answer questions will be provided in the passage; no outside knowledge of the topics is required.

According to the AAMC, the questions in the Critical Analysis and Reasoning Skills section test the following four specific skills:

- **Comprehension:** the ability to understand new information or to view facts or ideas in a new light.
- **Evaluation:** the ability to analyze ideas or arguments presented in a passage and to make judgments about their reasonableness, their credibility, and the soundness of supporting evidence.
- **Application:** the ability to apply information in a passage to new conditions or situations and to predict possible outcomes.
- **Incorporation of Information:** the ability to consider how new information affects the ideas presented in a passage, for example, whether it strengthens or weakens an argument or a hypothesis.

GENERAL TEST-TAKING STRATEGIES

The following sections present some general test-taking strategies that apply to the multiple-choice questions on the MCAT. These strategies can help you to gain valuable points when you take the actual test.

Take Advantage of the Multiple-Choice Format

All of the questions on the MCAT are in the multiple-choice format, which you have undoubtedly seen many times before. That means that for every question, the correct answer is right in front of you. All you have to do is pick it out from among three incorrect choices, called "distracters." Consequently, you can use the process of elimination to rule out incorrect answer choices. The more answers you rule out, the easier it is to make the right choice.

Answer Every Question

Recall that on the MCAT, there is no penalty for choosing a wrong answer. Therefore, if you do not know the answer to a question, you have nothing to lose by guessing. So make sure that you answer every question. If time is running out and you still have not answered some questions, make sure to enter an answer for the questions that you have not attempted. With luck, you may be able to pick up a few extra points, even if your guesses are totally random.

Make Educated Guesses

What differentiates great test takers from merely good ones is the ability to guess in such a way as to maximize the chance of guessing correctly. The way to do this is to use the process of elimination. Before you guess, try to eliminate one or more of the answer choices. That way, you can make an educated guess, and you have a better chance of picking the correct answer. Odds of one out of two or one out of three are better than one out of four!

Go with Your Gut

In those cases where you're not 100% sure of the answer you are choosing, it is often best to go with your gut feeling and stick with your first answer. If you decide to change that answer and pick another one, you may well pick the wrong answer because you have over-thought the problem. More often than not, if you know something about the subject, your first answer is likely to be the correct one.

Take Advantage of Helpful Computer Functions

On the MCAT, you have access to certain computer functions that can make your work easier. As you work through the on-screen questions, you are able to highlight relevant portions of the reading passages. This helps you save time when you need to find facts or details to support your answer choices. You are also able to cross out answer choices that you know are incorrect. This helps you use the process of elimination to pick the correct answer.

Use the Scratch Paper Provided

The MCAT is an all-computerized test, so there is no test booklet for you to write in. However, you are given scratch paper, so use it to your advantage. Jot down notes, make calculations, and write out an outline for each of your essays. Be aware, however, that you cannot remove the scratch paper from the test site. All papers are collected from you before you leave the room.

Because you cannot write on the actual MCAT, don't get into the habit of writing notes to yourself on the test pages of this book. Use separate scratch paper instead. Consider it an opportunity to learn to use scratch paper effectively.

Keep Track of the Time

Make sure that you're on track to answer all of the questions within the time allowed. With so many questions to answer in a short time period, you're not going to have a lot of time to spare. Keep an eye on your watch or on the computerized timer provided.

Do not spend too much time on any one question. If you find yourself stuck for more than a minute or two on a question, then you should make your best guess and move on. If you have time left over at the end of the section, you can return to the question and review your answer. However, if time runs out, don't give the question another thought. You need to save your focus for the rest of the test.

Don't Panic if Time Runs Out

If you pace yourself and keep track of your progress, you should not run out of time. If you do, however, run out of time, don't panic. Because there is no guessing penalty and you have nothing to lose by doing so, enter answers to all the remaining questions. If you are able to make educated guesses, you will probably be able to improve your score. However, even random guesses may help you pick up a few points. In order to know how to handle this situation if it happens to you on the test, make sure you observe the time limits when you take the practice tests. Guessing well is a skill that comes with practice, so incorporate it into your preparation program.

If Time Permits, Review Questions You Were Unsure Of

Within each test section, the computer allows you to return to questions you have already answered and change your answer if you decide to do so. (However, once you have completed an entire section, you cannot go back to it and make changes.) If time permits, you may want to take advantage of this function to review questions you were unsure of or to check for careless mistakes.

McGraw-Hill Education

MCAT

BEHAVIORAL AND SOCIAL SCIENCES & CRITICAL ANALYSIS

2015

PART 1

PSYCHOLOGICAL, SOCIAL, AND BIOLOGICAL FOUNDATIONS OF BEHAVIOR

UNIT I

Perception and Response

Foundational Concept: Biological, psychological, and sociocultural factors influence the ways that individuals perceive, think about, and react to the world.

CHAPTER 1

Sensing the Environment

Read This Chapter to Learn About

- Sensory Processing
- Vision
- Hearing
- Somatization: Tactile Sensation
- Taste
- Smell
- Perception

SENSORY PROCESSING

A **stimulus** is any signal from the environment that could potentially impact the senses. The signal is transmitted into a **sensation**, which describes the reception of environmental information by sensory organs. **Perception** is the final process of integrating sensations into the brain by selecting information from the environment to attend to, organizing that information, and interpreting the information to make it meaningful.

Thresholds

The study of how stimuli are translated into perception is called psychophysics. Human perception does not register every particle in the environment nor every change in intensity. For example, would you notice the weight of a flea on your skin? Or the taste of a single grain of sugar in your water? Your sensory ability acts as a filter, through which small enough changes in the world around you pass without detection, but larger changes are caught. In the 19th century, two psychophysicists discovered principles of human perception that shed (noticeable) light on the porousness of this filter. Gustav Fechner was a German psychophysicist associated with the concept of the **absolute threshold**: the absolute minimum intensity of a stimulus for human sensory perception 50 percent of the time. He discovered various absolute thresholds for different senses and stimuli (see the following table).

Examples of Absolute Thresholds

Sense	Absolute Threshold
Taste	1 teaspoon of sugar in 2 gallons of water
Smell	1 drop of perfume in the volume of a six-room apartment
Vision	A candle flame seen at 30 miles on a dark, clear night
Hearing	Tick of a watch at 20 feet in an otherwise silent room
Touch	The wing of an insect falling on the cheek from a height of 1 centimeter

Galanter, 1960

But what about a change from one intensity to another? Would an additional drop of perfume be noticeable in a six-room apartment if it were added to an existing cloud of perfume already sprayed seconds earlier? German physician Ernst Weber introduced the **just noticeable difference (JND)**, the amount by which a stimulus needs to *change* for a human to perceive a difference at least 50 percent of the time (see the following table). Weber observed that the JND increases in proportion to the intensity of the initial stimulus. For example, the brighter a light is, the greater an increase in luminosity is required for humans to notice the difference in brightness. **Weber's law** states that the JND of a stimulus is a constant proportion to the intensity or size of the initial stimulus. Each sense is associated with a different constant, referred to as **Weber's fraction**.

Sense	Examples of Just Noticeable Difference in Human Perception
Taste	20% saltier taste
Smell	Very complex
Vision	2% brighter
Hearing	10% louder
Touch	2% heavier

It should be noted that JNDs may change over the course of a person's life span and under certain medical conditions (e.g., olfactory JND increases significantly in dementia-related cognitive dysfunction). More recent research has supported Weber's law except at the very far ends of the spectrum (e.g., extremely heavy or extremely light). JND is also subject to **sensory adaptation**. Sensory adaptation refers to the gradual alteration in sensitivity with prolonged stimulation (e.g., music at a concert seems less loud at the end of the night) or absence of stimulation (e.g., when your eyes adjust to a dark room).

Signal Detection Theory

Signal detection theory seeks to describe how people make decisions. The brain receives and interprets signals. **Signals** are the information gathered from the environment with both the accurate information needed to make the correct decision, as well as the **external noise** that interferes with a person's ability to interpret the information and the **internal noise** from a person's own history, perceptions, and interpretations. When people make decisions about the truth value of a proposition, those decisions may be correct or incorrect:

	Decision—True	Decision—False
Actually—True	Hit	Miss
Actually—False	False alarm	Correct rejection

When signal detection theory is used in the context of Weber's law, this means that the greater the difference between comparison stimuli, the easier it is to make a correct decision about whether or not the stimuli are the same (hit or correct rejection). But with very similar comparison stimuli, it is more difficult to correctly identify differences, and it is more likely that incorrect decisions will be made (false alarm or miss).

When signal detection theory is used in the context of medical or psychological settings, it is often used to assess two different types of validity for tests.

- **Sensitivity** is the ability to detect a true signal. When the sensitivity of a test is increased, people are more likely to get both hits and false alarms. These types of tests are often useful as screening instruments that later more expensive and invasive tests will confirm or invalidate the original results (e.g., mammograms as a screening instrument for breast cancer).
- **Selectivity** is the ability to correctly reject a negative signal. Increasing the specificity of a test increases both correct rejections and misses. This is more useful for confirmatory tests (e.g., biopsy).

There is a give-and-take relationship between sensitivity and specificity of a test, so it is mathematically challenging to have both high sensitivity and specificity simultaneously within the same test.

Sensory Adaptation

Sensory receptors transform the environmental signals into stimulus energy that neurons can transmit to the central nervous systems. After firing, all neurons have a **refractory period** in which they cannot fire. During this time while the neuron recovers, no sensation will trigger a firing. As the neuron recovers, there may be a brief time period when only an increased sensory stimuli will trigger a response from the neuron, but a normal stimulation will not. The more frequently a receptor fires, the refractory and recovery period grows longer over time and stimulus adaptation occurs when only a new or significant stimulus triggers a response from the neuron. For example, the sensory nerve cells on the wrist of someone who wears a watch every day eventually stops firing in response to the stimulation from the pressure of the watch. Only a new or significant change to that pressure (e.g., hitting your wrist on a door) will trigger a response from the sensory neurons. Most sensory adaptations are reversible.

Sensory Pathways

Stimuli trigger a cascade of information flow from receptors, via nerve cells, to the brain, and sometimes to the spinal cord. All sensory information, except for smell, is routed through the thalamus. Then most of the information is sent to the cross-lateral side of the brain where it is processed:

- Auditory information is processed in the temporal lobe.
- Visual information is processed in the occipital lobe.
- Tactile information is processed in the somatosensory cortex, which is located in the parietal lobe.

One way to show how the parietal lobe processes sensory information from different areas of the human body is with a visual representation called a **homunculus** diagram. One such diagram is in Figure 1-1. Larger areas of the diagram indicate that there are more neurons processing sensory information for that area.

Types of Sensory Receptors

There are multiple types of sensory receptors, but modern science recognizes seven major classes of receptors. The first five are familiar and will be addressed later in this chapter: taste, touch, smell, sight, and hearing (i.e., the "five senses"). In addition, there are two other classes of sensors. The **vestibular** sensors help monitor how the body is responding to gravity and motion. They help the body maintain balance. These sensors are primarily located in the semicircular canals in the ear, which project information to be processed by the cerebellum. **Kinesthetic** sensors monitor the position of body parts in space. This type of receptor is overwhelmed during rapid growth spurts

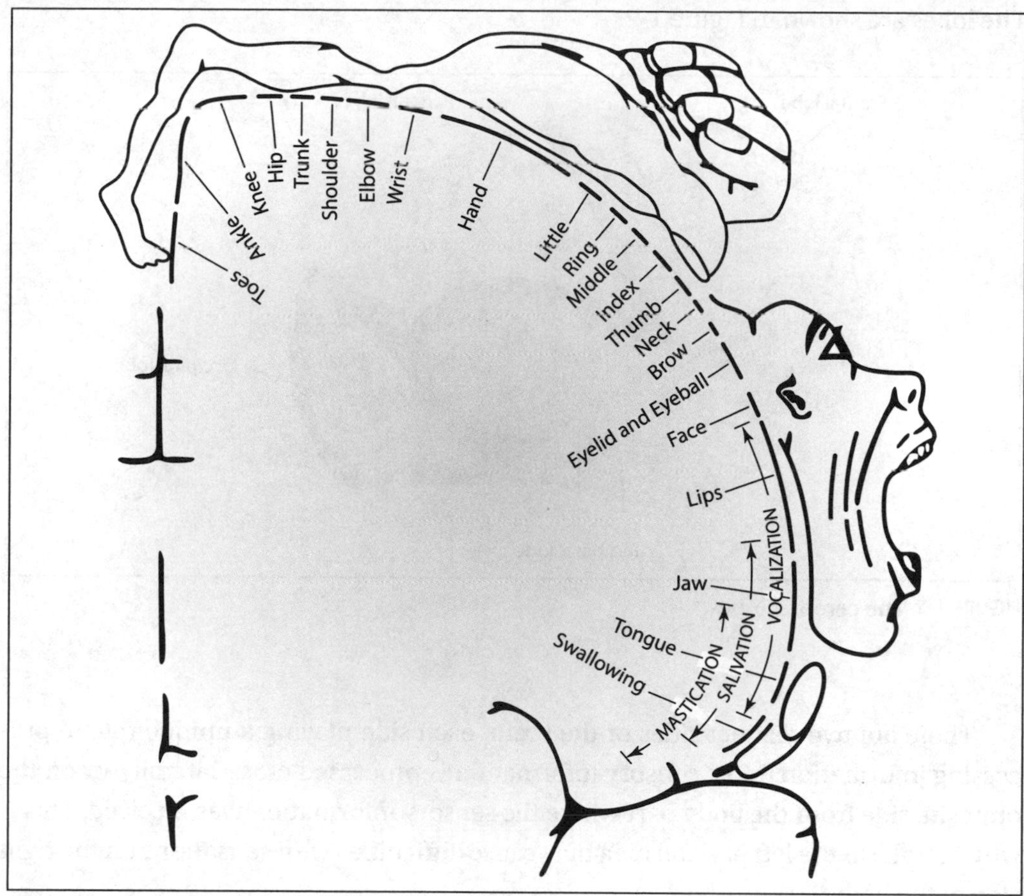

FIGURE 1-1 A homunculus diagram.

because the sensors have not caught up with the size of the body. Receptors of this type are spread throughout the body but are largely located in joints and muscles, which send information to the somatosensory cortex in the parietal lobe.

Information Processing in the Cerebral Cortex

The cerebral cortex is the surface of the brain. (The word *cortex* comes from the Latin word for "bark," as in tree bark.) The **cerebral cortex** controls voluntary movement, cognitive functions, and some memory storage. It is most heavily involved in higher-order cognitive processing, including language, sensory perception, voluntary motor functioning, and consciousness. The cerebral cortex is made up of four "lobes":

- frontal (attention, decision making)
- temporal (memory, language)
- parietal (movement, sensation)
- occipital (vision)

The lobes are shown in Figure 1-2.

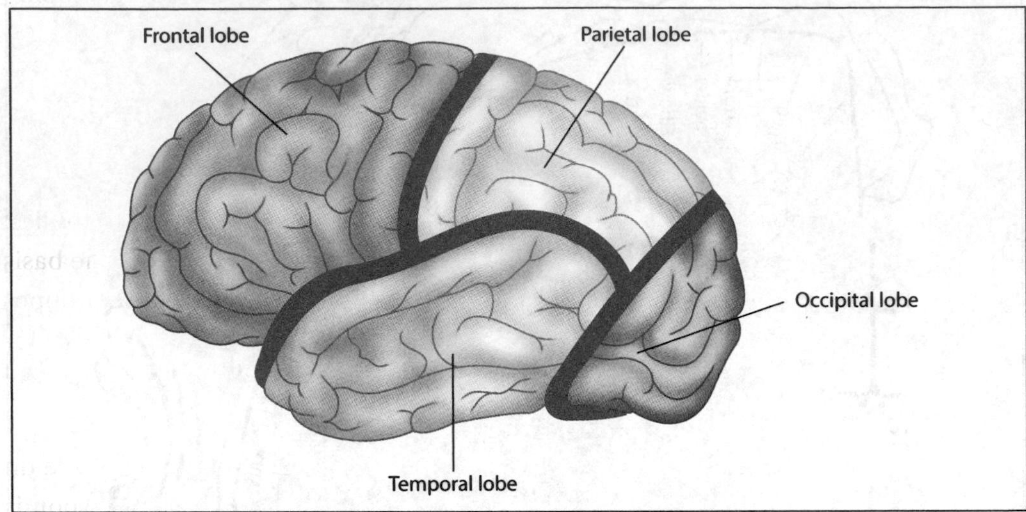

FIGURE 1-2 The cerebral lobes.

There are two distinct sides of the brain, each side playing a unique role in processing information. Most sensory information is processed cross-laterally, or on the opposite side from the body part where the sensory information was received. This is why a stroke in the left parietal area may cause difficulties with sensations on the right side of the body.

VISION

Vision is the sense that people best understand. The human eye can see only a small range of light frequencies (wavelengths between 400 nm and 700 nm). Within the visual system, there is a perception apparatus that organizes the visual light cues.

Rods and Cones

Light information is encoded in the brain via the retina of the eye. Two primary light receptors are involved: **rods** and **cones**. Both rods and cones work by catching photons and signaling this information to bipolar cells. Rods are more sensitive than cones, which allows for lower-light (scotopic) vision that is relatively low in acuity. Rods also have only one photopigment (rhodopsin), so they cannot sense differences in color and transmit only gray-scale visual information. Cones are activated in higher levels of light (photopic vision). They directly sense light and communicate data about light to the nervous system. Cones have lower sensitivity but higher acuity, and they are the source of color vision. When both cones and rods are activated, vision is said to be mesopic.

Visual Processing

There are two opposing views on how color vision works.

- **Opponent process theory** is based on three opposing color dichotomies: black–white, red–green, and yellow–blue. These are thought to provide the basis for all color vision. No single cone can provide information about both opposite colors at the same time. For example, if you stare directly at a red image for 60 seconds, then close your eyes, you will experience a green **after-image** thought to be caused by **vision fatigue** for the red color.
- **Trichromatic color theory** (also known as Young–Helmholtz theory) is based on the idea that the cones are divided into three specialized types. One type responds to short-wave light (blue), one to mid-wave light (green), and one to long-wave (yellow) light. In humans, mid- and long-wave cones are much more prevalent than short-wave cones. Precise discrimination among hues depends on relative levels of activity of different cones.

Color Blindness

The genes that code for mid- and long-wave cones are located on the X chromosome. Because color blindness is recessive, males are more likely than females to be color-blind, as a man has only a single X chromosome. The most common form of color blindness is red–green color blindness, but yellow–blue color blindness is also observed. Even less common is complete color blindness (monochromat), in which the individual sees only shades of gray.

A simple test can be used to identify color blindness. An individual is shown a diagram consisting of closely spaced dots of different colors and sizes. The arrangement is such that the dots of one color form a recognizable image. An individual with normal vision will see the image, constituted by dots of one color, stand out among dots of a different color. A color-blind individual will not see the image.

Parallel Processing

Once the retina of the eye transmits information to the visual cortex in the brain (occipital lobe), the brain divides up the signal (e.g., movement, straight lines of different orientations, color) and processes the pieces individually and simultaneously. This is called parallel processing.

Feature Detection

Within the visual processing system, certain specialized cells are uniquely tuned to see specific objects and to process the pieces of those objects, even in the midst of other complex stimuli. One of the most studied is the fusiform gyrus area of the brain, which solely processes information needed to identify faces. The ability to identify other individuals by their faces is thought to be an evolutionary advantage. It is also why your brain picks out the image of a face from other objects, such as an "emoticon" in which a colon, a dash, and a parenthesis looks like a smiling face on its side: :-). Individuals with damage to the fusiform gyrus demonstrate a specific deficit in the identification of human faces—a condition called prosopagnosia.

Higher-Order Visual Processing

Once the eye sends signals to the brain via the optic nerve, the brain begins higher-order processing and organizing of the information. The results may be affected by genetics, culture, age, and other influences on perception of environmental signals.

BINOCULAR CUES

Using input from the two eyes, the brain can determine many things about the environment based on the differences between the two views. These differences provide what are called binocular cues. The first binocular cue is **retinal disparity**. The retinas of the two eyes register two slightly different pictures due to the differences between the eye positions in the head. The closer the object is, the greater the disparity between the two views. The brain then reconciles the two pictures to create the experience of depth perception (this is also the system harnessed by 3-D movies). The second binocular cue is **convergence**, which incorporates the physical movement of the eyes. The individual eyes turn toward each other to focus on an object that is closer to the body.

MONOCULAR CUES

The input from just a single eye gives the brain many cues about depth perception in the environment, including:

- **Linear perspective.** Parallel lines stretching into the distance appear to move closer together.
- **Height in an image.** Objects higher in an image are assumed to be farther away.
- **Relative size.** Objects of the same type that are larger than others are assumed to be closer.

- **Light/shadow.** The interplay of light and shadow can create the image of three dimensions, even in a two-dimensional image.
- **Interposition.** If one object blocks the view of another object, the blocking object is assumed to be closer.
- **Texture.** The farther away an object is, the less distinct its texture becomes.

Many of these visual cues are believed to be innate or at least developed extremely early in life. Once the eyes have matured sufficiently, infants are able to see their environment clearly and seem to perceive depth. The classic experiment designed to assess depth perception in infants is the so-called visual cliff study. Psychologists Richard Walk and Eleanor Gibson in 1961 created a "visual cliff" to determine at what point in development infants use visual cues to perceive depth. They used a checkerboard pattern to provide depth cues, with one half of a table approximately 3 feet lower than the other half, but with a clear plastic top over the entire surface at the higher level, so an infant could crawl safely to the other side if she or he ignored the depth cues. In the experiment, the infant's mother stood on the far side of the table and called the child to her. Infants aged approximately 7 to 9 months consistently stopped at the edge of the visual cliff. Figure 1-3 shows an image of the study.

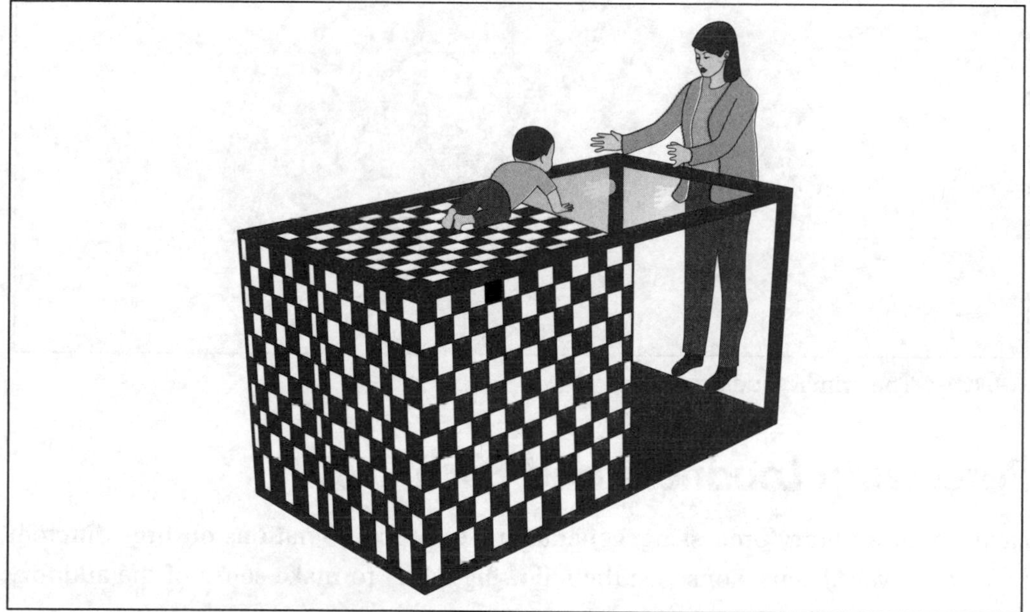

FIGURE 1-3 The "visual cliff" study.

Once the brain can account for where objects are in the environment, the higher-order processing begins to use shortcuts to process the environment more quickly and use less processing power. These shortcuts do not appear to be innate, but develop as a child increasingly learns about the environment.

CONSTANCY

The visual information processing system accounts for distance and shape so you continue to view objects as having a constant shape and size. For example, if you see a door, you are aware that it is a rectangle, regardless of how close you are or the angle at which you view it. If the door is open, your eye might sense a rhomboid shape, but you continue to perceive the door as a rectangle and maintain consistency of shape. Likewise, if you view an elephant from a distance, you will view it as a large object that is far away rather than a small object.

HEARING

Sound waves reaching the ear stimulate the vestibular nerve and cochlear nerves. These nerves combine into the vestibular-cochlear nerve (cranial nerve VIII). It projects into the brain stem, then through the midbrain, up into the thalamus. From there the signal is relayed to the primary auditory cortex in the temporal lobe (see Figure 1-4).

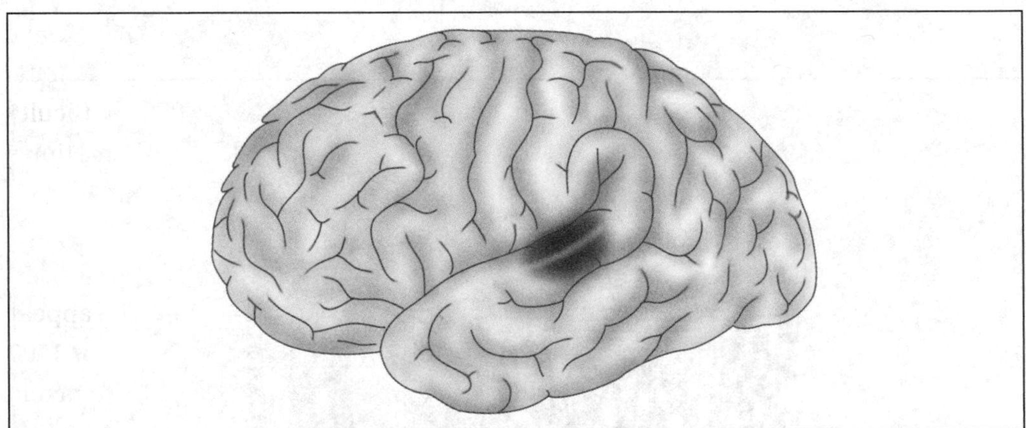

FIGURE 1-4 The primary auditory cortex.

Perceiving Loudness and Pitch

Hearing, or auditory processing, generally relies on combinations of three different types of physical sensations (see the following table) to make sense of the auditory world.

Physical Sensation	Measurement	Perception
Frequency	Hertz (Hz)	Pitch
Amplitude	Decibels (Db)	Loudness
Complexity	Harmonic structure	Timbre

The human ear is most sensitive to sounds at approximately 2000 Hz. The threshold of hearing is 0 decibels. Sounds between 80 and 120 decibels are dangerous with prolonged exposure. Sounds above 120 decibels are immediately dangerous and are perceived as painful. Loud sounds damage the delicate hair cells in the basilar membrane in the inner ear, and once these hair cells are damaged, they do not recover.

Hearing is a function of sensory reception by hair cells in the cochlea of the inner ear. There are three theories about how this reception takes place:

- **Place theory.** This theory is primarily associated with the German physicist Hermann von Helmholtz. According to this theory, pitch is perceived due to vibrations at specific locations along the basilar membrane in the inner ear. A specific frequency vibrates the hairs in a specific place on the basilar membrane, and the brain interprets the location of those vibrating hairs as a specific pitch.
- **Frequency theory.** Developed in the 1800s, this theory holds that the brain interprets pitch by the vibrating frequency of the entire basilar membrane. For example, a 2000 Hz vibration would cause the basilar membrane in the cochlea to vibrate 2000 times per second, which the brain would uniquely associate with the 2000 Hz pitch.
- **Reconciling the theories of hearing (volley theory).** Both theories proved to have some truth and some errors. The problem with place theory is that vibrating hairs at a single location are not independent of the other hairs in the area. The difficulty with frequency theory is that neurons have difficulty firing faster than 1000 times per second. The unification of these theories was achieved by the American psychologists Ernest Wever and Charles Brey in 1937, who developed the volley theory. They showed that neurons can work together using the functions described in both place and frequency theories to signal pitch. Sounds of less than 1000 Hz appear to rely more on the principles in frequency theory. Sounds in the range of 1000 Hz to 5000 Hz rely on a combination of frequency and place theories to encode sounds. Sounds greater than 5000 HZ rely solely on place theory principles (see the following table).

Frequency of Sound	Coding Principles
<1000 Hz	Frequency theory
1000 Hz–5000 Hz	Frequency + place theory
>5000 Hz	Place theory

How do you locate a sound in the environment? Similar in function to binocular depth perception cues, binaural cues can inform **auditory localization**, or the determination of location of a sound, by comparing the timing and strength of the same sound in each ear. This information is called binaural disparity. The distance between the ears and the ability to turn the head to change how the sound strikes each ear are both critical components of this process of locating the source of a sound in the environment.

SOMATIZATION: TACTILE SENSATION

Skin is the largest organ in the human body. It has at least six types of sensory receptors. Some of these receptors are specialized to respond to pressure, thermal, pain, or chemical stimulators, while some of the receptors are still a mystery. Pressure receptors in the skin, like all nerve cells, work using a "receptive field" (see Figure 1-5). These fields vary in size and shape depending on the part of the body. Each receptive field has an excitatory center with an inhibitory surround. Stimulating the center will cause the feeling of pressure, whereas stimulating the inhibitory areas inhibits pressure sensations.

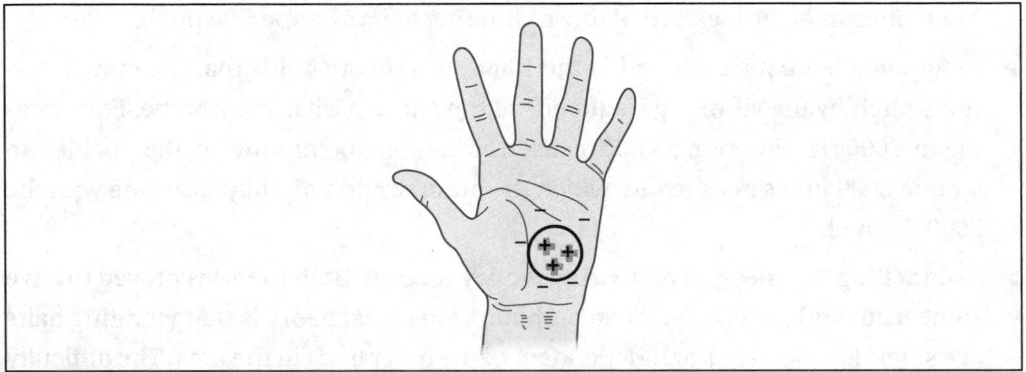

FIGURE 1-5 A receptive field for tactile sensation.

Once the stimulus activates the nerve fibers, the nerves run up the spinal cord ascending (sensory) pathways to the brain stem, where they cross to the other side of the brain. The tactile pathways then funnel through the thalamus on the way to the somatosensory cortex in the parietal lobe of the brain (see Figure 1-6).

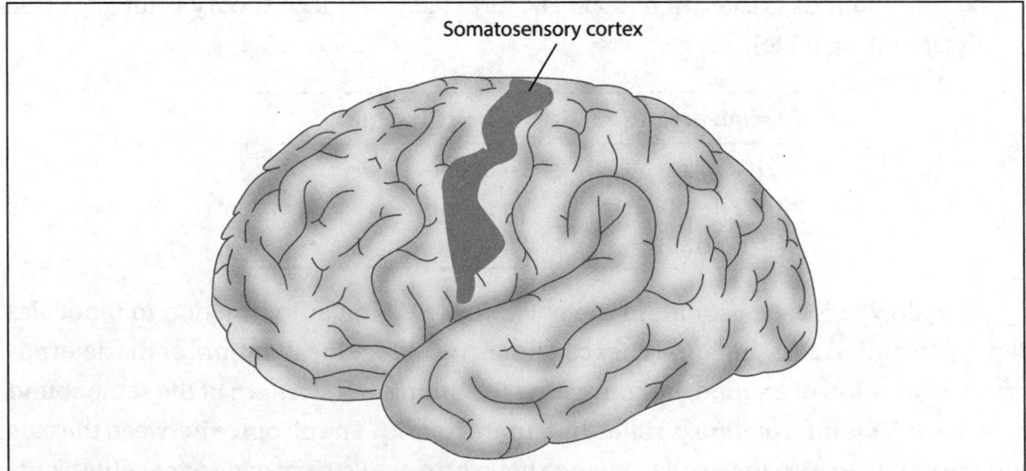

FIGURE 1-6 The somatosensory cortex.

Pain

Pain, or **nociception**, is transmitted to the brain via two pathways: "fast" and "slow." The fast pathway uses A-delta fibers, which are large myelinated neurons that can transmit signals quickly to the brain. This pathway transmits sensations such as a sharp pain when you cut your finger. In contrast, on the slow pathway, signals may lag up to 1–2 seconds behind signals transmitted via the A-delta pathways. The slow pathway uses the C-fiber neurons, which are small neurons that do not have a myelin sheath at all. The slow pathway transmits signals such as muscle pain.

> The famous duo of the Canadian psychologist Ronald Melzack and the British neuroscientist Patrick Wall developed the gate control theory of pain to explain this phenomenon. They postulated that descending pathways from the cortex act as a "gate" to the pain neurons. This gate is opened or closed by the descending pathways and reduces or exacerbates the level of pain signals that reach the brain.

Pain is a unique sensation. The same sensation will not cause the same experience of pain in different people. Psychological factors such as emotion and cognition play a crucial role in how much pain is perceived by an individual. Additionally, factors such as personality characteristics, a history of opioid medication use, and drug abuse will all affect pain levels. Endorphins also play a critical role in the perception of pain and may be another pathway linking psychological and physiological pain perception. Factors that affect endorphins will also affect perception of pain (see the following table).

Effects of Different Domains on Pain Perception

Domain	Exacerbate(s)	Reduce(s)
Mood	Depression, anxiety, anger, sadness	Laughter, good mood
Focus	Hyperfocus on pain	Distraction from pain
Beliefs	"I am powerless to stop it."	"I can handle this."
Expectations	"It will get worse."	"It will get better."
Culture/Gender	Complex: In general, it does not change pain levels but can change expression	

TASTE

Sense receptors on the tongue perceive five primary tastes: salty, sweet, sour, bitter, and umami, or savory. Taste perception is a chemical sense and varies greatly across individuals. The primary sensory mechanism is through taste buds, which have a brief life cycle (approximately 10 to 60 days). The density of taste buds on the tongue appears to be genetically determined. Twenty-five percent of individuals are labeled "supertasters." Supertasters have a greater density of taste buds (10,000 on the tongue) compared to "nontasters" (with as few as 500). Supertasters particularly have greater sensitivity to sweet and bitter flavors; for example, they experience more "burn" from chili peppers. Women are much more likely than men to be identified as "supertasters."

The facial and glossopharyngeal nerves (cranial nerves VII and IX, respectively) collect data from the tongue and send it through the medulla oblongata in the brain stem, and then up through the thalamus on the way to the gustatory area (insular cortex) in the frontal lobe. This area also has a close relationship with the limbic system and accounts for the emotional aspects of food and taste.

Taste buds can be acutely overstimulated, and *taste adaptation* occurs until the neurons recharge and can resume firing. Research has suggested that taste adaptation can occur in as few as four bites of the same food. For example, the fifth bite of a French fry does not taste as salty as the first bite. While tasting ability may be genetically or evolutionarily determined, taste and food preferences are clearly culturally determined. Some people love Hawaiian pizza, some love a plump beetle grub; it all depends on your culture of origin. At the present time, the only identified transcultural innate taste preference is a universal disgust for feces (Rozin, 1990).

SMELL

Smell, like taste, is a chemical sensory process. Researchers are still learning about how chemical sensations result in the perception of odors in the human brain. There is still much unknown about this process. It is estimated that humans can differentiate between approximately 10,000 scents. However, unlike taste, smell has no clear "basic" smells. In fact, it is estimated that 90 percent of the flavor of food is actually attributable to smell. Smell is unique because it is the only sense that is *not* routed through the thalamus. The olfactory nerve fibers (cranial nerve I) converge in the olfactory bulb in the brain. The olfactory system has projections into the amygdala, which is part of the limbic system (the emotional center of the brain) and the hippocampus (the memory center), which suggests an odor component to memory formation.

> **Anosmia** is the lack of the ability to smell. It can be caused by injury or disease. Famously, Ben Cohen of Ben and Jerry's ice cream has anosmia but enjoys the "rich and creamy" texture of his ice cream.

The sense of smell is largely underappreciated as a primary communication tool. Humans and other animals largely use the sense of smell (though potentially subconsciously) to communicate with one another. Pheromones are used by individuals to seek mates and by women to synchronize menstrual cycles to enhance evolutionary group dynamics. Other animals are perhaps less subtle about their use of smell, using urine, feces, or other substances to mark their territory. There do not appear to be any innate preferences for smell. All smell preferences appear to be culturally determined

(Bartoshuk). Cross-culturally, women appear to be slightly more accurate than men in accurately identifying odors in odor recognition tests (deWijk, Schab, & Cain, 1995).

PERCEPTION

Perception occurs when the brain processes the sensory stimuli and translates them in a way the person can understand. While these happen in multiple sensory systems, it is best explained in the visual system. The brain engages in two types of processing. In **bottom-up processing**, the brain examines pieces of a visual image and from those pieces puts together an entire image. There are "feature detectors" in the visual cortex that respond only to very specific stimuli (e.g., only vertical lines or only horizontal lines). Information from these feature detectors is put together by higher-order analyzer cells, which then finalize the whole image. In **top-down processing**, the brain uses *a priori* knowledge of the world to form fast percepts, or mental impressions. It then breaks down the total image into its constituent parts to check if the perceptual hypothesis is correct. Historically there were arguments about which kind of processing the brain uses, but as with many of these arguments, there is truth in both views. The brain appears to use both kinds of processing to understand the world.

Perceptual Organization

Gestalt perception is the concept that the whole is greater than the sum of its parts. There are five major principles of gestalt visual processing (see the following table). The **law of Pragnanz** is a related concept that states when things can be grouped together visually, they will be.

Principle	Example	Explanation
Proximity	You are more likely to see two groups of 6 than one group of 12. 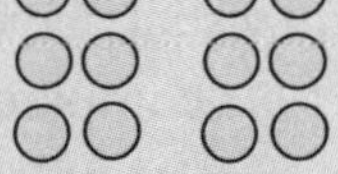	The closer objects are to one another, the more likely they will be grouped together.
Similarity	You are likely to see a cross because of the visual grouping of the squares as separate from the circles. 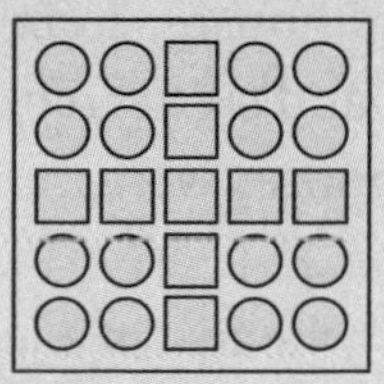	Objects that are visually similar (in size, shape, or color) are likely to be grouped together.

(continued)

Principle	Example	Explanation
Continuity	You will likely see a line from A to D and B to C rather than A taking a right turn at O and ending up at B. A C O D B	Humans visually continue a straight or curved line rather than transferring to another line.
Closure	You will likely see a white triangle that does not exist, because of the suggestion of lines.	When there are gaps in a picture, the perceptual system fills them in.
Common Fate	You will likely perceive these fish as members of a group rather than individuals.	When similar objects are moving together in the same direction, they are perceived as belonging to a single group (e.g., schools of fish).

Cultural Influences on Visual Perception

While there is a shortage of data on cultural influences on visual perception, there are a few key studies. Darhl Pedersen and John Wheeler in 1983 compared the responses of two subgroups of Navajos to the Müller-Lyer illusion, a pair of diagrams with center lines that appear to have different lengths but in fact are exactly equal. The difference in perception is caused by short lines that are attached at different angles. (See Figure 1-7.) One group of Navajos lived in round houses, so in early childhood they had little exposure to visual angles, straight lines, and 90-degree corners. Another group who grew up in more European-style angular houses were more susceptible to the illusion.

Similar responses have been recorded from Zulus who live in a less "carpentered" world with few rectangular structures (Segall, Campbell, & Herskovits, 1966). This

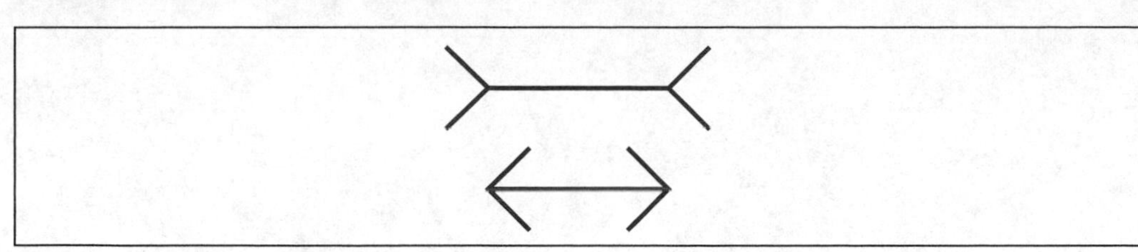

FIGURE 1-7 The Müller-Lyer illusion.

group is less likely to view the illusion as the corner of a building as Americans typically do. Education can also alter perceptions within a culture (Hudson, 1960), with those with more education being better able to use visual depth cues to comprehend a flat picture.

CHAPTER 2

Making Sense of the Environment

Read This Chapter to Learn About

- ➤ Attention
- ➤ Cognition
- ➤ Culture, Environment, and Biology in Cognitive Development
- ➤ Problem Solving
- ➤ Decision Making
- ➤ Intelligence
- ➤ Nature, Nurture, and Intelligence
- ➤ Measuring Intelligence
- ➤ Memory
- ➤ Language

ATTENTION

The human brain may have a seemingly unlimited capacity to process sensory inputs, but the individual can focus only on a small percentage of those sensations at any one time. Attention must occur before cognition. **Selective attention** occurs when an individual focuses on one element in an environment while ignoring others. Attentional focus can be voluntary (such as reading this paragraph) or involuntary (roommate slamming a door).

COGNITION

Cognition has not been fully explained by science. Some researchers, such as cognitive psychologists, engage in a "top-down" approach by approaching cognition as a wholistic function, attempting to understand how cognitive processes occur in the brain and then examining how neural networks that are used in that process. Other researchers, such as neuroscientists, use a "bottom-up" approach by attempting to understand how neurons create neural networks that lead to thought. It is hoped that researchers will eventually meet in the middle by approaching the problem from each direction.

Stages of Cognitive Development

The following table summarizes the stages of cognitive development identified by the Swiss psychologist Jean Piaget.

Piaget's Stages of Cognitive Development

Stage	Age*	Purpose	Key Terms for This Stage
Sensory Motor	Birth–2 years	Coordination of sensations with voluntary motor movement	**Object permanence:** knowledge that an object continues to exist even if hidden from view
Preoperational	2–7 years	Increased use of mental images and symbols	**Ego centrism:** difficulty sharing another person's viewpoint **Animism:** the belief that all things are living
Concrete Operational	7–11 years	Increased problem-solving abilities; mastery of conservation; much of cognition and mental operations are limited to tangible objects and actual events	**Conservation:** the amount inside a container is the same even if the dimensions of the container change **Reversibility:** the ability to understand that actions can be reversed **Decentration:** the ability to focus on multiple aspects of a problem simultaneously
Formal Operational	11–Adult	Begin to understand and mentally manipulate abstract constructs (e.g., ethics, free will, love)	**Hierarchical classification:** the ability to focus on multiple types of classification simultaneously

* Cross-culturally, children progress through the stages in the same order, but the timeline/ages may be different.

Other researchers have identified the **information processing approach** as an alternative to Piaget's developmental stages. According to this cognitive development theory, people are active problem solvers who make decisions based on environmental demands. The theory attempts to explain how the same biological brains can lead people to take very different approaches to life. It also explains how cognitive development can continue into adulthood. After age 60, the human brain shrinks both in size and in the number of active neurons. While that loss sounds concerning, it is not directly correlated to dementia. On average, cognitive speed declines. However, problem-solving ability remains steady. The higher the original cognitive capacity and the more cognitively active an older individual stays, the slower the cognitive decline; this is true for both age-related and disease-related (e.g., Alzheimer's).

CULTURE, ENVIRONMENT, AND BIOLOGY IN COGNITIVE DEVELOPMENT

A number of biological factors may impact a child's cognitive development. Some of these may be genetic (e.g., trisomy 21), due to the health of the mother (e.g., nutrition status or drug use), or environmental (e.g., exposure to lead paint in the home). However, beyond these factors, there continues to be a great deal of argument about how much of cognitive development is innate and how much is learned or environmental.

Cultural environment certainly plays a role in cognitive development. The stages of cognitive development appear to occur in the same order cross-culturally, but the timeline for developing different cognitive process may be different across cultures because different cultures provide different learning opportunities for cognitive development. A culture that values reading will expose children at a young age to the skills and learning experiences that develop the ability to read, whereas hunter-gatherer cultures will expose a child to experiences to help them develop spatial reasoning and psychomotor skills.

PROBLEM SOLVING

There are two general problem-solving methods. The first is the **generate-test method** (also known as "trial and error"). This can be useful when there is a small set of possible solutions, but it is very time-consuming for large possible solution sets. The second is **means-end analysis**. This method uses heuristics and breaks larger problems into subgoals. The solver then works each subgoal to completion.

The American psychologist James Greeno has identified the following three basic types of problems:

1. Problems that require inducing structure (e.g., analogies, pattern series). This type requires the solver to identify patterns and relationships among parts of the problem.
2. Problems that require arrangement of problem items (e.g., anagrams). This problem type requires a rearrangement of visual or spatial parts of the problem in order to form a solution. The solver often uses the generate-test problem-solving approach.
3. Problems that require transformation to change aspects of the problem from an initial state to a final state (e.g., the Tower of Hanoi problem in cognitive psychology). For this type of problem, the solver often uses the means-end problem-solving approach.

There are cultural differences in problem solving. Generally, Eastern Asian cultures are more likely to rely on a holistic cognitive style that focuses on context and relationships. Western European cultures are more likely to use an analytical cognitive approach that focuses on individual aspects of the problem.

Psychologists have identified a number of specific approaches that humans use cross-culturally to solve problems. The use of **algorithms** and **heuristics** allows for mental "shortcuts" based on the individual's previous knowledge. A similar approach is using **analogies** to previous experiences or to turn abstract ideas into more concrete problems to solve the problem (e.g., "achieving world peace is like trying to reduce sibling rivalry"). These analogies are not always appropriate to the problem at hand, but they can give the individual a jump start on problem solving. Another common approach is breaking down a larger problem into subgoals and working toward solutions to the subgoals. When an outcome is known, working backward from the outcome to the current state can be useful. One more common approach is changing the representation of the problem, such as changing written word problems to visual diagrams.

Barriers to Problem Solving

A number of barriers to effective problem solving have been identified. Some of these are external and some are internal to the problem solver. Externally, irrelevant or **extraneous information** can interfere with the efficient solution of a problem, and there may be **unnecessary constraints** that reduce the number of possible solutions. Internally, the individual may have **rigid mental sets** that reduce the ability to view a problem from another perspective. Another internal cognitive bias that interferes is **functional fixedness**, in which an individual has difficulty manipulating aspects of the problem and can use objects or ideas only in a traditional way.

DECISION MAKING

Decision making is more than simple logic. Often emotion and previous experiences create biases and heuristics that play a role in how an individual makes and maintains a decision. Heuristics and algorithms are cognitive shortcuts that involve scripts and "mental flow charts" that an individual has developed from previous experiences. Research has shown that the more tired people are, the more heavily they rely on these mental shortcuts to base their decisions on because the shortcuts reduce the cognitive load. However, the chosen heuristic may not be appropriate to the situation. By contrast, **intuition** and **insight** are more likely to occur when people have the capacity for a greater cognitive load because these techniques may use subconscious processing of information that informs their decision making and problem solving. You also cannot underestimate the impact (both positive and negative) of emotion on decision making, including allowing the person to make a rapid decision in line with his or her values (e.g., running into the street to save a child from an oncoming car), altering the ability to make any decision (e.g., paralysis from fear), or altering the ability to maintain a decision once it is made (being either resistant to change or unable to maintain a decision). It is also noteworthy that recent research has suggested that individuals are best at making decisions when only three or four options are available. When choosing among more than three or four options, individuals take longer in their decision making and are not necessarily happier with their choice. This is referred to as the "paradox of choice."

Cognitive Dissonance

Cognitive dissonance occurs when a person's beliefs are not in line (discongruant) with his or her actions or with reality. This dissonance is uncomfortable for most individuals, so the brain develops an explanation to bring beliefs and actions into harmony. The psychologists Amos Tversky and Daniel Kahneman produced a famous series of studies examining how individuals develop explanations for their behavior even when no real explanation exists. Once an individual develops an explanation for his or her behavior, that individual will often be hesitant or uncomfortable with changing that reason even when faced with factual information that conflicts with it. This can lead to extremely strong belief perseverance, overconfidence, and even occasional belligerence.

INTELLIGENCE

Multiple researchers have developed a number of differing theories on intelligence.

- The **triarchic theory of intelligence**, proposed by the American psychologist Robert Sternberg, focuses on intelligent "behavior" as the measurable component of intelligence. Sternberg identified three critical components to intelligence: (1) **contextual**, culturally based determination of intelligent behavior; (2) **componential**, the cognitive processes that determine intelligent behavior; and (3) **experiential**, how the environment and intelligent behavior interact and how the person learns from this interaction.

- The theory of **eight intelligences**, proposed by the American psychologist Howard Gardner, identified eight different domains: logical/mathematical, linguistic, musical, spatial, interpersonal, intrapersonal, naturalist, and bodily-kinesthetic. Gardner's theory has not yet been widely supported in the research literature.
- In cognitive testing, the integration of multiple areas of intelligence is referred to as the "G-factor," or simply "g," and identifies the domain of **general intelligence** across multiple dimensions. This idea was developed in the early 1900s by the British psychologist Charles Spearman, who noted most people who do well in one area of testing do well in multiple areas of testing (and similarly, those who do poorly are also likely to do poorly across multiple areas of testing). The British psychologist Raymond Cattell broke down the G-factor into crystallized G(*c*) and fluid G(*f*) intelligence. G(*c*) is the ability to use information already learned and includes skills, knowledge, and vocabulary. G(*c*) improves with age. G(*f*) is the ability to analyze complex situations, use logical reasoning, and solve problems. This type of intelligence decreases with age and is more susceptible to loss through stroke or brain injury.
- A small but growing understanding of intelligence also involves **emotional intelligence (EI)**. EI involves the ability to understand emotional expression (within a culture) and to use emotion as an effective tool to engage in social interactions. EI research has gained more momentum recently due to the rise in diagnosis of autism spectrum disorders.

NATURE, NURTURE, AND INTELLIGENCE

Genetics/heredity and the environment work together to determine the individual's adult level of intelligence. However, measuring intelligence across cultures can be difficult because of the need to determine what is being defined as "intelligence." The use of a Western-education based definition and poor testing methods were responsible for the spread of a number of incorrect racial and ethnic stereotypes during the 20th century.

Identical twins who were adopted separately at birth are often studied in an attempt to determine how much of intelligence is due to genetics and how much is due to environment. However, research has shown a wide range of estimates on how much of intelligence is attributable to genetics (estimates vary from 40 to

80 percent) and how much is attributable to the environment (from 20 to 60 percent). A few environmental factors are known to affect intelligence, including socialization and gender roles, observational learning, and operant conditioning (being rewarded for some behaviors, such as those that support and increase intelligence, and not for others). Genetically, abnormalities such as trisomy 21 (Down's syndrome) can have a known effect on intelligence. However, there seems to be evidence that each subsequent generation does better on intelligence testing than the previous generation. While this phenomenon has been most widely studied in the United States, there is evidence that it is also occurring in multiple cultures around the world. This is known as the Flynn effect, named for the researcher who discovered it.

MEASURING INTELLIGENCE

IQ, or **intelligence quotient**, is an attempt to quantify the intelligence of an individual. Modern IQ test scores are based on a normal bell curve where the score of 100 is always the mean and the standard deviation is 15 (see Figure 2-1). Therefore, a person of "average" intelligence is anyone who scores between 85 and 115. This indicates that the person's intelligence quotient lies within the normal distribution of intelligence. Individuals who score two standard deviations below the mean (<70) are classified as intellectually disabled. Individuals scoring two standard deviations above the mean (>130) are classified as gifted. One definition of an individual with a learning disability

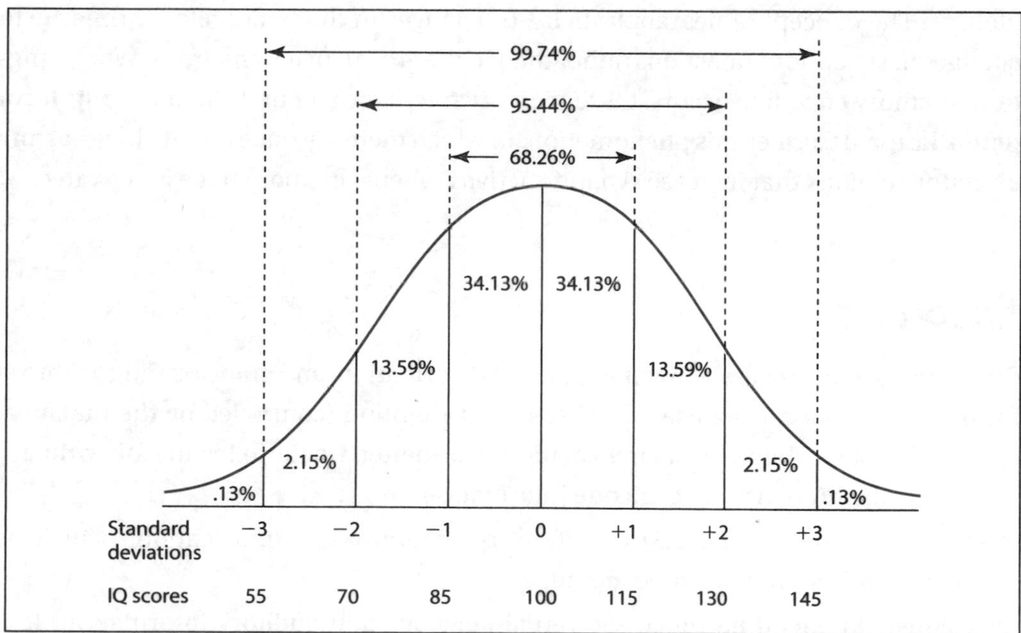

FIGURE 2-1 Distribution of IQ scores along a normal bell curve.

is a person demonstrating average or above average intelligence who scores 1.5 to 2 (varies based on state law and educational standards) standard deviations below his or her IQ in one specific domain (e.g., IQ = 100, verbal processing = 65 would be a verbal processing disability).

MEMORY

There are a number of different types of memory:

- **Declarative memory** handles factual information. Within declarative memory, there is a separation between **episodic memory** and **semantic memory**. Episodic memory is focused on personal facts and chronological information connected to your individual recollections (e.g., you can recall and consciously reexperience the birthday party where your friends sang "Happy Birthday" to you for the first time). By contrast, semantic memory is more focused on factual information that is not connected to individual recollection (e.g., you can remember the words to "Happy Birthday" but not recall and consciously reexperience the first time you heard the song).
- **Procedural memory** is more focused on psychomotor memory and the ability to recall psychomotor skills (e.g., throwing a baseball).

Synaptic connections are selectively strengthened during the process of encoding, and these changes in synaptic connections form the basis for memory and learning. Unlike what was once thought, the brain does continue to grow new neurons, prune synaptic connections, and develop new connections throughout an individual's lifetime. The concept of neural plasticity, or changes in the brain, refers primarily to changes in synaptic connections rather than to the growth of new neurons. When long-term memory encoding occurs, these memory traces form neural circuits. **Long-term potentiation** describes this phenomenon, in which memory traces create long-lasting excitatory circuits that increase synaptic activity when a memory trace is activated.

Encoding

Encoding is the process of taking external information and transforming it into a format that the brain can use. The first step is attention (controlled by the thalamus and frontal lobe). Then sensory information is formatted via the following four primary pathways that humans use to encode information.

- **Visual encoding** processes written or figure-based information, which is temporarily stored in **iconic memory**.
- **Acoustical encoding** processes verbal language and auditory information. It is often aided by the **phonological loop**, which repeats this information in a person's

echoic memory for improved storage and retrieval. Repetition may also include self-vocalizations to enhance auditory encoding (such as repeating a phone number out loud).

- **Tactile encoding** encodes touch-based information via the somatosensory cortex.
- The **semantic** pathway encodes sensory information that is associated with a particular meaning or context rather than strictly a sensory input.

Enhancing Encoding

There are a number of common methods that people use to enhance encoding and improve memory.

- **"Chunking,"** or combining information, is a useful tool to aid in encoding information in short-term memory. Short-term memory is known to have a limited amount of storage (7 ± 2 items), as shown by the work of psychologist George A. Miller. However, chunking allows for more information storage (e.g., recalling the numbers 177614921812 is difficult, but chunking the same information into the more familiar formats of 1776-1492-1812 turns the same numbers into much easier-to-remember chunks.).
- **Mnemonics** are also frequently used to recall information. Acronyms (e.g., common medical acronyms such as *ABC* for airway, breathing, and circulation) and physical cues (e.g., using the knuckles on your hand to recall short versus long months) are two of the most popular.
- **State-dependent memory** is a unique encoding/recall process that uses environmental cues to enhance encoding and recall of information. Research into this type of memory shows that if you learn information in a specific environment and body state, you will better recall that information when you are in the same state (e.g., you will recall testing information better if you learn the information in the same type of situation and body state as when you take the test).
- **Elaborative** or **connective** encoding is a process that assists with memory by attaching novel information to information that is already known. Making connections to already known information enhances an individual's ability to encode new information and store it in long-term memory.

Memory Storage

There are three types of memory storage.

- **Sensory memory** is the first stage of memory consolidation. It is extremely brief, 0.5 seconds (visual) to 2–3 seconds (auditory), storage of the information people take in from their senses. Only critical information from the vast amounts that people take in is passed on to short-term, or working, memory.

- **Short-term memory, or working, memory** was classically defined by the American psychologist George A. Miller. He found that the human brain can typically hold 7 ± 2 items at any one time, though that amount may be increased with "chunking." Short-term, or working, memory (what you hold actively in your mind at any one time) generally lasts about 30 seconds. Acoustic encoding is strongly associated with this form of memory (e.g., repeating someone's telephone number out loud until you can write it down). Biologically, this process involves making biochemical changes to create proteins that enhance already existent synaptic connections.
- In **long-term memory**, information is transmitted from short-term consciousness to longer-term storage. It is believed that long-term memory is essentially unlimited and can last a lifetime. Semantic/meaningful coding is primarily associated with this type of memory. Biologically, this type of memory is associated with the development of new synaptic connections called **long-term potentiation**. Development of these connections is associated with REM stage sleep. The hippocampus in the temporal lobe is thought to be critical in consolidating long-term memories. But this process also includes a number of areas called the "medial temporal lobe memory system." The amygdala is critical to forming and retaining memories associated with fear, anxiety, and the development of phobias. And memory storage is scattered across multiple areas in the cortex.
- **Semantic networks** are the memory connections made by an individual's lived history and the individual's memory of events that occur during his or her lifetime. **Spreading activation** occurs when the recall of one meaningful piece of information triggers the recall of other pieces of information (e.g., the recall of a childhood memory leads to remembering other details of your childhood).

Retrieval

Retrieval is the process of getting stored information back into conscious memory. There are two types of retrieval processes. **Recognition** is the more basic retrieval process; it requires only that the individual identify that he or she has learned this information in the past (e.g., the answers to multiple-choice test questions). This process is simple and requires little cognitive load. The more complex version of retrieval is **free recall**; this requires more cognitive load. **Recall** is the ability to access the information directly from the memory (e.g., fill-in-the-blank test questions).

Humans use a number of **retrieval cues** to help with the recall of information and to relearn information. Examples are context cues (where the information was learned) or activating the semantic network of that information. When you cannot freely recall a piece of information, retrieval cues can assist by activating other neurons associated with that information (e.g., you cannot recall someone's name, but you begin to think about other people in that social network and the name pops back into your mind). Because of the spreading activation that occurs via semantic networks, retrieval can also take the form of "relearning." **Relearning** happens when a person learns the same information a second time. There is a more rapid gain of information when it is relearned than when it is learned initially. It is always easier to relearn a piece of information than to learn a new piece, because it is only a matter of reactivating dormant connections in the brain.

Strong emotions may enhance the encoding and retrieval of **emotion-congruent** information. This is known as "flashbulb memory," in which powerful emotions create a vivid recollection (e.g., "Where were you during the 9/11 attacks?"). These memories degrade at the same rate as other memories, but humans often (incorrectly) continue to believe that the flashbulb memories are accurate. This can create difficulties with eyewitness testimony that occurs years after the event, as cognitive psychologist Elizabeth Loftus has found in her research. Emotions can also create difficulties with the recall of emotional-discongruent information (e.g., it can be difficult recall information learned during a happy experience when you are sad).

Forgetting

Memory dysfunctions can occur naturally. A retrieval failure may occur due to failure of the encoding specificity principle, in which the retrieval cue does not correspond well to the encoded memory. It could also be due to ineffective coding and low attention levels during learning. Either of these could result in the "tip of the tongue" phenomenon in which the individual cannot recall needed information. Memory dysfunctions can also occur due to brain injury, stroke, or disease. Two of the major disease processes associated with memory loss include Pick's and Alzheimer's diseases, in which beta-amyloid plaques interfere with synapse transmission allowing recall of information, and Wernicke-Korsakoff syndrome, in which prolonged alcohol use results in difficulty encoding new information and recalling previously learned information. Encoding and retrieval begin to decline after the age of 60. Aging individuals who maintain their cognitive activity show significantly less decline than those who do not. The effectiveness of working memory and episodic memory do show age-related declines. However, crystallized memory and procedural memory do not appear to be significantly affected in normal aging.

Measures of **retention** assess how humans hold onto information and how quickly they forget learned information. **Decay theory** states that forgetting occurs when the memory synapses degrade with disuse over the passage of time. The German psychologist Hermann Ebbinghaus was famous for establishing the empirical **forgetting curve** to show how quickly information degrades in the human memory (see Figure 2-2). He showed that recall degrades more rapidly than recognition memory.

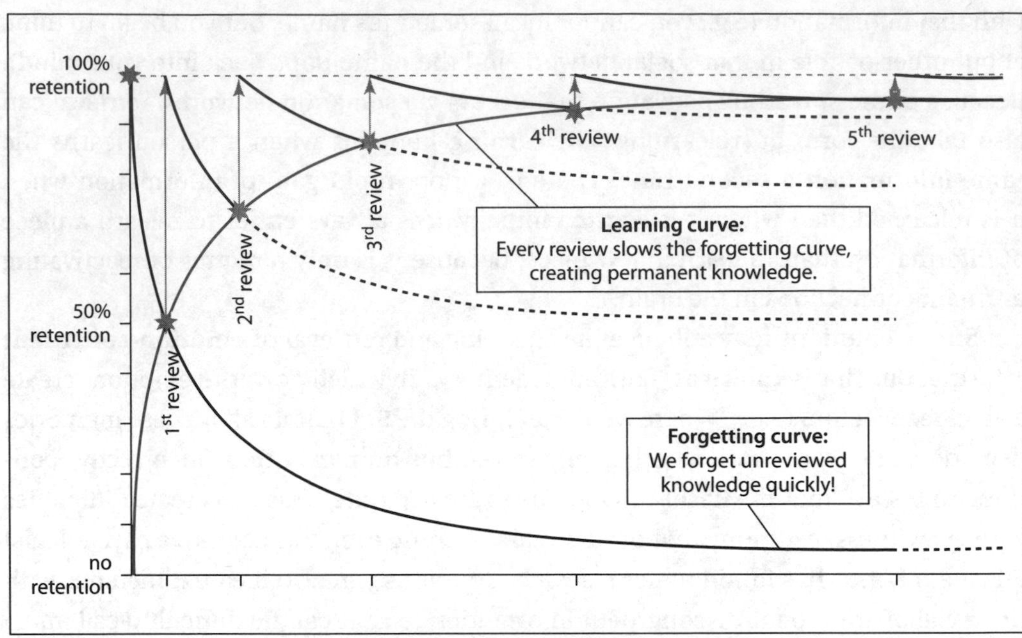

FIGURE 2-2 The learning curve and the forgetting curve.

Interference

Memory interference can also impact memory when the encoding of information is interfered with or prevented. **Retroactive interference** occurs when new information interferes with previously learned information. **Proactive interference** occurs when the old information prevents learning of new information. Both retroactive and proactive forms of interference can prevent encoding or retrieval of appropriate information (see Figure 2-3).

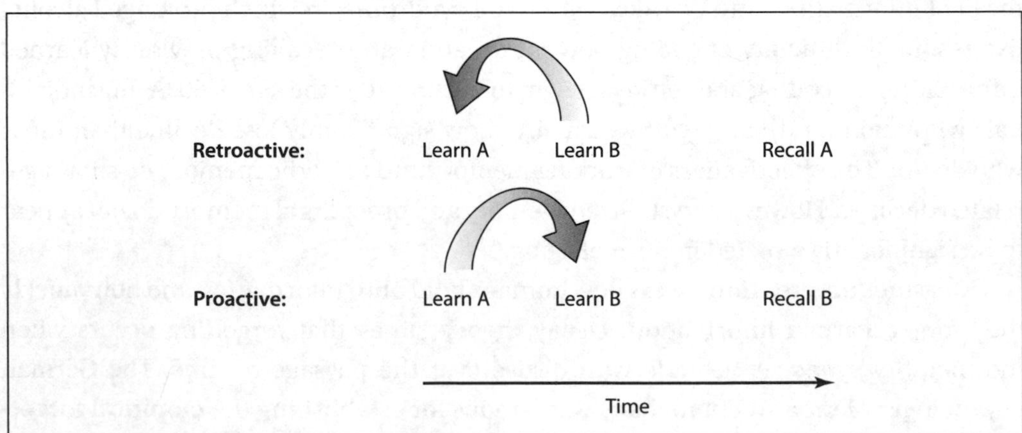

FIGURE 2-3 Retroactive and proactive interference.

LANGUAGE

There are three major theories of language development: learning/behaviorist, nativist, and interactionist. Each of these theories addresses the relative roles of nature versus nurture in language development.

- **Learning/behaviorist.** This theory was proposed by the American psychologist B. F. Skinner, who stated that children learn language in the same manner that they learn every other cultural norm, by observing and imitating those around them. Adults shape children's vocalizations by reinforcing with praise or providing the requested object. Children then learn to imitate the adults around them and develop language skills. Learning theory holds that brain structures may have emergent properties that grow as language vocalizations are shaped by external experiences.
- **Nativist.** The American linguist Noam Chomsky challenged the learning approach by claiming that children could not possibly learn every word combination and sentence before using it, and therefore language must have innate properties. Proponents point to research that shows that language acquisition in children occurs the same way across cultures. They argue that the basic structure and drive for language development is a function of the **language acquisition device (LAD)** in the brain. Chomsky has argued that language is unique to humans. When a research team taught a chimpanzee sign language, the animal was humorously named "Noam Chimpsky"; reportedly, Dr. Chomsky was not amused. The nativist-LAD approach is supported if an innate drive for language explains why children will often develop a means to communicate even when they do not speak the same language. A famous example is the development of the French Creole language in Louisiana by children placed in a nursery from different language cultures.
- **Interactionist.** Later researchers have combined these two earlier approaches and support the idea that some aspects of language are inherent to humans, while other aspects are learned. However, the specifics of which aspects are inherent and which are learned are still controversial.

Influence of Language on Cognition

Cross-culturally, children usually speak their first words at the age of 10 to 12 months. The first 10 to 15 words are slow in developing, but then between 1 and 2 years of age, children go through a vocabulary spurt. Research shows that bilingual children do not develop language more slowly. They may initially have a smaller vocabulary in each language, but they have a greater total vocabulary across both. By around 8 years old, bilingual children have approximately the same vocabulary level as their monolanguage peers. When socioeconomic status is controlled, research shows that bilingual children tend to have greater analytical ability, selective attention, and cognitive flexibility, but slower language-processing speed than their monolanguage peers.

The form and structure of the language you use shapes how you view the world. Language can change your attitudes, worldviews, and self-identity. In a study by American sociolinguist Susan Ervin-Tripp, bilingual Japanese women were asked to complete a set of sentences. When responding in English, the women communicated more North American-European values in relation to a woman's role in society and the economy. When responding in Japanese and using the same statements, the women communicated more traditional Japanese views on women's self-identity and cultural roles. So even the language used moment-to-moment can alter how someone interacts with the world.

Different Brain Areas Control Language and Speech

The neurons involved in language are generally located in the left hemisphere of the brain. Broca's area in the left frontal lobe is predominantly responsible for the production of speech (see Figure 2-4). Someone with damage in this area would understand language but would have difficulty producing the words to respond. In contrast, Wernicke's area in the left temporal lobe is responsible for the understanding of language.

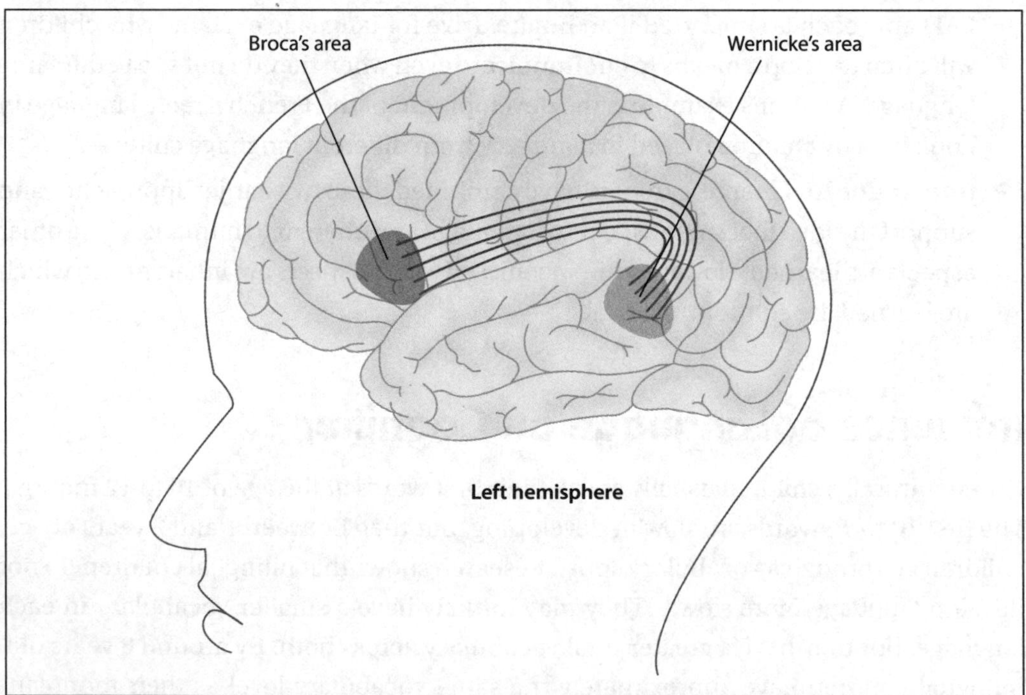

FIGURE 2-4 Broca's area (speech) and Wernicke's area (language).

A person with damage in the Wernicke's area could produce words, but it would be "word salad," or a string of words that do not make sense together. That person would also have difficulty understanding statements made to him or her.

However, do not confuse Wernicke's area (anatomical location) with Wernicke's encephalopathy and **Wernicke-Korsakoff syndrome**, which is the result of prolonged thiamine (Vitamin B_1) deficiency, usually in the context of alcohol addiction. Wernicke's encephalopathy does not primarily affect Wernicke's area. Karl Wernicke was a very prolific German neurologist who put his name on many of his discoveries. His work was great for science, but confusing for students.

CHAPTER 3

Responding to the World

Read This Chapter to Learn About

- Emotion
- Stress

EMOTION

Emotions are more than a simple, one-dimensional experience. They comprise cognitive, behavioral, and physiological components, although there is significant scientific debate about which component is the primary (first or strongest) component. The **cognitive** component involves the cognitive appraisal of the situation. This appraisal is partially automatic and partially under individual control. The **behavioral** component refers to the activities that relate to the cognitive component of emotion. This aspect of emotion is under individual control, and the behaviors may exacerbate or diminish the experience of the emotion (e.g., honking your horn loudly to someone who cuts you off in traffic or taking slow, deep breaths). The **physiological** component of emotion reacts via the autonomic nervous system (ANS). The sympathetic component of the ANS system activates the body during extremes of emotion, particularly during instances of the fight-or-flight response: releasing stress hormones, increasing heart rate, and increasing breath capacity. The parasympathetic system reverses the changes of the sympathetic system and returns the body to normal. It can be activated by the individual via diaphragmatic breathing, meditation, or other relaxation exercises. The sympathetic and parasympathetic nervous systems are generally in homeostatic equilibrium.

Universal Emotions

Anthropology research has identified a number of **universal emotions**. Originally developed from research by Paul Ekman, the list typically includes from four to seven "basic" emotions. The generally accepted emotions are fear, anger, happiness, surprise, joy, disgust, and sadness.

Similar facial expressions that match these emotions have been shown to exist across different cultures. While expression of emotions does have cultural components, it is possible that there is a genetic component to understanding those expressions. Some research indicates that these seven emotions also occur in animals, particularly primates. Humans from different cultures, and primates as well, can separate and categorize facial expressions for each of the seven basic emotions. Emotional expression across cultures is certainly adaptive. Being able to recognize friendly or threatening behavior would be critical when encountering people from other cultures. It is also adaptive within a community as a way to communicate emotions. Some evolutionary psychologists believe that emotional expression developed before language as a proto-language to share knowledge of dangerous and safe items in the environment.

Other researchers examining how emotional memories are stored and retrieved prefer the **biaxial theory of emotions**. This theory identifies emotions based on valence (positive or negative) and the level of arousal it causes (elevated or neutral). These factors then determine how memories are stored in the brain and the emotional status that makes it easier to retrieve these memories. These researchers place all human emotions on these two axes rather than the distinct "basic" emotions of Ekman's theory.

There are three major theories of how humans consciously experience emotions and label which emotion they are experiencing. These theories attempt to answer the question "Which comes first, the experience or the label?"

- According to the **James–Lange theory**, the experience of emotion stems from a person's perception of autonomic arousal. A stimulus creates autonomic arousal, which the individual labels as "fear." Emotion misattribution to physiological arousal may occur, but generally it assumes that humans can (subconsciously) differentiate among physiological arousal caused by fear, anger, or excitement.

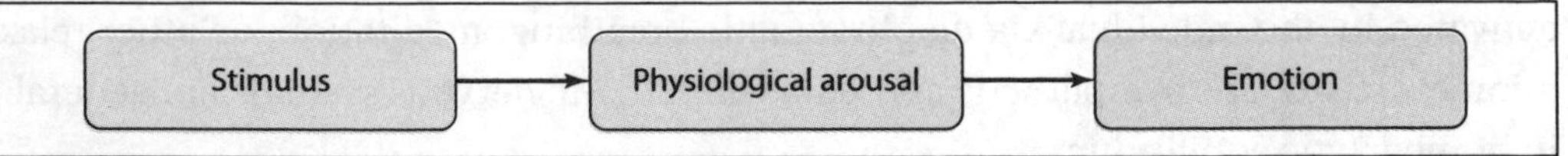

➤ The **Cannon–Bard theory** of emotion differs from the James-Lange theory in claiming that the experience of physiological arousal can occur without the emotion (e.g., while exercising). According to this theory, a stimulus triggers the thalamus (and other subcortical brain structures) to simultaneously create autonomic arousal and cause the individual to label the emotion.

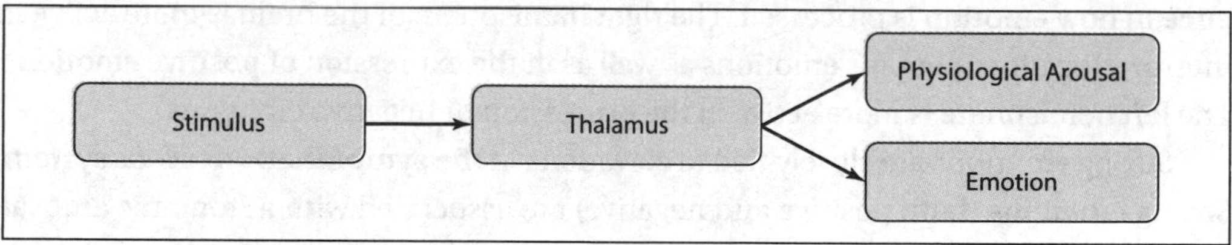

➤ The **Schachter–Singer theory** of emotion is a combination of the two previous theories. It posits that a stimulus (e.g., a threatening dog) triggers an autonomic arousal in the body (e.g., via the sympathetic nervous system). That causes the person to appraise the environmental context, and based on that appraisal to interpret the emotion (e.g., fear). This is the only theory that involves active appraisal of the environmental context, which is critical because the same autonomic experience in a different context may trigger a different emotion to be identified (e.g., a roller-coaster ride would be interpreted as "thrilling"). This emotional theory has gained precedence in recent research.

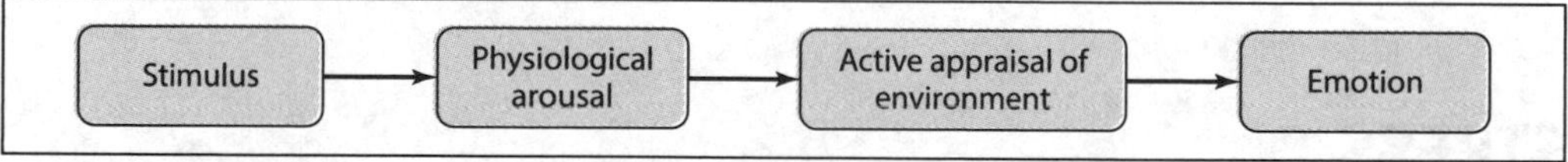

Biology and Emotional Perception

The development, identification, and experience of emotions involve a number of different brain areas. The **limbic system** comprises the amygdala, hypothalamus, and adjacent structures. The amygdala is particularly associated with negative emotions such as fear and anger. Sensory inputs potentially related to emotion arrive in the thalamus. Those inputs that could relate to a threat are "fast tracked" directly to the amygdala, while those that are determined to not be a threat are "slow tracked" to the appropriate area of the cortex for analysis (e.g., visual-occipital lobe). In addition to the limbic system, the **prefrontal cortex** is critical to voluntary control of emotions relating to cognitive, behavioral, and physiological factors. In addition, the prefrontal cortex is critical for processing emotional experiences, planning responses to emotional experiences, and relating emotional experiences to temperament and decision making. The **anterior cingulate cortex** functions to identify the level of threat from pain and the emotional distress related to that pain level (e.g., short-term injury versus long-term injury). The **mesolimbic dopamine pathway** is also critical in regulating emotion; this pathway is activated by pleasant or rewarding events. During the use of drugs of abuse, this pathway is "hijacked." There is also a **hemispheric difference** in how emotion is processed. The right hemisphere of the brain is more active in interpreting other people's emotions as well as in the expression of positive emotions. The left hemisphere is more active in the expression of negative emotions.

Strong emotions are closely tied to elevations in the **sympathetic nervous system**. Strong emotions (both positive and negative) are associated with autonomic arousal. Excitement and fear both cause increased heart rate, increased respiration rate, release of cortisol and other stress hormones, and increased galvanized skin response. In contrast, feeling calm or mildly happy activates the **parasympathetic nervous system** with reduced heart rate, reduced muscle tension, and slowed breathing. However, there are some unique physiological markers of emotion as well. For example, asking an individual to shift facial muscles to a smiling or frowning position can actually create positive or negative mood shifts, respectively.

The links between emotions and autonomic nervous arousal are also likely related to episodic memories. Strong emotional experiences can be integrated into episodic memories. Those episodic memories can then be triggered by strong emotions that are similar to those in the memory of the original event. Post-traumatic stress disorder flashbacks are an example of how emotions can repeatedly trigger episodic memories.

STRESS

Stress has behavioral, cognitive, and physiological components. Austrian-Canadian endocrinologist Hans Selye was the father of stress research. He found that stress can be caused by both positive and negative events, and that the stress caused by both kinds of events can have similar physiological, behavioral, and cognitive effects. Selye identified the body's primary stress system as the hypothalamus-pituitary-adrenal axis (HPA axis). (See Figure 3.1.) He found that the HPA axis goes through three states:

1. The **alarm state** is the initial activation after an acute stressor.
2. The **resistance state** is prolonged activation during a chronic stressor.
3. In the **exhaustion state**, the HPA axis and the body's ability to respond to stress begin to break down.

The new and growing field of positive psychology examines positive stress, as well as positive emotions in general and the positive psychological processes that keep humans mentally healthy and resilient to stress.

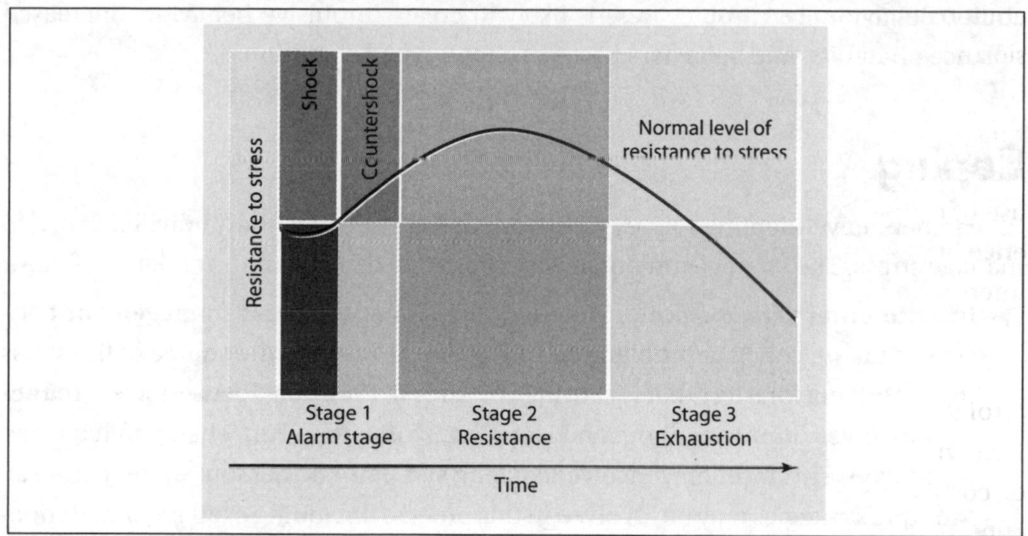

FIGURE 3-1 Selye's general adaptation syndrome. *Source*: Adapted from *J. W. Santrock. Adolescence,* 15th ed., McGraw-Hill Education, 2014.

Stress occurs when people experience events that they judge as being beyond their ability to handle. It is this critical appraisal that can activate the fight-or-flight response. Stress can occur in acute situations (e.g., a car running a stoplight and heading for your car), or it can be chronic (e.g., long-term financial difficulties). Stressful events can be cataclysmic and shared with many other people (e.g., the 9/11 attacks), or they can be very personal (e.g., divorce).

Responses to Stressors

Response to stressors depends on the chronicity of the stressor. Acute stress heightens the individual's ability to respond to the stressful situation. By contrast, chronic stress takes a toll on the individual. Physiologically, stress causes acute activation of the sympathetic nervous system. Over time in the context of chronic stress, other issues begin to develop. Chronic stress causes the body to experience decreased sleep quantity and quality, reduced immune response to infections, weight gain, increased insulin resistance (and resulting increased susceptibility to type II diabetes), fatigue, and slowed wound healing. Emotionally, chronic stress can create a burnout experience in which the individual feels chronically fatigued, has difficulty with positive emotional responses, and experiences a decreased optimistic outlook. Cognitively, acute stress can enhance cognitive abilities. By contrast, chronic stress impairs memory encoding and can interfere with recall. It also can produce increased stereotyping and pigeonholing because making judgments based on superficial attributes rather than on individualized assessments requires less cognitive load. The individual with chronic stress also begins to experience slowed cognitive speed and decreased problem-solving ability. Behaviorally, chronic stress is likely to create impulsive behaviors, increased reliance on habits, and behaviors based on stereotyped cognitions.

Coping

Researchers have identified many different coping strategies that individuals use to manage stress. The strategies are typically grouped in dichotomous models, as follow:

- **Instrumental versus emotion-focused. Instrumental stress management** consists of taking concrete problem-solving actions to reduce the source of the stress (e.g., studying for a test that is causing you stress). **Emotion-focused stress reduction** involves improving the mood state (e.g., going for a run when you have had a bad day). This form may involve reducing sympathetic nervous system arousal. Multiple strategies may be involved in this process, including exercise, meditation, diaphragmatic breathing, and spiritual resources. Both instrumental and emotional forms of stress management are active stress-control techniques. For most stressors, the ideal combination involves a combination of the two strategies.
- **Approach versus avoidance.** Another dichotomous coping model is approach versus avoidance. In this model, an individual copes with a stressor by using a problem-solving (approach) method to address the stressor and resolve it. In avoidance coping, the individual may attempt to escape the situation through alcohol, drugs, distraction, or other means to attempt to avoid facing the stressor. Both approach and avoidance coping strategies can be considered active or passive depending on the situation.
- **Passive versus active.** Active coping involves actively engaging the stressor in some way. This may be in an approach or avoidance manner, but it requires the individual to acknowledge the stressor and attempt to reduce the impact of the stressor on his or her life (by engagement or disengagement). Passive coping strategies are often associated with avoidance strategies; the individual takes no active steps to reduce the impact of the stressor on his or her life but just waits for it to go away.
- **Adaptive versus maladaptive.** Adaptive and maladaptive forms of coping are generally defined by their outcomes, and these may be environmentally or situationally determined. Coping strategies that may be adaptive and enhance outcomes in one situation (e.g., going for a run to reduce stress and improve long-term health outcomes) may actually impair outcomes under different environmental pressures (e.g., going for a run outside in Beijing or Los Angeles during "hazardous" air pollution alert days). Therefore, research into adaptive and maladaptive coping strategies clearly outlines the individual, environment, and situation that is being studied to identify how these strategies may help or hurt individuals who are in these situations.

Unit I Minitest

16 Questions **30 Minutes**

This minitest is designed to assess your mastery of the content in Chapters 1 through 3 of this volume. The questions have been designed to simulate actual MCAT questions in terms of format and degree of difficulty. They are based on the content categories associated with the foundational concept that is the theme of this unit. They are also designed to test the scientific inquiry and reasoning skills that the test makers have identified as essential for success in medical school.

In this test, most of the questions are based on short passages that typically describe a research study or some similar process. There are also some questions that are not based on passages.

Use this test to measure your readiness for the actual MCAT. Try to answer all of the questions within the specified time limit. If you run out of time, you will know that you need to work on improving your pacing.

Complete answer explanations are provided at the end of the minitest. Pay particular attention to the answers for questions you got wrong or skipped. If necessary, go back and review the corresponding chapters or text sections in this unit.

Now turn the page and begin the Unit I Minitest.

Directions: *Choose the best answer to each of the following questions. Question 1 is not based on a passage.*

1. The theory of hearing that best explains perception of low pitched sounds is called ___________. The theory of hearing that best explains perception of very high pitched sounds is called ___________.
   A. place theory, frequency theory
   B. frequency theory, place theory
   C. auditory gate theory, place theory
   D. place theory, auditory gate theory

Questions 2–5 are based on the following passage.

Passage I

Researchers studying signal detection have documented various magnitude differences necessary to detect the presence of stimuli (absolute threshold) and to detect changes in the perceptual experience of the stimuli (just noticeable difference). These differences are dependent on the type of sensory experience being measured and can be characterized by proportional differences in magnitude rather than absolute amounts.

A recent study examined the just noticeable difference necessary to perceive tempo changes. In this experiment, signal detection methods were used to examine the amount of change necessary to detect a difference between an initial/target tempo and a comparison stimulus. Two test conditions were evaluated. The initial/target tempo

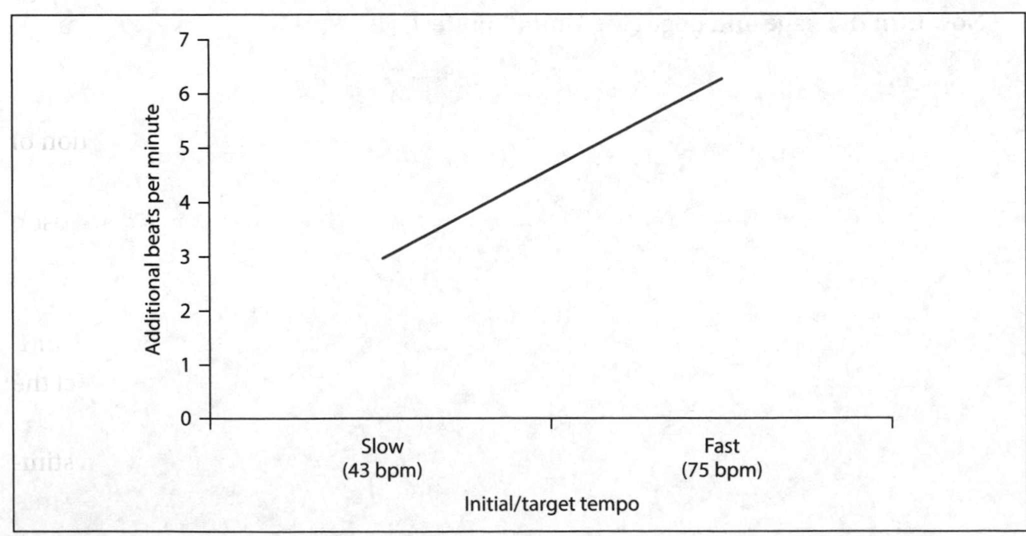

Detecting tempo change (beats per minute). *Source*: Adapted from Thomas, K. (2007). "Just noticeable difference and tempo change." *Journal of Scientific Psychology*, 2, 14–20.

speed was either *slow* (43 beats per minute [bpm]) or *fast* (75 bpm). Comparison tempos were presented that were either sped up or slowed down relative to the initial/target tempo. Participants were asked to identify whether the comparison tempos were the same tempo or a different tempo from the initial/target tempo. The accompanying graph depicts the tempo changes necessary for detection for both the *slow* and *fast* initial/target tempos.

2. If a third initial/target tempo of 60 beats per minute was tested, which of the following would you expect to be TRUE based on the results of this study?
   A. It would take a change in magnitude greater than the *fast* tempo for participants to detect a change.
   B. It would take a change in magnitude smaller than the *slow* tempo for participants to detect a change.
   C. It would take a change in magnitude greater than the *slow* tempo but less than the *fast* tempo for participants to detect a change.
   D. The magnitude of the change necessary for participants to detect a change more than 50 percent of the time would be exactly the same regardless of the target tempo.

3. Suppose this study used a forced-choice signal detection method. Which type of signal detection response would be MOST likely as the speed of the comparison tempo increased, regardless of the initial/target tempo?
   A. a miss
   B. a false alarm
   C. a correct rejection
   D. a hit

4. Which of the following statements BEST describes Weber's law?
   A. The just noticeable difference (JND) necessary to detect a change in the magnitude of a comparison stimulus (i.e., the tempo) is a constant proportion of the initial/target stimulus.
   B. The JND necessary to detect a change in the magnitude of a comparison stimulus (i.e., the tempo) is a fixed amount, independent of the initial/target stimulus.
   C. The JND necessary to detect a change in the magnitude of a comparison stimulus (i.e., the tempo) is always the same as the absolute threshold to detect the stimulus.
   D. The JND necessary to detect a change in the magnitude of a comparison stimulus (i.e., the tempo) is exactly half of the magnitude necessary to perceive that the stimulus is present.

5. Which of the following conclusions is supported by this study?
   - **A.** The faster the tempo of the initial/target stimulus, the greater the difference required between the initial and comparison tempos for participants to perceive a difference.
   - **B.** The faster the tempo of the initial/target stimulus, the greater the proportion of change needed for participants to perceive a difference.
   - **C.** The slower the tempo of the initial/target stimulus, the greater the difference required between the initial and comparison tempos for participants to perceive a difference.
   - **D.** The slower the tempo of the initial/target stimulus, the greater the proportion of change needed for participants to perceive a difference.

Question 6 is not based on a passage.

6. A researcher inserts electrodes into the brain of a monkey. When the monkey is shown lines aligned at different orientations, the cells respond preferentially to lines of certain particular orientations. It is MOST likely that the researcher has inserted the electrodes into which region of the brain?
   - **A.** occipital lobe
   - **B.** temporal lobe
   - **C.** frontal lobe
   - **D.** parietal lobe

Questions 7–10 are based on the following passage.

Passage II

Jean Piaget, a prominent figure in developmental psychology, believed that the development of all cognitive abilities occurred during the first two years of life. Piaget devised various procedures for examining development in young children. These activities focused on how children (and people) think and how they interact with the world around them. Piaget asserted that biological changes interacted with childhood experiences, resulting in unique developmental stages characterized by schemas, or mental structures.

The following table lists the four stages of development identified by Piaget and their function.

Stage	Age	Purpose
Sensory Motor	Birth–2 years	Coordination of sensations with voluntary motor movement
Preoperational	2–7 years	Increased use of mental images and symbols
Concrete Operational	7–11 years	Increased problem-solving abilities; mastery of conservation; cognition and mental operations are mostly limited to tangible objects and actual events
Formal Operational	11–Adult	Begins to understand and mentally manipulate abstract constructs (e.g., ethics, free will, love)

7. Two children, Tommy and Janet, watch a researcher pour water from a short, wide glass into a tall, narrow glass. When asked, Tommy confidently states that there is now more water in the tall, narrow glass than there was in the short, wide glass. Janet asserts that the amount of water has not changed. Based on Piaget's stages of development, which answer BEST represents this example?
   A. Tommy and Janet are exhibiting egocentrism because they are unable to share each other's viewpoints.
   B. Tommy is not aware of the continued existence of the water once it is poured from one glass to the other, while Janet has developed object permanence.
   C. Janet has developed reversibility and understands that the water can be poured back into the original container, while Tommy has not yet developed reversibility.
   D. Janet has developed conservation and is aware that the amount of water inside a container is the same even if the dimensions change, while Tommy has not yet developed conservation.

8. Amanda's mother hides Amanda's toy rattle beneath a blanket. Amanda does not search for the rattle and appears to be unaware of its existence. Based on Piaget's model, what stage is Amanda in and what concept has she NOT yet mastered?
   A. sensory motor, object permanence
   B. sensory motor, conservation
   C. preoperational, object permanence
   D. preoperational, conservation

9. Based on Piaget's model, what concept is characterized by the ability to absorb new ideas and what concept is characterized by the process of modifying previously developed mental processes?
   A. Accommodation is characterized by the ability to absorb new ideas; assimilation is characterized by the process of modifying previously developed mental processes.
   B. Assimilation is characterized by the ability to absorb new ideas; accommodation is characterized by the process of modifying previously developed mental processes.
   C. Coordination is characterized by the ability to absorb new ideas; consolidation is characterized by the process of modifying previously developed mental processes.
   D. Consolidation is characterized by the ability to absorb new ideas; coordination is characterized by the process of modifying previously developed mental processes.

10. On a rainy day, Juan is asked why it is raining. He replies that it is raining so that he can "play with his toy boat." What developmental stage is Juan likely in, and what concept has he yet to master?
   A. formal operational, decentering
   B. sensory motor, transitivity
   C. preoperational, egocentrism
   D. concrete operational, classification

Question 11 is not based on a passage.

11. Which field of psychology examines positive stresses as well as positive emotions in general?
   A. psychodynamic approach
   B. human-focused psychology
   C. positive psychology
   D. motivation and emotion approach

Questions 12–15 are based on the following passage.

Passage III

The study of emotional experience is often characterized by the attempt to answer the question, "Which comes first, the experience or the label?" Some researchers suggest that the physiological arousal occurs, then the individual contextualizes the experience based on his or her environment, resulting in emotion such as "fear" or "happiness."

Other researchers suggest that humans can subconsciously identify the difference in arousal caused by various emotional states or that the arousal and classification occur in parallel.

Recent research has examined the relationship between culture and emotion. One such study examined the differences between how American and Japanese participants contextualize emotion. The researchers examined athletes' use of emotion-related words in interviews. Compared to American athletes, Japanese athletes were found to be more likely to identify emotions with others than with themselves. Based on these findings, the researchers conducted a second experiment in which they asked Japanese and American participants to describe typical emotions experienced by Olympic medalists. The researchers counted the number of emotion-related words and assigned them to either self-focused or self+other–focused groups for comparison.

The results of the second study are shown in the following graph.

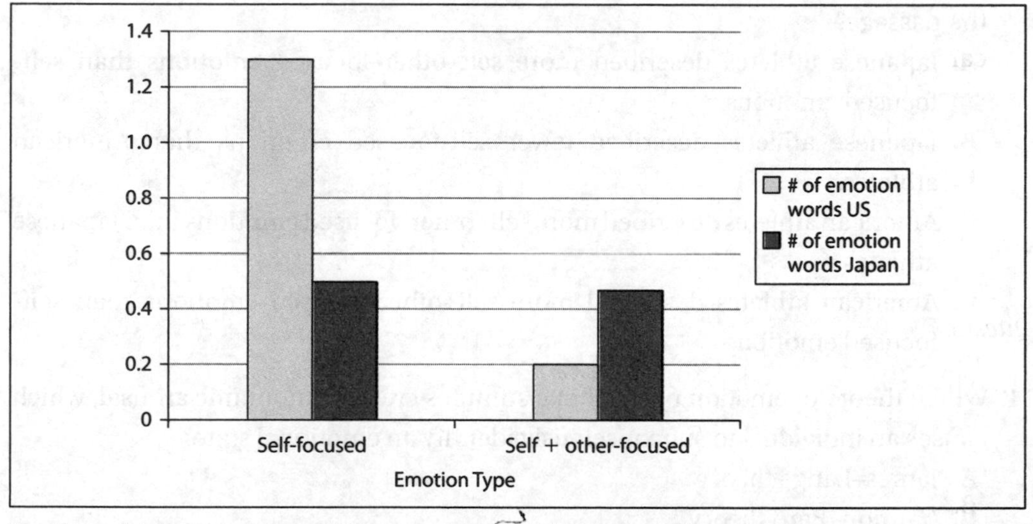

Number of emotion words used by American and Japanese participants. Responses assigned to self-focused and self + other-focused groups. *Source*: Adapted from Uchida, Yukiko, et al. "Emotions as within or between people? Cultural variation in lay theories of emotion expression and inference." *Personality and Social Psychology Bulletin 35*(11), (2009): 1427–1439.

12. Which statement describes BEST how the Schachter–Singer theory of emotion could be used to interpret the results of this study?
    - **A.** The experiences triggered physiological arousal, which caused specific emotions. Because the physiological arousal conditions were similar, the responses between the cultural groups were similar as well.
    - **B.** The experiences triggered autonomic arousal, which the participants then appraised. Each group interpreted their emotional experiences based on cultural differences as a result of the appraisal process.
    - **C.** The experiences activated the thalamus, which simultaneously created both physiological arousal and the emotion. Any differences observed were due to different types of arousal in participants from different cultures.
    - **D.** Experiences between cultures occur in different ways and use different brain regions. The observed cultural differences represent different theories of emotion.

13. Which of the following BEST describes the results of the second study described in the passage?
    - **A.** Japanese athletes described more self+other–focused emotions than self-focused emotions.
    - **B.** Japanese athletes described fewer self-focused emotions than American athletes.
    - **C.** American athletes described more self+other–focused emotions than Japanese athletes.
    - **D.** American athletes described more self+other–focused emotions than self-focused emotions.

14. Which theory of emotion posits that a stimulus creates autonomic arousal, which causes an individual to subconsciously identify an emotional state?
    - **A.** James–Lange theory
    - **B.** Cannon–Bard theory
    - **C.** Schachter–Singer theory
    - **D.** James–Singer theory

15. What additional experiment could be included in future research to further investigate emotion and cultural differences between populations?
    - **A.** asking participants to complete a memory recall task prior to indicating the emotions that they believed the athletes exhibited
    - **B.** conducting the experiment on additional groups from different cultures and comparing the results between them
    - **C.** conducting the experiment on the same group of participants over time but changing the narrative scripts
    - **D.** asking participants to wear heart rate monitors and measuring their arousal while reading narrative scripts

Question 16 is not based on a passage.

16. Jane is able to remember and consciously reexperience her 15th birthday party when her parents gave her a Beatles album. She also remembers the Beatles' classic look because her parents described it to her in detail. Which type of memory BEST characterizes the first example, and which type of memory BEST explains the second?
    A. episodic memory, procedural memory
    B. episodic memory, semantic memory
    C. semantic memory, procedural memory
    D. procedural memory, explicit memory

This is the end of the Unit I Minitest.

Unit I Minitest Answers and Explanations

1. **The correct answer is B.** According to frequency theory, pitch perception corresponds to the frequency of vibration of the entire basilar membrane in the inner ear. According to place theory, pitch perception corresponds to the vibration of specific locations along the basilar membrane. Frequency theory cannot account for neurons firing over 1000 times per second, so it is associated only with lower-pitched sounds. The volley theory reconciles the two theories by showing that the neurons work together using the functions described in both place and frequency theories to signal pitch.
2. **The correct answer is C.** If a third tempo of 60 bpm was introduced, it would be in between the *slow* tempo condition (43 bpm) and the *fast* tempo condition (75 bpm). According to Weber's law, a proportional difference in the initial/target and comparison tempos would be necessary for a person to detect a difference. Therefore, the magnitude (number of beats per minute) of the change would need to be greater than the *slow* tempo but less than the *fast* tempo.
3. **The correct answer is D.** If this study used a forced-choice signal detection method, responses could be classified into four categories: miss (failing to identify a changed stimulus), false alarm (identifying an unchanged stimulus as changed), correct rejection (identifying an unchanged comparison as the same as the initial/target stimulus), or hit (correctly identifying a comparison stimulus that differs from the initial/target stimulus). As the magnitude of the comparison tempo increased, the greater would be the likelihood that a participant would perceive a change and the greater the chance that he or she would identify the comparison tempo as different from the initial/target tempo.
4. **The correct answer is A.** According to Weber's law, the JND of a stimulus is in a constant proportion to the intensity/size of the initial/target stimulus. Therefore, the JND must be a constant proportion of the initial/target stimulus. While the absolute threshold is a similar concept, that term refers to the minimum intensity/size necessary to perceive the existence of a stimulus and does not indicate the amount of change in an existing stimulus necessary to perceive a difference.
5. **The correct answer is A.** The faster the initial/target tempo, the greater the difference needed for detection between the initial and the comparison stimuli. The slower the initial/target tempo, the smaller the difference needed to be between the initial and the comparison stimuli. The magnitude of the change necessary to perceive differences increased in proportion to the magnitude of the initial/target stimuli. The proportion of difference necessary is constant because the results were consistent with Weber's law.
6. **The correct answer is A.** The occipital lobe is responsible for processing visual images. Further, research examining line orientation has found that specific

neurons selectively fire in response to lines of different orientations. This is also consistent with feature integration theory (bottom-up processing).

7. **The correct answer is D.** Janet is displaying an understanding of conservation, while Tommy has yet to develop conservation. Conservation is characterized by the ability to understand that the amount of a substance within a container remains the same even if the dimensions of the container change. Egocentrism is characterized by difficulty in sharing another person's viewpoint, a problem that is not necessarily represented in the question. Reversibility is not necessary for an understanding of conservation and is associated with a more complex understanding about state changes in objects and numbers. Object permanence is developed earlier, during the sensory motor stage.
8. **The correct answer is A.** The sensory motor stage is associated with the development of motor coordination and a memory of past events. During this stage, children master the concept of object permanence. Object permanence is characterized by the knowledge that an object continues to exist even when out of view of the child.
9. **The correct answer is B.** Assimilation is characterized by the ability to absorb new ideas and experiences and to incorporate them into existing mental structures. Accommodation is the process of modifying previously developed mental structures and behaviors and adapting them to new experiences.
10. **The correct answer is C.** The preoperational stage is characterized by the increased use of mental images and symbols. A key characteristic of the preoperational stage is egocentrism, in which the child is unable to see the world externally. To the child, the world does not exist by itself and only exists to satisfy the child's interests and needs.
11. **The correct answer is C.** Positive psychology is a growing field that examines positive stress and emotions and how positive psychological processes keep humans mentally healthy and resilient.
12. **The correct answer is C.** The Schachter–Singer theory of emotion posits that a stimulus triggers an autonomic arousal in the body (sympathetic nervous system), which causes a person to appraise the environmental context, and based on that appraisal, to interpret the emotion. This is the only theory that requires active appraisal of the environmental context, which is critical because the same autonomic experience in a different context may trigger a different emotion to be identified.
13. **The correct answer is B.** Japanese athletes described fewer self-focused emotions than American athletes. Additionally, Japanese athletes described more self+other–focused emotions than American athletes. However, Japanese athletes described slightly more self–focused emotions than self + other–focused emotions.
14. **The correct answer is A.** The James–Lange theory posits that a stimulus creates autonomic arousal, causing the individual to identify an emotional state. The

Cannon–Bard theory of emotion posits that a physiological arousal can occur without the emotion and that the stimulus simultaneously triggers autonomic arousal by the thalamus and the labeling of the emotion. The Schachter–Singer theory posits that stimuli trigger an autonomic arousal in the body, which causes the individual to appraise the environmental context in order to determine the emotional response.

15. **The correct answer is** B. Conducting the experiment on additional groups from different cultures could yield more information about culture specific differences in populations. A memory recall task and repeated measures of the same group would most likely not reveal any new information. Likewise, measuring arousal would not be very likely to result in new information.
16. **The correct answer is** B. Episodic memory is characterized as the ability to remember and consciously re-experience past events. Semantic memory is characterized by memory of facts.

UNIT II

Behavior

Foundational Concept: Biological, psychological, and sociocultural factors influence behavior and behavior change.

CHAPTER 4

Individual Influences on Behavior

Read This Chapter to Learn About

- The Nervous System
- The Endocrine System
- Behavioral Genetics
- Personality
- Psychological Disorders
- Motivation
- Sleep
- Attitudes

THE NERVOUS SYSTEM

Neurons are the basic building blocks of the nervous system. Each **neuron** is a cell that can receive information, transform it, and transmit that information. The neuron receives information from other neurons as it is transmitted across the synapse (the junction between two neurons). The **dendrites** receive the information and forward it to the soma. The **soma** (cell body) is the location of the cell nucleus and the general functioning of the cell. The signal then travels down the **axon** away from the soma to the **terminal buttons** that release neurotransmitters into the synapse to transmit the signal to the dendrites on the next cell. See Figure 4-1.

Neurons only fire in an "all-or-nothing" pattern. When a neuron is in its resting state, positively charged sodium and potassium ions are actively pumped out, while negatively charged chloride ions are kept inside. This creates an electrochemical

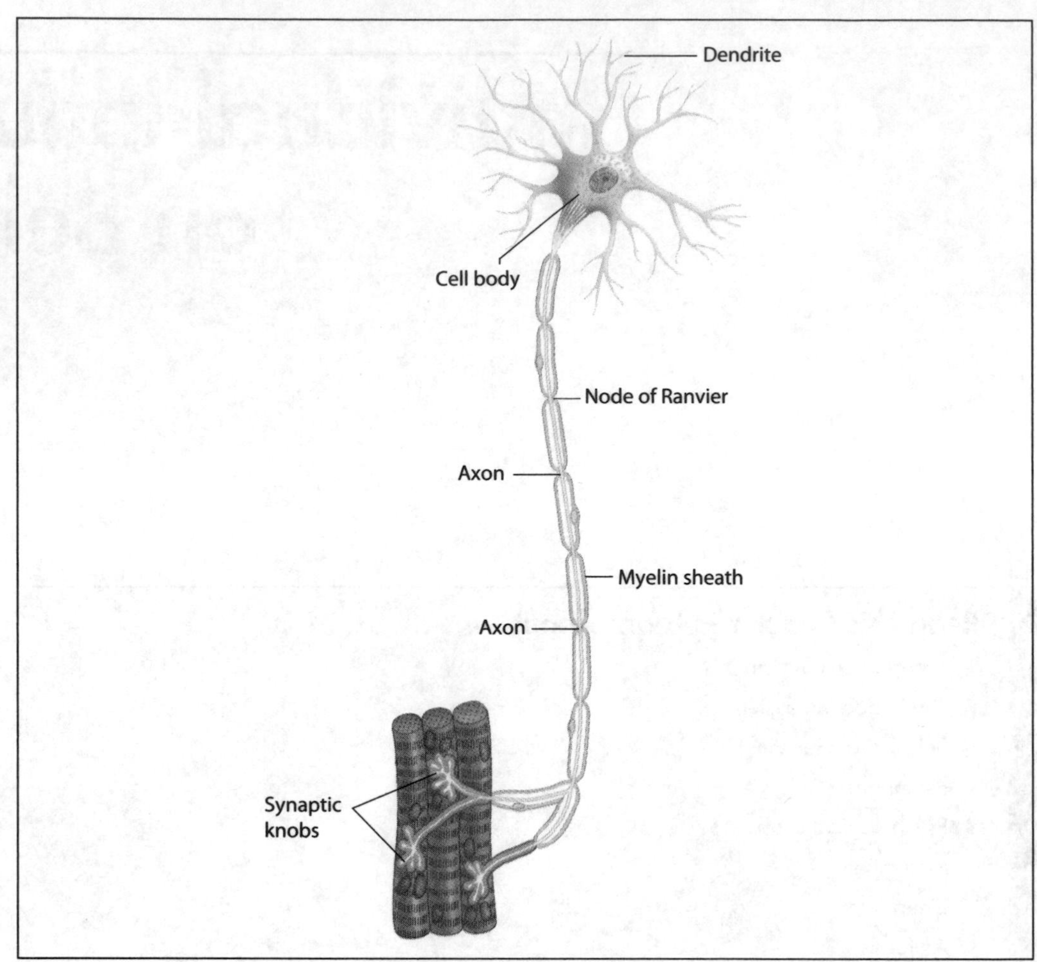

FIGURE 4-1 Neuron structure. A typical neuron consists of dendrites, a cell body, and an axon. *Source*: From Sylvia S. Mader, *Biology*, 8th ed., McGraw-Hill, 2004, reproduced with permission of The McGraw-Hill Companies.

gradient that stores potential energy. A neuron that is in its stable, charged state and is not firing or recovering has a **resting potential** of approximately −70 millivolts. In this state, the neuron has the ability to fire if stimulated. During firing, the "windows," or **ion channels**, of the neuron briefly open, allowing the positively charged ions to flow inside. This process is called **depolarization**, indicating a reduced electrical differential between the inside and outside of the neuron. Then the windows close, and the neuron begins to actively transport the K+ and Na+ ions back out of the cell in order to regain its −70 mv charge. The **action potential** reflects a very brief alteration in the neuron's electrical charge as the signal moves down the axon. After firing, the neuron undergoes an **absolute refractory period**, during which it cannot fire, followed by a **relative refractory period**, when only a very large stimulus will trigger a firing.

If the axon is covered with a **myelin sheath** (an insulating material that surrounds axons), the signal will travel more quickly than if the axon is unmyelinated. The myelin sheath is an outgrowth of **glial** cells. In the peripheral nervous system, a subtype of glial cell is called a Schwann cell; in the central nervous system, oligodendrocytes myelinate the neurons. Though much smaller than neurons, oligodendrocyte glial cells make up about 50 percent of the brain's volume and provide various support activities for the neurons (e.g., nourishment, removal of waste, insulation).

Neurotransmitters are the primary means by which cells communicate with each other across the synapse (see Figure 4-2). Neurotransmitters are chemical messengers that transmit signals from one cell to another.

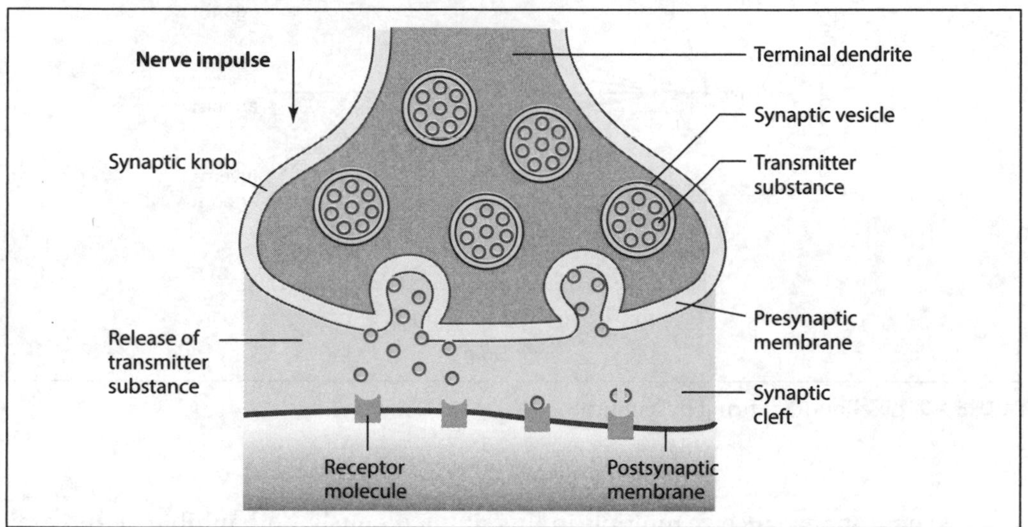

FIGURE 4-2 Communication across a synapse.

Neurotransmitters are packaged in **vesicles** by the neuron. When the cell fires, the vesicles merge with the presynaptic membrane and release the neurotransmitter into the presynaptic cleft. When a neurotransmitter is dumped into the synapse by the presynaptic cell, it fits into the receptors on the postsynaptic cell. It should be noted that neurotransmitters from a presynaptic neuron and exogenous chemicals (drugs) may perform one of four different actions on the postsynaptic neuron:

- Cause a neuron to fire by attaching to a postsynaptic receptor and triggering depolarization (**agonist** creating an **action potential**).
- Encourage a neuron to fire by attaching to a receptor but with only partial efficacy to activate it, allowing some positively charged ions into the neuron and making the neuron less negatively charged (e.g., −60 mv). This, in conjunction with the same "fire" message from other neurons within a short period of time, will build up until a critical **threshold** is reached (around −55 mv) and the postsynaptic neuron fires (**partial agonist creating excitatory postsynaptic potential**).
- Inhibit a neuron from firing by attaching to and blocking the receptor molecules on the postsynaptic membrane, which means agonists cannot attach to the receptor (**antagonist** blocking any effects on internal neuron polarization).

➤ Encourage a neuron not to fire by attaching to a postsynaptic receptor that makes the neuron more negatively polarized (e.g., −80 mv) (**inverse agonist** creating **inhibitory postsynaptic potential**).

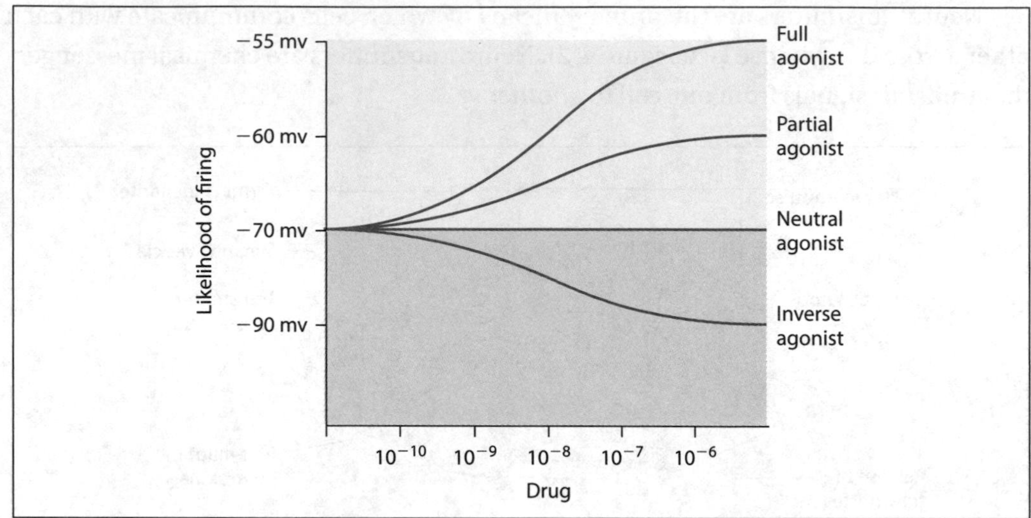

FIGURE 4-3 Likelihood of firing by a neuron.

The neuron may receive multiple inputs simultaneously, both inhibitory and excitatory, and it is the summation of these inputs that ultimately determines if the neuron reaches the firing threshold to produce an action potential. Figure 4-3 diagrams the likelihood of firing by a neuron.

The influence of the neurotransmitter ends when the neurotransmitter (1) is removed from the synaptic cleft as an intact neurotransmitter and returned to the presynaptic cell in a process called **reuptake** (most common), (2) is broken down by enzymes in the synaptic cleft and the pieces returned to the presynaptic cell, or (3) floats away into the fluids surrounding the neuron (minimal).

To be a neurotransmitter, (1) a chemical must be produced inside the neuron, (2) all of the precursor enzymes must be located in the neuron, (3) there must be enough of the chemical in the presynaptic neuron to produce an effect on the postsynaptic neuron if released, (4) the presynaptic neuron must be able to release the chemical and the postsynaptic neuron must have receptors for it to bind to, and (5) a biological mechanism such as reuptake or removal from the synaptic cleft must be possible to stop the effect on the neuron. There are also some molecules that act like neurotransmitters but do not obey all of these rules, including some neuropeptides or gases. While there are currently more than 50 identified neurotransmitters (or molecules such as neuropeptides that act like neurotransmitters), there are six major neurotransmitters and one major neuropeptide in the human body. They are listed in the following table.

Six Major Neurotransmitters and One Major Neuropeptide		
Name	**Symbol**	**Activities**
Acetylcholine	ACh	Most often in the periphery: motor neurons for skeletal muscles Learning, memory, problem solving, attention REM stage sleep onset
Dopamine*	DA	Controls voluntary movement (lack of DA is associated with Parkinson's) Involved in goal-directed behavior and motivation Reward and pleasant feelings Addiction: cocaine, amphetamines, and other drugs of abuse elevate DA Schizophrenia: elevated DA Depression: some antidepressants increase DA
Norepinephrine*	NE	Associated with mood and arousal (fight-or-flight response) Depression: some antidepressants elevate NE Addiction: some drugs of abuse elevate NE
Serotonin*	5HT	Most often found in the brain (#1) and in the gut (#2) Involved in biological regulation (sleep, eating, sex, pain perception) Involved in cognition (memory, learning) Involved in mood (aggression, depression, anxiety) Most medications for depression and obsessive-compulsion increase 5HT
Histamine*	H	Affects arousal and attention Affects immune response Influences food and water intake May affect blood flow in the brain
Gamma-aminobutyric acid	GABA	Primary inhibitory neurotransmitter in the body Many antianxiety, antiseizure, and sleep medications affect this system Many drugs of abuse (e.g., alcohol) affect this system
Endorphins		Neuropeptide Similar to opiate drugs in structure and its effects on the body Released by exercise, pain, positive social contact Creates pain relief, pleasurable emotions Many drugs of abuse hijack this pathway (e.g., heroin)

* Belong to a class of neurotransmitters called "monoamines" due to the shape of a single amino group connected to an aromatic ring

Within the nervous system, there are two major divisions: the peripheral and the central nervous systems. The **peripheral nervous system (PNS)** refers to the nerves that lie outside of the brain and spinal cord. Within the PNS, there are two subdivisions: the somatic and the autonomic systems. The **somatic nervous system** is made up of the nerves that control voluntary muscle movements (efferent nerves) and receive sensations from the body (afferent nerves). The **autonomic nervous system** is often referred to as the "involuntary" system, although recent research has shown that humans do have some control over these processes. Within the autonomic system there is the **sympathetic** system (which responds to stress to mobilize the body's resources) and the **parasympathetic** system (which returns the body to its normal state of balanced functioning, or **homeostasis**, after the stressor has passed). See the diagram in Figure 4-4.

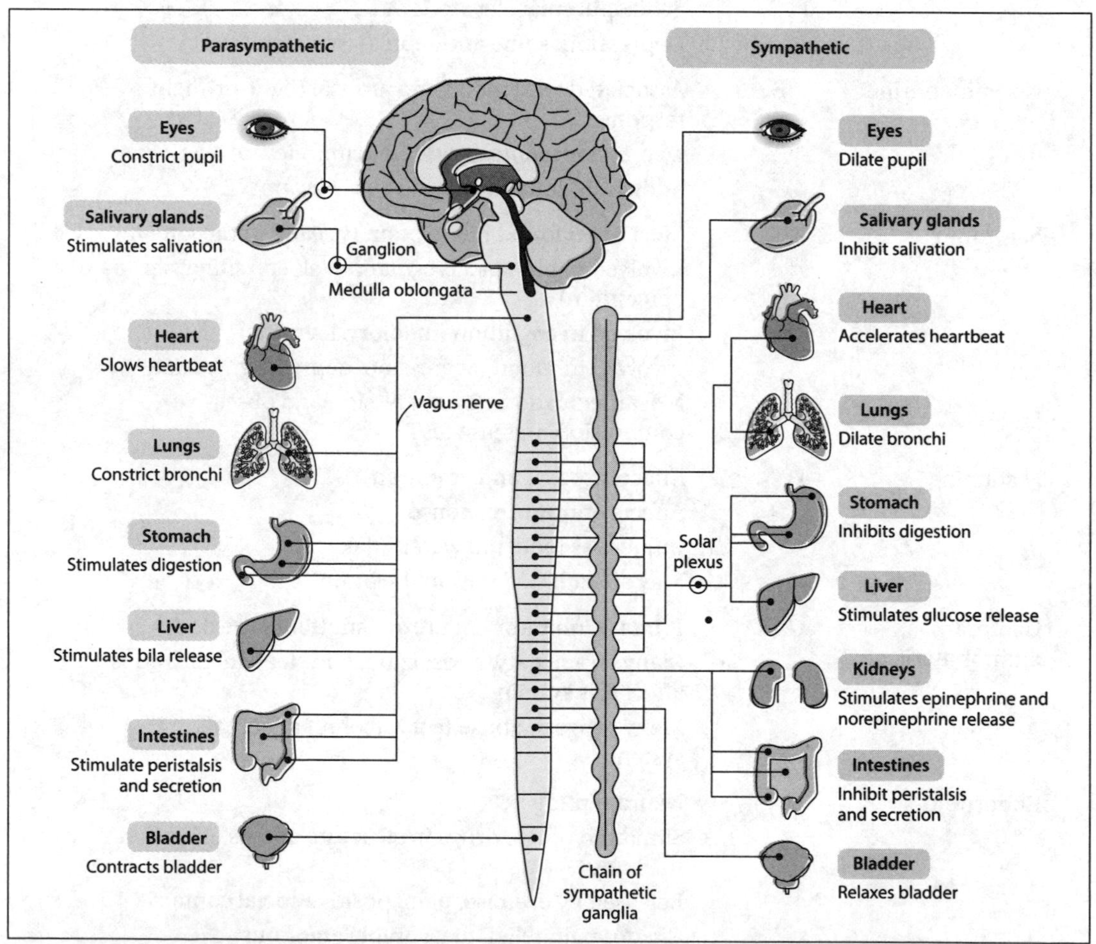

FIGURE 4-4 The parasympathetic and sympathetic nervous systems regulate organ function.

The **central nervous system** refers to the nerves that constitute the brain and spinal cord. The spinal cord carries both afferent (to the brain) sensory signals and efferent (from the brain) motor signals. The brain itself is divided into three major components based on their likely evolutionary development (see Figure 4-5).

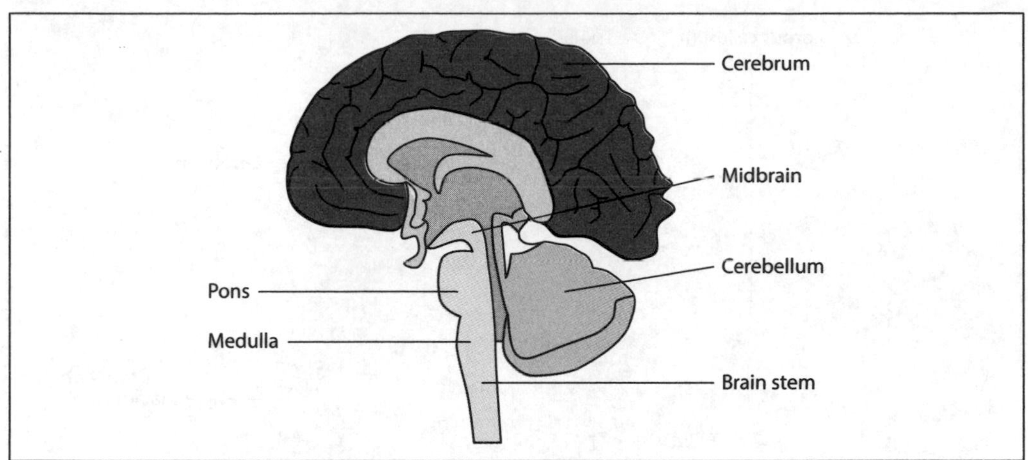

FIGURE 4-5 Sections of the brain.

- The **hindbrain** (or **brain stem**) is composed of the cerebellum, medulla, and the pons. The **medulla** controls many unconscious processes vital for life, including blood circulation, breathing, muscle tone, and reflexes. The **pons** includes areas involved in sleep and arousal. The **cerebellum** coordinates balance, movement, and the sense of equilibrium.
- The **diencephalon** sits between the brain stem and cerebrum in adult humans. It primarily comprises the **thalamus**, which acts as the primary relay station between the incoming sensory signals (except smell) and the brain, as well as the outgoing motor signals to the body. This is also the location of the **hypothalamus**, which is responsible for basic biological needs such as hunger, thirst, and temperature control for the body.
- The largest portion of the brain is called the **cerebrum** (or **forebrain**); this part sits under the skull and is responsible for sensing, thinking, consciousness, emotion, memory, and voluntary movements. The **limbic system**, the system closely associated with emotions, lies in the subcortical region of the cerebrum as do some structures such as the **hippocampus**, which is associated with memory. The cerebral cortex is the outer layer of the cerebrum with its many folds; it houses complex thought and consciousness. The right and left hemispheres are connected by the corpus callosum, a bundle of axon fibers that facilitates communication between the two sides of the brain. (See Figure 4-6.)

  The brain has four lobes (see Figure 4-7):

- The **occipital lobe** processes visual information.
- The **parietal lobe** receives the afferent signals from the body and processes physical sensations via the **somatosensory cortex**.
- The **temporal lobe** contains the **primary auditory cortex**, which processes auditory signals. **Wernicke's area**, the part of the brain responsible for language and speech comprehension, is located in the left temporal lobe.

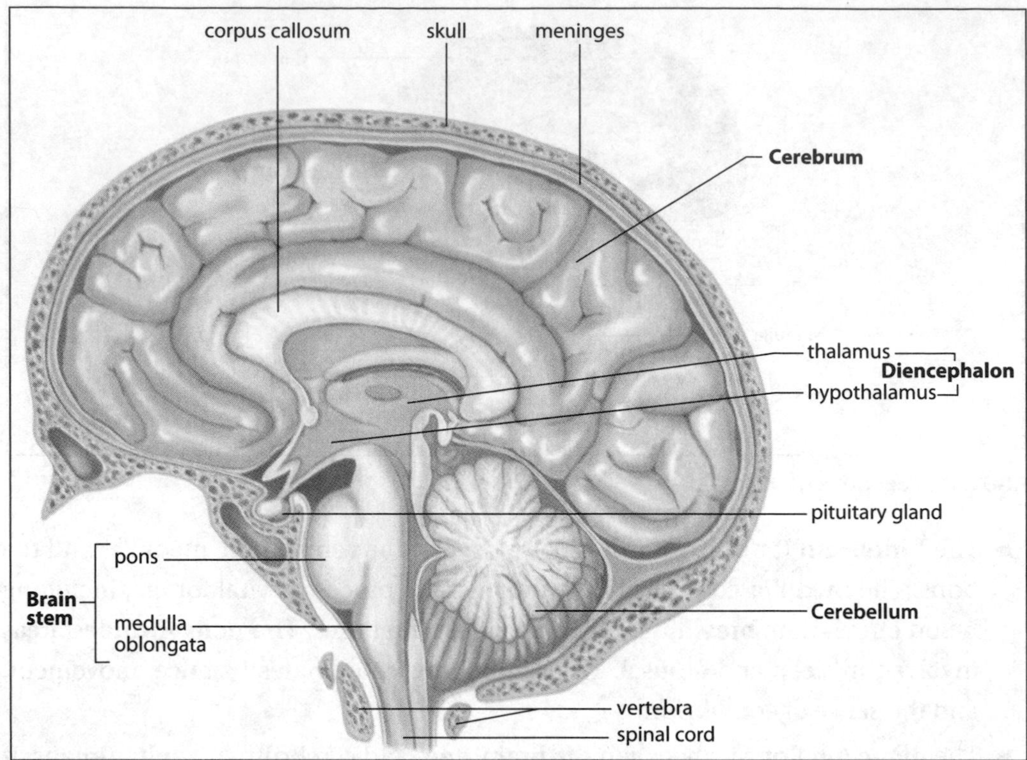

FIGURE 4-6 Brain structure. The cerebrum of the brain is divided into right and left hemispheres connected by the corpus callosum. *Source*: From Sylvia S. Mader, *Biology*, 8th ed., McGraw-Hill, 2004, reproduced with permission of The McGraw-Hill Companies.

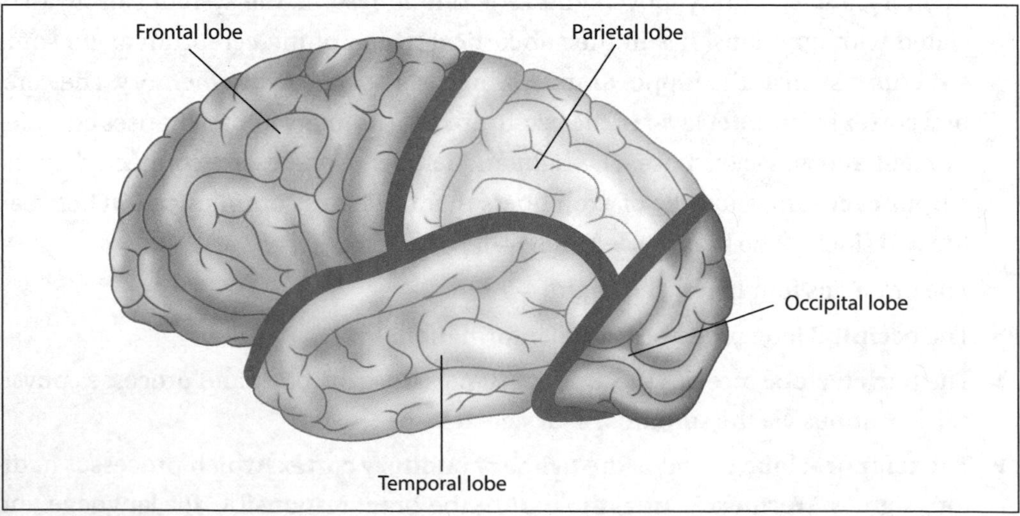

FIGURE 4-7 The cerebral lobes.

- The **frontal lobe** is responsible for "everything else." It contains the **primary motor cortex**, which lies adjacent to the parietal lobe's sensory cortex. The frontal lobe also houses the **prefrontal cortex** at the anterior portion of the brain. The prefrontal cortex is associated with a wide variety of higher-order cognitive functions, including judgment, problem solving, working memory, and attention. In general, it acts as the control system of the brain that determines how to synthesize complex information into organized and coherent thoughts.

THE ENDOCRINE SYSTEM

The endocrine system is a collection of glands that release hormones into circulation, sending signals to a wide variety of tissues, including organs, muscles, neurons, and even other glands, some of which are relatively far away from the glands (see Figure 4-8). The **hormones** are chemical communicators that travel through the bloodstream and transfuse into target cells. They are usually released in small pulsating bursts, sometimes based on circadian rhythms for regular maintenance of body systems, or in brief bursts that last only a few minutes for unusual situations. The **pituitary gland** is often called the master gland. It is located in the hypothalamus and often releases hormones that control how other glands release hormones. The endocrine system can have a strong influence on behavior. During times of stress, the fight-or-flight reaction is mediated by the pituitary gland, causing the adrenal glands to release adrenaline/epinephrine, which then prepares the body for an emergency. The gonadotropin hormones from the pituitary affect the gonads or sexual glands (testes and ovaries) during adolescent development, creating secondary sexual characteristics and heightened sexual interest. The thymus plays a critical role in the immune system. The thyroid controls energy use, protein production, and bodily sensitivity to other hormones. The parathyroid controls calcium use in the body. The pineal gland was once thought by the 17th-century French philosopher René Descartes to be the sole link between the mind and body. Today, however, it is recognized as having the critical role of releasing melatonin and assisting with the circadian rhythms of the body.

Some organs also have secondary endocrine functions and release hormones that affect distal tissues in the body. The pancreas releases insulin. The kidney releases hormones affecting blood pressure and urine concentration, which should not be confused with the adrenal glands that sit on top of the kidneys and release glucocorticoids among other hormones. The liver produces hormones that affect multiple areas of digestion and iron use in the body. The heart produces hormones to affect blood pressure and blood volume. Even adipose (fat) tissue releases hormones that affect energy storage and usage; recently it was also discovered that it releases low levels of the hormone estrogen as well.

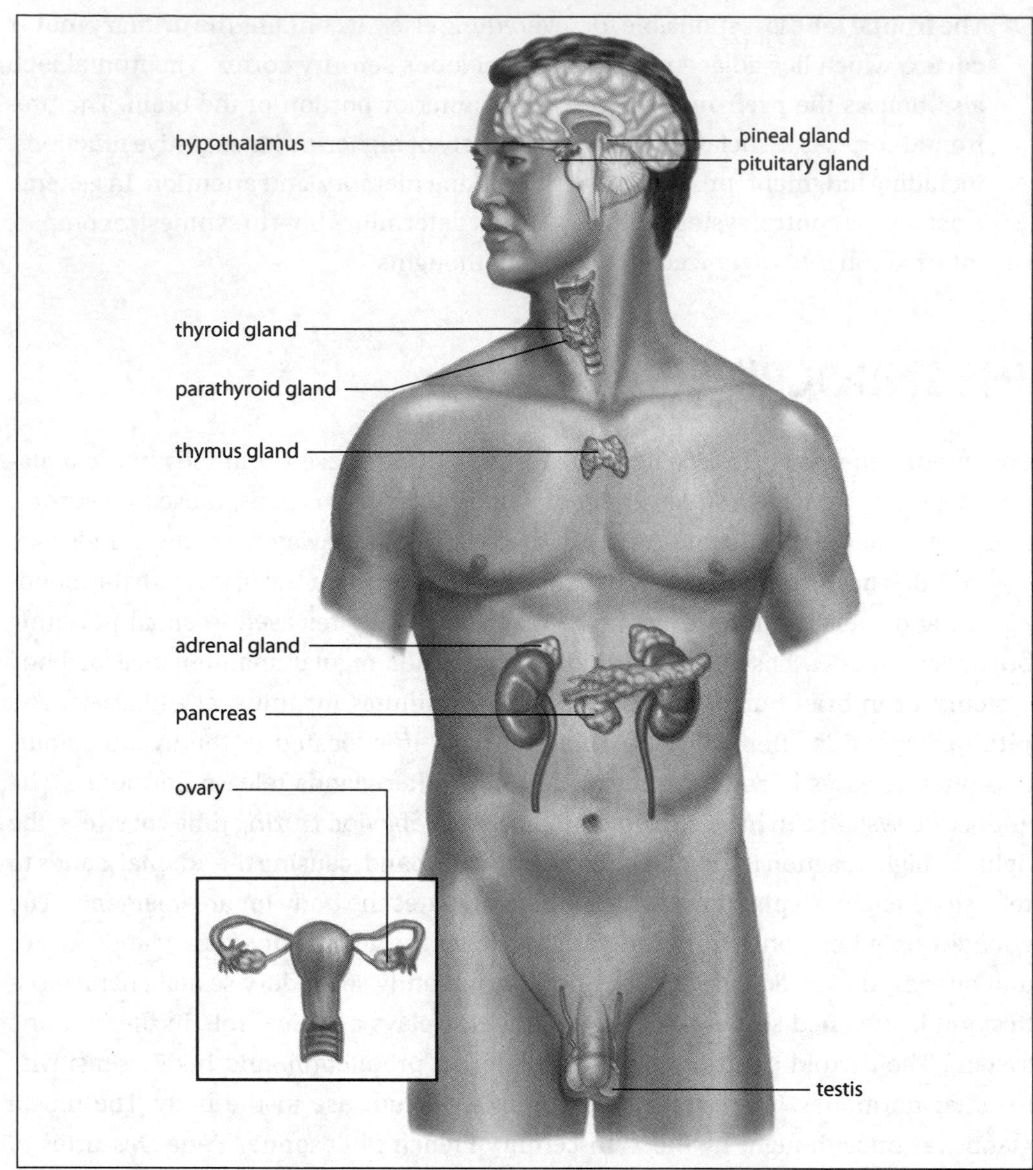

FIGURE 4-8 The endocrine system. Anatomic locations of major endocrine structures of the body. *Source*: From Sylvia S. Mader, *Biology*, 8th ed., McGraw-Hill, 2004, reproduced with permission of The McGraw-Hill Companies.

BEHAVIORAL GENETICS

Your genes interact with the environment to create temperament, behaviors, and cognitive ability, thus forming your physiological and psychological makeup. Heredity material is made up of chromosomes. Humans have 46 chromosomes (23 pairs). Each parent contributes one chromosome to each pair, which means that a child has 50 percent genetic relatedness to each parent. Identical twins share 100 percent of their genetic material as a single zygote split into two separate individuals. Fraternal twins come from two separately fertilized eggs and share genetic similarity as any two siblings (50 percent). Each chromosome contains thousands of genes. Genes are biochemical components of DNA that are key in transmitting hereditary material. Your **genotype** is your genetic makeup. Your **phenotype** is the observable expression of those genetics.

It should be noted that behavioral genetics has a difficult history. Sir Francis Galton, one of the first behavioral geneticists in the 1800s, believed that all of an individual's mental and physical health could be described by his or her genetic makeup. He proposed behavioral genetics in order to "explain" why the British upper class was supposedly more intelligent and enlightened than other ethnicities. Galton pioneered the field of eugenics that 20th-century fascist states later put to cruel misuse.

Abandoning the early history of the field, modern behavioral genetics is focused on how genetics affect behavior, cognition, and physiology and vice versa. There continues to be active discussion of "nature versus nurture" regarding how much of a person's character is caused by genetics and how much is caused by upbringing and environment. The most fundamental answer is that it appears to be the combination of genetics and environment that determines how an individual develops psychologically, behaviorally, and physically. It is likely that these characteristics are not controlled by a single gene, but are rather **polygenic traits**, determined by multiple genes. This means that adopted identical twin studies are the best way to answer nature–nurture questions. Identical twins (same genetic code) who have been adopted into different families (changing the environment of upbringing) are studied to identify correlations between temperament, cognitive ability, physical strength, and other individual factors. From these studies it has been determined that identical twins appear to have a 0.8 correlation for intelligence and a 0.5 correlation for personality traits. Interestingly, however, whether they are biological or adopted, children have only around a 0.2 correlation for intelligence with the parent(s) who raised them. Thus it appears to be a combination of genes and environment that governs the development of personality, physical skills, and behavior. Environment includes experiences, upbringing, and other external influences. The **diathesis-stress model** explains the relative impact of genes on mental health and behavior. This model proposes that an individual is set up with certain genetic characteristics that influence mental health (e.g., a susceptibility for depression). However, if external stressors (e.g., loss of a job, divorce) exceed the individual's protective factors (e.g., good self-esteem, social support), the genetic susceptibility may become a reality.

Of course, within any population there is a natural genetic variability. Some regulatory genes (genes that control the expression of other genes) may produce specific behaviors across cultures. These regulatory genes are more widely researched in nonhuman animals because techniques such as gene knockouts and cross-breeding make it much easier to control the genetic makeup and genetic expression of animals. However, regulatory genes are a likely factor in human behaviors such as basic facial expressions.

PERSONALITY

Personality can be defined and measured in a number of different ways. But across all definitions, it is generally seen as a robust set of reactions that make up how an individual interacts with the world. There are continuing disagreements between the major theories regarding how much a personality can be changed, and how much is due to nature versus nurture.

The **psychoanalytic** theory of personality was famously first espoused by Sigmund Freud. Under this model, the personality comprises three factors. The **id** is the most basic element of personality (e.g., What do I want?). It is the primary information processor and is strictly ruled by the pleasure principle. The id is largely unconscious and cannot be changed. The **ego** is the secondary level of processing. It is based in the reality principle (e.g., What can I get away with? or What do I need to do?). The individual is marginally conscious of this level of processing, but the ego cannot really be changed. The third and highest level of processing is the **superego** (e.g., What should I do?). It is somewhat conscious and the most susceptible to change via psychotherapy. The superego often mediates the relationship between the id and the ego.

Humanistic personality theory arose in reaction to Freud's psychoanalytic personality models. The American psychologist Carl Rogers is known as founder of this field. He based his personality model on five primary statements:

1. Humans can be viewed only as gestaltic beings, and cannot be broken into independent parts.
2. Humans exist within their human community and within the larger cosmos.
3. Humans are self-aware and conscious, which makes them unique among animals.
4. Humans can choose their behavioral reactions to situations, and because of that awareness, they are also responsible for their behavioral choices.
5. Humans are continually pursuing future self-actualization by expanding their creativity and finding meaning in events.

Under this theory, mental health issues occur when individuals either do not take responsibility for their actions (4) or they are hampered from developing and growing as a human (5). In Rogers' view, psychotherapy can be very useful in changing negative personality characteristics to positive.

One problem with these two personality trait theories is that they rarely had research to support the assumptions they were based on (although there have been attempts to perform such research in the modern era). In contrast to the preceding theories, the **five-factor model** by Robert McCrae and Paul Costa was based on empirical research from the earliest development of the model. According to this model, personality includes multiple durable traits that explain behavioral reactions, and these reactions are maintained even across a wide variety of situations. Furthermore, personality characteristics group into five basic dimensions: extraversion, neuroticism, openness to new experience, agreeableness, and conscientiousness. A person's personality is defined based on his or her scores on each of the five factors. This model is widely used in industrial-organizational psychology, human resources, and career counseling.

The **social-cognitive theory**, developed by Albert Bandura, grew out of behaviorism. It was originally called social-learning theory, but the name was changed as the researchers came to understand how social influence affected cognition in general, not just learning. Bandura's model identifies how personality is shaped by social reaction to the individual. In this model, three aspects interact with each other to develop personality: behavior, environment, and cognitive factors. Bandura also emphasizes the importance of people's ability to understand how current actions affect the future and to plan accordingly. The individual's feelings of **self-efficacy**, or beliefs that his or her actions will achieve some planned future outcome, have gained increasing attention. A person who believes that his or her actions can affect the future, and who can apply future planning to the interacting three factors, can not only express a personality but also change that personality. Under this theory, a person who chooses to make personality changes can do well in psychotherapy.

While genetics likely interact with environmental characteristics to develop personality (as discussed in the previous section), it is unclear to what extent various aspects of biology impact personality. The German-born psychologist Hans Eysenck was a strong believer that personality is determined by a person's genes. His model proposes that there are only three personality factors: extraversion (sociable, outgoing), neuroticism (nervous, anxious), and psychoticism (egocentric, antisocial). Eysenck's model has mixed support. His three personality factors are not widely supported, but his view of the influence of genetics on personality is supported. Some adopted twin studies suggest that 40 to 58 percent of personality traits are genetically heritable.

PSYCHOLOGICAL DISORDERS

The definition of psychological disorders is somewhat culturally bound. There are some disorders that seem to occur only in specific cultural contexts (e.g., Hwa-Byung in Korean culture, or anorexia nervosa in affluent Western cultures), while others seem to cut across cultures (e.g., depression). When psychological disorders do arise, there are two major approaches to treatment.

The **biomedical approach** identifies genetic and chemical reasons for the disease state and attempts to counter these dysfunctions solely with medications. This approach has been the traditional approach in medicine, but it is losing ground as people develop a better understanding of the multiple factors that affect human health.

As medicine and psychology have grown increasingly sophisticated, there is a recognition that the old Cartesian dualistic belief that the body and the brain do not interact is completely faulty and may in fact do patients more harm than good. Today the increasingly supported approach to mental and physical health is the **biopsychosocial approach**. This approach is based on the idea that one needs to understand a person's biological, psychological, and social circumstances in order to identify the appropriate treatment for that person. It also includes the understanding that the appropriate treatment may not involve any biochemicals. For example, there is significant research that shows that cognitive-behavioral therapy is more effective in the treatment of depression than antidepressant medication. These studies also show that both psychotherapy and antidepressants create the same changes in the brain as measured by fMRI. However, after stopping both treatments, the positive brain changes caused by psychotherapy persist for at least one year, whereas the similar changes caused by medication stop within two weeks. With serious and persistent mental illness such as schizophrenia, the best treatment approach is a combination of medication and psychotherapy, which is far more effective than medication alone to increase treatment adherence and improve rehabilitation.

Proponents of medications and psychotherapy, though taking differing approaches to treating mental health, have pragmatically agreed on classifying major psychological disorders. The ***DSM* (*Diagnostic and Statistical Manual*)** published by the American Psychiatric Association was the primary means for diagnosing mental health disorders up through version 4 (*DSM-IV*). However, the publication of version 5 (*DSM-5*) created a great deal of controversy due to what some felt was overwhelming influence on the diagnostic criteria by pharmaceutical companies, and it has since lost a great deal of its following among mental health providers. Instead, many mental health providers are moving to the ***International Classification Diseases* (version 10; *ICD-10*)** manual published by the World Health Organization. This publication is viewed as less influenced by pharmaceutical companies and more reflective of culturally bound mental health diagnoses.

The estimated prevalence rate of mental health conditions varies by country. Further, prevalence rate should not be confused with diagnosed rate as there are many individuals in the United States who do not receive a diagnosis or treatment for their mental health condition due to stigma, economics, or availability of treatment providers. Estimated annual prevalence rates for the US population are found in the following table. Note that more than one-quarter of US adults qualify for some type of mental health (emotional, behavioral, cognitive, and/or substance abuse) diagnosis.

Psychological Disorders Among US Adults	% of US Adults
Qualify for any mental health diagnosis	26.2%
Nonsubstance-related mental health diagnosis	18.6%
Major depressive disorder	6.9%
Bipolar disorder	2.6%
Schizophrenia	1.1%
Anxiety disorder (PTSD, panic, general anxiety)	18.1%
Personality disorder	9.1%
Drug or alcohol abuse/dependence	8.7%

Data from National Institutes of Health

Types of Psychological Disorders

Anxiety disorders are associated with inappropriate escalations of the hypothalamus-pituitary-adrenal (HPA) axis that trigger the flight-or-flight response. There are increased feelings of being threatened and fearful emotions that the individual cannot control. There are multiple subtypes of anxiety disorders. Disorders that fall under this category include post-traumatic stress disorder (PTSD), panic disorder, phobias, obsessive-compulsive disorder, and generalized anxiety disorder. Neurochemically, this pathway is often associated with dysfunctions in the GABA system (the primary inhibitory system in the brain) or the serotonin system (the "feel good" pathway).

Somatoform disorders describe disorders that link physiological and psychological mental health. Somatoform disorders are often mistaken for disorders that some people intentionally create in order to gain something. For example, some people fake medical symptoms in order to support a lawsuit (**malingering**). Other people hurt themselves in order to create real medical symptoms, such as by injecting themselves with harmful bacteria in order to gain sympathy (**factitious disorder**; what used to be known as Munchausen's syndrome). True somatoform disorders are *not* intentional. The individual actually experiences the symptom (sometimes in the context of a diagnosable medical condition) which can be exacerbated or alleviated by the individual's psychological condition. Conversion disorder is an example of this; the individual experiences a severe trauma and then loses function in a body part. It should also be noted that *all* pain conditions (even those in diagnosed disease states) include a somatoform component because a person's emotional state, depression, anxiety, social support, and other psychosocial factors have been shown to strongly affect that person's pain experience.

The term **mood disorders** includes any mental health diagnosis that is affected by depression (e.g., major depression disorder, dysthymia, bipolar depression, seasonal affective disorder). Symptoms of these disorders can be classified into two categories, emotional-cognitive and vegetative symptoms. Emotional-cognitive symptoms include feelings of sadness, irritability, anger, low self-esteem, slowed processing speed, and low motivation. Vegetative symptoms include changes in sleep, sex drive, appetite, and increased fatigue. When assessing depression in patients who are medically ill, it is important to focus on the emotional-cognitive symptoms because the vegetative symptoms of depression may be caused or exacerbated by the medical illness. The etiology of mood disorders may be related to structural changes in the brain, genetic prevalence, and cognitive patterns. The idea that has received the most attention for pharmacological treatment is the monoamine hypothesis. This is related to the concept that mood disorders are related to too small or too large amounts of monoamines. Monoamines are a class of neurotransmitters that include serotonin, dopamine, and norepinephrine. These three neurotransmitters are the basis for most pharmacological treatments of depression.

Schizophrenia disorders involve a complex series of symptoms that are divided into positive and negative symptoms. Positive symptoms are those that are "additive"—and seen with greater prevalence among those with schizophrenia; these include hallucinations, delusions, emotional disturbance, and disorganized speech. Negative symptoms are those that show diminished functioning compared to healthy individuals; these include cognitive symptoms such as diminished problem solving and diminished adaptive behavior, social symptoms such as social withdrawal and diminished humor appreciation, and emotional symptoms such as flat emotions and apathy. Pharmacological treatment is generally better at addressing positive symptoms than negative symptoms. Schizophrenia usually occurs in early adulthood (before 25 years old). Full onset is colloquially known as a **schizophrenic break**, though often **prodromal** symptoms occur before the full onset of schizophrenia. Remission of symptoms can occur. An individual has a better chance of remission if onset is fast and later in life with few negative symptoms, and if the individual had good social and occupational engagement prior to onset. There does appear to be a genetic component. Those who have a first-degree relative with schizophrenia have a 9 percent chance of developing the disorder, with up to 80 percent chance among identical twins if one twin is diagnosed with schizophrenia. By contrast, the general population risk level is 1 percent. Neurochemically, schizophrenia has been traditionally associated with the **dopamine hypothesis**, which suggests that overactivity is related to a specific receptor subtype of dopamine (D_2), especially in the mesolimbic dopamine pathway, and too little dopamine in the mesocortical pathways. Glutamate (a major excitatory neurotransmitter in the brain) has also been implicated in recent research, as has serotonin and GABA (a major inhibitory neurotransmitter). There has also been some research implicating malfunctioning sodium channels.

Drug addiction, substance abuse, and other addictive behaviors affect approximately 9 percent of the US population. Frequently, addiction is to substances, but more recently, researchers have begun looking into addictive behaviors (e.g., gambling, internet addiction). Both substance addiction and addictive behaviors hijack the dopamine pathways and increase transmission of dopamine. Dopamine pathways are associated with the brain's reward system. Increasing dopaminergic activity makes the individual feel good and desire to keep repeating the behavior or substance use.

There are also a number of progressive nervous system disorders that show a gradual loss of functioning. **Alzheimer's disease** is a progressive dementia that affects a patient's memory and cognition. Most diagnoses of Alzheimer's occur after the age of 65; however, some early-onset cases can occur in the late forties. Early-onset cases appear to have a more genetic component compared to late-onset cases, and some specific genetic risk factors have been identified. Short-term memory is initially affected, and as the disease progresses, the individual will eventually have difficulty with encoding and recalling long-term memories as well. Other symptoms that arise as the disease progresses include mood swings, confusion, irritability, and aggression, and in the advanced stage, communication difficulties. The body appears to "forget" how to function over time. Therefore, while Alzheimer's is rarely a direct cause of death, its presence contributes to a number of other physical maladies (e.g., infected bedsores, pneumonia) that can be a direct cause of death. Multiple etiologies for Alzheimer's have been proposed and are being actively pursued in research. At present, two possibilities appear to have the most support. The first is that inefficient enzymes fail to adequately break down beta-amyloid, which develops into fibrillar plaques that inhibit learning and enhance neuronal decay. The second hypothesis posits that abnormal tau-amyloid proteins develop into neurofibrillary tangles within the cells that disrupt intracellular communication and cause cell death.

Parkinson's disease is officially identified as a movement disorder. It is characterized by tremors when a patient is not actively moving. Onset usually occurs in the fifties; however, early onset is also possible (e.g., actor Michael J. Fox's publicized battle with early-onset Parkinson's). Over time, the tremors progress to difficulty with motor movement, motor "freezing," and a shuffling walk. Cognitive changes are likely to occur as the disease progresses, including difficulty with executive functioning (e.g., planning, organization), difficulty with attention and memory, and slowed processing speed. Visual-spatial abilities also decrease. Psychologically, depression, apathy, and anxiety are common comorbidities. The symptoms of Parkinson's are triggered by the death of dopamine-producing cells in the substantia nigra. The cause of the cell death is unknown, although smoking, genetic heredity, and exposure to some pesticides are risk factors. As the dopamine-producing cells die, there is too little dopamine (D_2 again) in the nigrostriatal pathway that is associated with motor control. Pharmacological treatment attempts to increase the amount of dopamine in the system. However, the delivery systems for medication are difficult. The medicine may be intended for the nigrostriatal dopamine pathway, but it can also affect the mesolimbic dopamine pathway (associated with schizophrenia, addiction, and impulse control behavior). So pharmacological treatment of Parkinson's is a delicate balancing act between controlling the symptoms of the disease and the unintended side effects of treatment.

Research for each of these disorders is ongoing. Particularly exciting is the potential use of stem cells to slow down or stop disease progress. It may be possible to regenerate neurons in the central nervous system (something thought almost impossible only 20 years ago) to slow the progress of the disease. Research also continues to focus on identifying the etiology of these diseases, because if researchers do not understand the cause of the cell death, they may not be able to stop the same process from occurring with the new neurons. Regardless, stem cells show great promise in future treatment of these diseases. Even if stem cell use only slows the progress of the disease, it would provide significantly improved quality of life for patients.

Autism spectrum disorders (ASD) have gained increased attention in the past 20 years and have become the focus of many educators, researchers, and child advocates. They are a combination of developmental disabilities that affect communication abilities, social interactions, and stereotypic or repetitive behaviors. In the past, ASDs were referred to separately as pervasive developmental disorder, childhood disintegrative disorder, autism, and Asperger's disorder. The Centers for Disease Control and Prevention (CDC) estimates that approximately 1 in 68 children will be born with ASD, with a five times greater prevalence in boys (1 in 42) than girls (1 in 168). The exact cause of ASD is unknown, though it is believed to have a combination of environmental and genetic causes. Some research has found structural irregularities in the brain, and other research has implicated neurotransmitters (e.g., serotonin) or hormones (e.g., oxytocin). ASD is known to have a heritable component, and an identical twin's likelihood of diagnosis when the other twin was diagnosed is up to 90 percent. However, research is preliminary and ongoing. Treatment for ASD is usually a combination of educational or behavioral interventions (such as applied behavioral analysis), family psychotherapy, and medications such antidepressants, antianxiety drugs, anticonvulsants, antipsychotics, and stimulants. Some early research supports the use of nutritional or dietary interventions to address disruptive or aggressive behavior.

MOTIVATION

A number of theories attempt to explain what motivates people to achieve certain actions. The theories range in coverage from basic motivations to more complex ones, and they are not necessarily mutually exclusive. As has been seen in other areas of research, often each theory contains a piece of the truth, which is then folded into newer theories as a field develops.

Instinct is the most fundamental motivator. It may be completely unconscious, but it impels humans to act and respond in specific ways. Evolutionary psychologists often point to genetics and evolutionary pressures to identify the role of instinct in human behaviors. The human sexual drive may be considered an instinct. The fight-or-flight response may also be instinctual. Both of these instincts push people to preserve their lives and propagate their genes.

Beyond basic motivation, **drive reduction** serves as a higher-level motivator for human behavior. A drive is an internal state of discomfort. A person who wants to relieve that discomfort will set out to accomplish the tasks necessary to reduce the discomfort. Discomfort may occur at a basic level (e.g., "I'm cold, so I need to find my coat."), or it may be more complex (e.g., "I need to achieve X level of productivity so I'll feel comfortable that I won't lose my job."). Discomfort may be related to elevation in the hypothalamus-pituitary-adrenal axis, with increases in stress hormones (e.g., adrenaline, cortisol) applying some of the biological pressure.

Positive arousal may also serve as a complex motivator. Increased goal-directed activity resulting in a positive outcome is likely to release a dopamine cascade in the brain (e.g., the "reward pathway"). Thus an individual experiences significant neurochemical arousal as a reward (along with possible social and psychological rewards) that reinforces the goal-directed behavior. This pathway may also be hijacked and used for drug or alcohol abuse. If the goal-directed behavior produces an artificial flood of dopamine due to drug use, the goal-directed behavior "get more cocaine" will be reinforced.

Other aspects of motivation also need to be considered. The presence of possible **incentives** (external rewards that can motivate behavior) can motivate a person to achieve certain tasks (e.g., "If I win that scholarship, I will be able to go to the school I want."). There may be **affiliation** motivators (e.g., "I don't want to go to that movie, but my friends want to go and I want to be with my friends.") and **cognitive** motivators based on active processing and weighing information from past experiences (e.g., "I know that if I eat a candy bar now, it will just be unhealthy quick energy and I will be hungry and uncomfortable again soon. So I will wait until dinner.").

Some theories attempt to explain human needs and motivations on a larger scale. One of the most famous was developed by the American psychologist Abraham Maslow and is known as **Maslow's hierarchy of needs** and is shown in Figure 4-9. Maslow postulated that a person's ultimate motivation is for self-actualization, but self-actualization cannot occur if more fundamental needs are not fulfilled first. The needs listed in Maslow's hierarchy move upward from basic physiological needs (food, water), to safety concerns, to social connections, to self-esteem, and finally to self-actualization. Only when a lower level of the pyramid is attained can an individual focus on progressing to the next step.

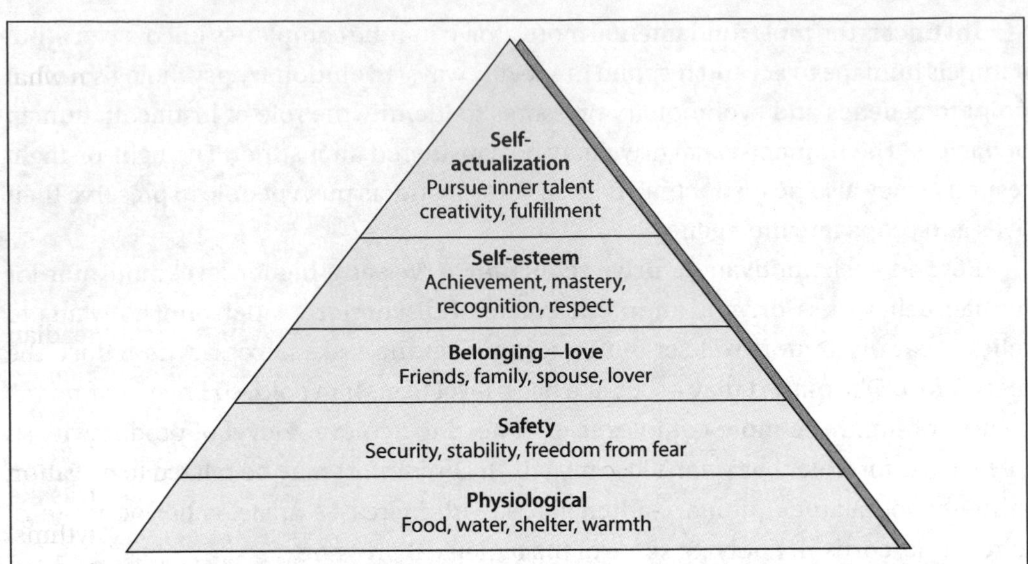

FIGURE 4-9 Maslow's hierarchy of needs.

Many of these motivators have biological underpinnings. The biological drive for food is located in the hypothalamus. In rats, when the lateral hypothalamus was lesioned, the rats showed no interest in eating. However, when the ventromedial nucleus of the hypothalamus was lesioned instead, the rats ate constantly regardless of calorie need. There are also a number of hormonal feedback loops that govern hunger levels and energy usage. Three hormones appear to have the strongest influence on food intake and fat storage: **insulin** (energy usage/storage), **leptin** (satiety hormone), and **ghrelin** (craving hormone).

Sexual activity and mate seeking are basic goal-directed behaviors that are strongly influenced by biology. Attraction to a sexual partner is at least partially related to pheromones and genetics. Research has shown that women during the fertile phases of their menstrual cycles prefer genetically different partners (e.g., nonfamily), but during pregnancy, they prefer genetically similar men (e.g., family), a preference that may be evolutionarily related to safety during pregnancy. However, the advent of modern hormonal birth control may cause some difficulties. Hormonal birth control causes the female body to mimic pregnancy and may change the focus of attractions. The scientific study of sexuality was initiated by the research team of William Masters and Virginia Johnson in the mid-1900s. Their groundbreaking research into human sexual behavior broke many taboo rules that existed at the time.

Many sociocultural factors also affect the expression of these motivational behaviors. For example, culture affects not just food choices, but also people's perceptions of what foods are palatable, their eating patterns (e.g., frequency, portion sizes), and their social interaction during meals. Culture also affects sexual expression. Culture may identify sexually taboo partners (e.g., a person married to someone else), influence sexual behavior (e.g., encourage or discourage kissing in public), or govern what behaviors are permissible (e.g., in approaching potential partners).

SLEEP

The biological rhythms of the body affect behavior and physiology. The circadian rhythms cause changes in the body based on the light and dark portions of the typical 24-hour day. The brain's "timekeeper" for these rhythms is the suprachiasmatic nucleus, which responds to light/dark information from the environment. Cognitive functions such as alertness and attention, as well as physiological functions such as the release of growth hormone and body temperature, are affected by circadian rhythms. Today those natural rhythms may be disrupted by electric lighting and by the light from television and computer screens. Circadian rhythms are also disrupted when people fly rapidly across multiple time zones. Research with rats even suggests that repeated or constant "jet lag" can cause premature death because of the elevated stress on the body. All of these artificial shifts in circadian rhythms create sleep difficulties and increased physiological stress on the body. They cause the body and brain to think that they should be awake, even when the nighttime goal is sleep. That causes confusion across a wide variety of physiological systems including cardiac functioning, digestion, hormone release, and other body functions.

The second system that affects sleep is the neurochemical-homeostatic system. When humans are awake, they use adenosine-triphosphate (ATP) for energy by breaking the bond of the adenosine molecule. When adenosine builds up in the body, it affects the suprachiasmatic nucleus and humans get sleepy. Further, caffeine is an adenosine receptor blocker, so the sleep messages cannot reach the suprachiasmatic nucleus. Adenosine continues to build up in the body, but there are no feelings of sleepiness until the "caffeine crash." The sleep researcher William C. Dement is the founder of the field of sleep medicine.

Within sleep there are four stages:

- The first stage is a light "cat nap" type sleep.
- The second stage is a deeper stage of sleep.
- The third stage is a critical stage called **slow wave sleep**. It is characterized by **delta wave EEG** readings. In this stage the body slows as much as possible, and achieves the slowest heart rate and lowest body temperature. It is during this stage that the greatest release of growth hormone, the most effective wound healing, and the most active immune responses occur. The third stage is critical to help maintain the body system. In the sleep laboratory, when this stage is disrupted, symptoms of nausea, muscular-skeletal pain, and headaches can occur. After the slow-wave

sleep stage, the body appears to begin to start waking up with increased blood pressure and heart rate.

- The fourth stage is REM stage sleep (rapid eye movement). This final stage of sleep is characterized by active (and occasionally bizarre) dreaming, **sleep paralysis** for the major muscle groups of the body, and quick darting movements of the eyes behind closed eyelids. This stage is thought to be particularly critical to memory consolidation, and the active dreaming experienced by the sleeper is part of this process.

Each sleep cycle takes 90 to 120 minutes on average, with more time spent in slow-wave sleep early in the night and more in REM stage sleep as the night progresses. In infancy, newborns will go through six to eight sleep cycles in a 24-hour period, and REM sleep accounts for 50 percent of the time in those sleep cycles, with an increased amount of time also spent in slow-wave sleep. As the individual grows to adulthood, 20 percent of sleep is spent in REM sleep and 20 percent is spent in slow-wave sleep.

Sleep deprivation is often underrecognized as a critical component to psychological and physiological well-being. Most humans need 7 to 9 hours of sleep per night. It is important to understand that not just sleep quantity, but sleep *quality* and coherent sleep architecture are critical to well-being. Most modern pharmaceutical sleep aids can be problematic in this regard because they may increase the quantity of sleep but decrease the quality of sleep. Sleep deprivation can have both psychological and physiological consequences. Psychologically, the individual experiences fatigue, irritability, decreased memory functioning, difficulty with decision making and problem solving, and increased stereotyping of others. Physiologically, there is an increased risk of obesity and type II diabetes, risk of heart disease, impaired immune response, and diminished growth or healing.

Insomnia is one cause of sleep deprivation. Stress is the most common culprit, with approximately 32 percent of Americans losing sleep at least one night per week due to stress. Other common etiologies of insomnia include caffeine overuse, late night electronics use with bright lights (e.g., TV, computer, smart phones), and sleep disorders. Polysomnography testing, psychotherapy (cognitive behavioral therapy for insomnia, or CBT-I), and sleep hygiene can each be useful for assessment and treatment of insomnia and other sleep disorders. Pharamacology can be useful in some instances but can cause sleep architecture disruption and should be monitored closely for potential abuse and dependence.

ATTITUDES

Attitudes can also be a large influence on behavior. An attitude is not a single factor. It is made up of three components. The cognitive component is made up of one's beliefs and ideas about the world. The affective component is the emotional reasoning that affects an attitude. Behaviors are made up of habits and activities that result from the attitude. It is important to note that behaviors derived from attitudes may be unconscious (or habitual) or they may be intentional.

Advertisers have long taken advantage of these attitude-behavior connections. They have used them to develop effective advertising techniques. One such technique is called **foot in the door**. In this technique, the prospective customer is first asked to accept a small and obvious proposal (e.g., "Do you want a nice car?"). A customer who accepts that proposal is then more likely to accept a greater (and more costly) proposal (e.g., Would you be willing to pay $50,000 for a Brand X car?). Another popular technique is called **door in the face**. In this technique, the prospective customer is first presented with an outrageous demand. Once the customer rejects the demand, he or she is then more likely to accept a lesser (and seemingly more reasonable) request. Even the offer of "free samples" to create a feeling of obligation to make a purchase (or provide a donation) is often used to encourage customers to buy. An additional frequently used technique is body language. Decreasing the amount of personal space between two individuals can increase an individual's persuasive power, so sellers may stand closer to perspective customers to persuade them to buy. These types of techniques can create changes in both attitudes and behaviors without customers realizing that they are being manipulated by their own cognitive defenses.

Cognitive dissonance theory was developed by the American social psychologist Leon Festinger. According to Festinger, individuals prefer to view themselves as acting in line with their beliefs (this is known as **self-perception theory**). When there is a disconnect between a person's beliefs and actions, the person will often change those beliefs or attitudes to align them with the actions. In the classic study exemplifying this theory, individuals were paid either 1 dollar or 20 dollars to tell other participants that a boring task is fun. Because people do not like to view themselves as misleading others, they searched for reasons for their behavior. Individuals who were paid a lot of money were able to point to the money as the reason for their behavior. But individuals who were paid only 1 dollar showed significant attitude changes, and during the post-experiment interview they reported they actually thought the task was fun. These people did not show any awareness of the influence of money on their change in attitude. This same effect has been shown repeatedly in multiple other studies.

CHAPTER 5

Social Processes That Influence Human Behavior

Read This Chapter to Learn About

- How Groups Affect Individuals
- Culture
- Socialization

HOW GROUPS AFFECT INDIVIDUALS

Humans are by nature socially oriented. The presence of others often affects how humans behave. The type of group situation (e.g., workplace), the number of people in the group (e.g., few versus many), and the individual's relationship to those in the group (e.g., strangers versus familiar people) all can consciously or unconsciously affect how individuals react.

Groups can create changes in the amount of effort an individual puts into a task. If the task is easy, performing it in a group increases the effort a person puts into completing a task. With simple tasks (e.g., single-digit math problems on a timed test), the individual performs tasks faster and more accurately in a group situation (**social facilitation**). However, if the task is more complicated, this often leads to **social loafing**, where the individual reduces his or her efforts on the assumption that other members of the group will step up to complete the task. (Anyone who has completed a group project in school has probably witnessed this effect firsthand.)

Even in critical situations such as an emergency, the presence of a large group will often cause individuals to delay stepping forward to help. This phenomenon is termed the **bystander effect**. Thus if you have an emergency, it is better to have only one or two people nearby to help rather than a crowd. With a crowd, you are likely to get a slower response because there is a **diffusion of responsibility** across the people in the crowd. The bystander effect often has to be drummed out of medical students early in their training, because in an emergency, the initial reaction is to stay back if there are others around.

The group can also alter how people view themselves. The larger the group, the greater the **deindividuation**, and the more likely an individual is to comply with the group and lose his or her inhibitions regarding participating in the group's activities. Large groups increase the feeling of anonymity and expand the **diffusion of responsibility**, making individuals less likely to consider the moral or long-term consequences of the group activities in which they participate. This phenomenon can be seen when individuals who would not normally behave in an antisocial way suddenly damage property, injure other people, and set cars on fire when they join fans rioting after a football team loses.

CULTURE

The definition of **culture** includes the customs, values, beliefs, and behavioral norms that are shared among a community and passed down to the next generation. Culture can play a major role in human responses, and multiple cultures may influence an individual at the same time. Culture, both singular and multiple, definitely affects human behavior, but which values are emphasized and how culture is expressed may differ from individual to individual. The culture into which a child is born is the **culture of origin** (e.g., natal family culture). For some multicultural individuals this may be a combination of two cultures (mother's natal culture + father's natal culture). The second culture type is one of **assimilation**, which is a culture that an individual immigrates to and consciously or unconsciously picks up (e.g. the new culture's language, values, and behavioral norms). Assimilation of this type is often a two-way street. Immigrants who assimilate into a dominant culture bring with them ideas, language, religious beliefs, and culinary choices that effectively leave their mark on the dominant culture as well. In a culture of **accommodation**, an individual understands and lives in a culture different from his or her own, but does not endorse the values and cultural norms of that culture. Finally, a culture of **adoption** is one intentionally chosen by an adult who consciously adopts those cultural norms and integrates into the lifestyle of the chosen culture.

The culture of origin affects how an individual initially views him- or herself and can have a lifelong effect on concepts such as self-worth and self-identity. Even if the individual later intentionally disengages from the natal culture, that culture remains the identity that the individual is rejecting; it is the stable cultural point that the individual is using as a reference for self-differentiation.

SOCIALIZATION

Cultural norms, values, and beliefs can be taught explicitly or implicitly. **Socialization** describes the process of disseminating and adopting cultural norms. There are multiple agents of socialization. The earliest is parental and family influence. As an individual ages, his or her peers and the media take a more active role in socialization. As the individual ages further, the choice of profession and workplace takes on a large role in socialization; the profession offers a specific set of behavioral norms and values. Actions taken within socially accepted norms are subtly (and sometimes more obviously) rewarded, encouraging the individual to continue to act and believe in a way that aligns with the group's social norms.

In addition to socialization, there are a number of other group-focused factors that may affect an individual's attitude and behaviors. **Conformity** to a group due to social pressures may cause an individual to adjust both internal attitudes and external behaviors. Solomon Asch performed a famous series of research studies that has shown that conformity (or peer pressure) can actually cause someone to change a correct answer on a task to a blatantly incorrect answer in order to conform to group norms. See Figure 5-1.

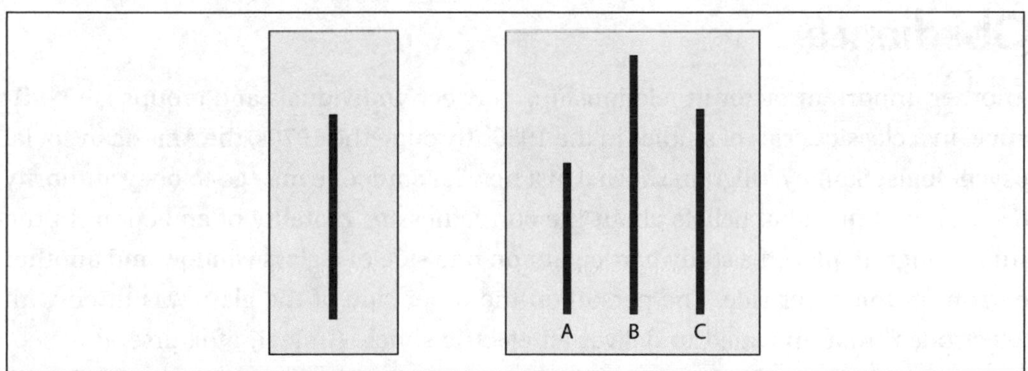

FIGURE 5-1 Solomon Asch's research study. Individuals were asked to match the length of the specimen line to one of the three next to it.

In his study he had individuals state whether lines were the same length or different lengths. When individuals performed the task alone, they had no difficulty identifying the correct answer. However, when there was one participant in a group with three confederates who chose the incorrect answer, the participant would change their answer to an obviously incorrect answer to conform to the group's response. The desire for the group to agree, even in the face of incorrect information, is also known as **group think**.

Groups can change how people solve problems and develop opinions. **Group polarization** is the process by which individuals in groups are likely to form opinions that are more extreme than those they would develop if they were considering the problem or opinion alone. This phenomenon can be viewed on a large scale in political rallies or on a small scale in class discussions. In both situations it has been observed that individuals leaving those group events are likely to espouse more extreme opinions than those they had prior to attending.

Deviance

People who deviate from social and cultural norms can feel out of step with those around them. Deviance can be either a form of individual expression or a type of antisocial behavior. Some psychologists recognize the concept of **positive deviance**, in which individuals break social rules in response to positive moral or values reasoning (e.g., a whistle-blower at a company that is dumping toxic waste into the city water supply). However, it is not uncommon for social deviants (even positive deviants) to experience punishment by the group in the form of social isolation, financial penalties, or other hardships.

Obedience

Another important factor in relationships between individuals and groups is **obedience**. In a classic series of studies in the 1950s through the 1970s, the American social psychologist Stanley Milgram showed just how far someone may go to obey authority regardless of personal beliefs about the correctness or morality of an action. In the study, Milgram placed a study participant on one side of a glass window and another person on the other side. The person on the other side of the glass was fitted with "electrodes" that appeared to deliver an electric shock. (In fact, of course, the electrodes were fake and the person wearing them was a research confederate.) The study participant was given an electric switch supposedly attached to the electrodes and told to punish the other person with increasingly powerful shocks (up to "XXX DEATH") every time that person answered a math question incorrectly. A surprising number of study participants obeyed the commands of the researcher to deliver electric shocks, even when they knew the shocks could or would harm the other individual. It should be noted that this study would not be allowed in modern times due to the extreme negative mental health impact on participants, and in fact it was one of the studies used to mandate the implementation of university institutional review boards (IRBs) to oversee research ethics.

There are certainly cultural influences on how far someone will go to obey authority. Even today, cultural obedience to authority has been implicated in tragedies ranging from airplane crashes to military actions. In general, while the United States has become a more individualistic society since the 1940s, the powerful influence of authority does not appear to have changed as much as people might have thought. Obedience can be reinforced further in some hierarchical professions.

Situational or **social power** can also have a surprisingly strong influence on attitudes and behaviors. In the Stanford prison experiment in the 1970s, Philip Zimbardo divided ordinary college students into two groups, the “guards” and the “prisoners.” By the end of the study, the guards were abusing the prisoners, even developing punishments not specified in the study. Thus even typical, educated young adults can quickly change attitudes and behaviors to conform to the situations, and those changes can lead to surprisingly cruel behaviors.

CHAPTER 6

Attitude and Behavior Change

Read This Chapter to Learn About

➤ Associative Learning
➤ Observational Learning
➤ Theories of Attitudes and Behavior Change

ASSOCIATIVE LEARNING

Associative learning is a specific type of learning. In this type of learning the individual learns to "associate" or pair a specific stimulus with a specific response based on the environment around them. This association is not necessarily a conscious process and can include involuntary learned responses (e.g., children in a classroom becoming restless at 2:55 pm on a Friday before the 3 pm bell). This category of learning includes classical conditioning and operant conditioning.

Classical Conditioning

Classical conditioning is one of the first associative learning methods that behavioral researchers understood. Classical conditioning has now been shown to occur across both psychological and physiological processes. Classical conditioning is a form of learning in which a response originally caused by one stimulus is also evoked by a second, unassociated stimulus. The Russian physiologist Ivan Pavlov and his dogs are most famously associated with this type of conditioning. Pavlov noticed that as the dogs' dinnertime approached (**unconditioned stimulus**, or **UCS**), they began to salivate (**unconditioned response**, or **UCR**). He found this unusual because the dogs had not eaten anything, so there was no physiological reason for the increased salivation before the dinner was actually served. Pavlov then experimented with ringing a bell (**neutral stimulus**) before feeding his dogs. As a result, the dogs began to associate the (previously neutral) bell sound with food and would salivate upon hearing the bell. The bell became a **conditioned stimulus (CS)**, and the salivation response became a **conditioned response (CR)**. This experiment is diagrammed in Figure 6-1. The learning process needed to connect previously unconnected stimuli (neutral stimuli) and responses is what changes a UCS to a CS and a UCR to a CR.

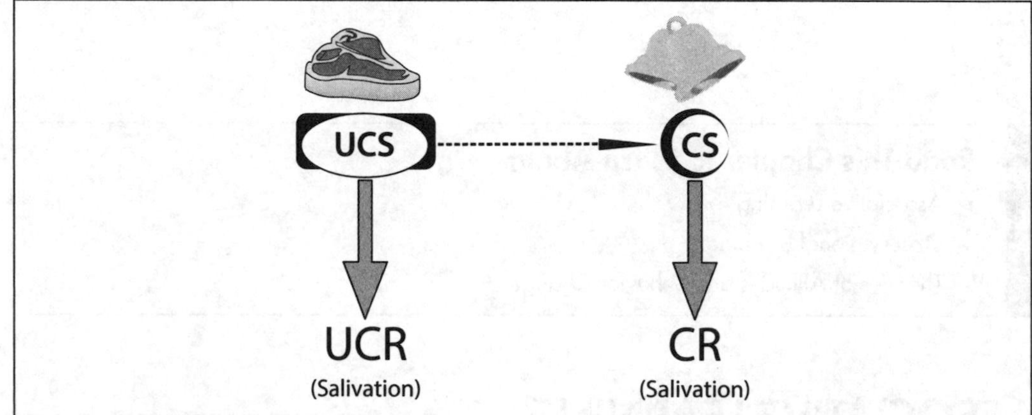

FIGURE 6-1 Classical conditioning.

Learning to connect neutral stimuli to a conditioned response is the process of **acquisition**. If the CS and CR are repeatedly connected, the CR will remain strong. However, if the CS (e.g., the bell sound) occurs repeatedly without the UCR trigger (e.g., the food), eventually the CR will diminish in response to the CS and then stop altogether in a process known as **extinction** (and the CS will once again become a neutral stimulus). **Spontaneous recovery** can occur if there is a delay in which the CS does not occur and the CS is presented again. After the delay, when the CS is again presented, the CR will occur again, weaker than before but still present.

Generalization can also occur with the CS. This is the process of expanding the parameters of the CS to include other stimuli (e.g., the dogs begin to show CR in response to a bell, a clicking noise, and a tone). The psychologist John B. Watson and the case of Little Albert is a classic example of this phenomenon. Dr. Watson gave 11-month-old Albert a white rat. The child was playful with the rat until Watson struck a loud gong (UCS) near the child's head, which caused pain (UCR). Quickly the child began to associate the rat with the pain of the gong and began to show a fear response (CR) to rats (CS). Soon he also **generalized** this fear response (CR) and began to show fear in the presence of white rabbits, white fur coats, a white dog, and Santa Claus beards, even though the gong was never used in the presence of those items. The process of generalization is the opposite of **discrimination**, in which the individual shrinks the parameters of the CS, requiring it to be more specific to show the CR.

Classical Conditioning in Advertising

The concept of classical conditioning is widely used in advertising. A new product is initially a neutral stimulus. In a commercial, the product (neutral stimulus) is shown being used by young, active healthy people having a great time (UCS), whom the viewer desires to emulate (UCR). Over time, the previously neutral product becomes associated with the desire to be like the people in the commercial. At that point the product becomes a conditioned stimulus, and the desire to emulate the people in the commercial is a conditioned response. Figure 6-2 shows a diagram of this example.

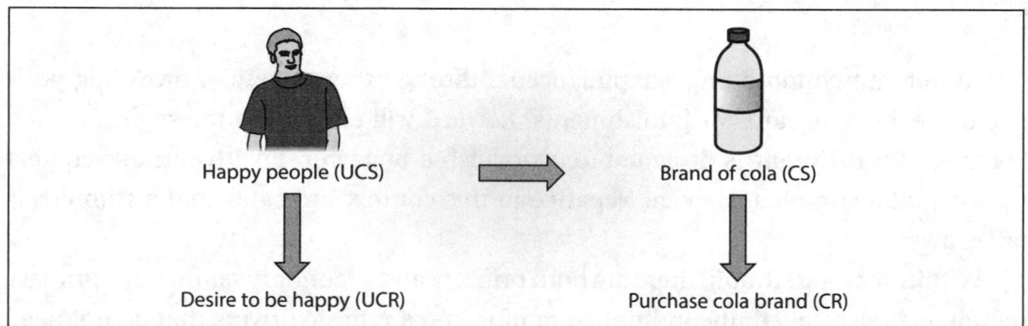

FIGURE 6-2 Classical conditioning in advertising.

Acquired fears or phobias are also often explainable through classical conditioning. For example, suppose an individual on an airplane flight experiences turbulence (UCS) and has a fear response (UCR). The individual generalizes from that one flight to all flights and has a severe fear response (CR) at every thought of another airplane flight (CS). Unlike other types of learning, phobias can be acquired quickly (often after one negative experience), generalize rapidly, and resist normal extinction.

Even physiologically, a person who experiences morning sleepiness is more alert (UCR) after drinking caffeinated coffee (UCS). After a while, just walking into the coffee shop (CS) where he or she buys morning coffee makes that individual feel more alert and awake (CR). The CS of the coffee shop creates the CR of wakefulness even before that first sip of coffee.

Operant Conditioning

Operant conditioning is a slightly more complex form of associative learning, but it is very visible in daily living as a way in which individuals connect behavior to positive and negative outcomes to create behavioral change (see the following table). Operant conditioning is defined as a method of learning that shapes behavior via rewards and punishments for individual actions. The individual learns that consequences are experienced as a result of certain actions and then shifts behavior to gain more positive consequences. The behaviorists Edward Thorndike and B. F. Skinner are most closely associated with the current understanding of this type of learning.

Operant Conditioning		
	Positive	**Negative**
Reinforcement	Giving a pleasant experience (giving a favorite food)	Taking away an unpleasant experience (removing a shock)
Punishment	Giving an unpleasant experience (shock)	Taking away a pleasant experience (removing a favorite food)

In operant conditioning, shaping occurs through the process of providing positive or negative rewards or punishments. **Reward** will encourage the repetition of a behavior. **Punishment** is designed to extinguish a behavior. **Positive** in this context means that a stimulus is given. **Negative** in this context indicates that a stimulus is taken away.

Within shaping stimuli, there are both primary and secondary reinforcers. Primary reinforcers (also called unconditioned reinforcers) are basic drivers that do not need to be taught (e.g., food, sex, comfort). Secondary reinforcers (also called conditioned reinforcers) are reinforcers that the individual has learned to value (e.g., getting an A on a test).

Through the use of appropriate reinforcement or punishment, an individual's or animal's behavior can be **shaped**. Behavior can be reinforced and expanded, and it can also be **extinguished** with the use of punishment in response to the behavior. Reinforcers and punishments can be provided on a number of **reinforcement schedules** that can determine the speed of adoption or extinction of a behavior (see the following table).

There are many examples of operant conditioning in daily life. Casinos often use this technique to reinforce gambling behavior. The use of variable ratio reinforcement schedules (e.g., payouts) increases customers' gambling behavior and makes it more difficult for them to stop.

Variable and Fixed Reinforcement Schedules			
	Variable	**Fixed**	**General**
Ratio (behavior)	Reinforcer given after a varying number of displays of the behavior (e.g., a rat receives food after hitting the bar 1, 5, or 7 times)	Reinforcer given after a certain number of instances of the behavior (e.g., a rat receives food after every 3 bar presses)	Higher ratios (e.g., 1 food pellet for every 5 bar presses) result in higher response rates but are harder teach initially than lower ratios (e.g., 1 pellet for 1 bar press)
Interval (time)	Reinforcer given after a varying amount of time (e.g., food is released for a random amount of time that a rat spends in a particular space)	Reinforcer given after a fixed period of time (e.g., food is released for every 15 minutes that a rat spends in a particular space)	Shorter intervals (30 seconds vs. 2 minutes) creating a higher response rate
General	Variable schedules resulting in greater resistance later to extinguishing of the behavior	Behaviors shaped by fixed ratios being easier to extinguish later	

When an individual is in a distressing situation, the Hypothalamus-Pituitary-Adrenal (HPA) axis is activated, creating physiological discomfort. The individual then reviews the initial reason for the fear, creating psychological and cognitive discomfort. This combination of psychological and physiological distress creates an experience that the individual wishes to escape. This kind of operant learning is thus called **escape learning**, in which the individual learns to reduce exposure to a negative experience by escaping from a situation. The escape acts as a negative reinforcement of the escape behavior, a pattern that the individual is then likely to repeat. **Avoidance learning** is another powerful kind of conditioning. An individual may begin to avoid situations that cause fear and anxiety because avoidance reduces physiological arousal and psychological discomfort. Both escape learning and avoidance learning are very pertinent to the development and (later) treatment of anxiety disorders. If an individual is placed in conditions that create physiological and psychological distress, he or she learns to escape and later avoid the situation. Escape and avoidance then become reinforcing behaviors that can develop into phobic and anxiety disorders.

Operant conditioning is common as children grow and learn from their environment. For example, if a child has a temper tantrum and the parent gives in, the child learns that a temper tantrum will gain him or her something desirable, so this behavior is reinforced and the child is more likely to repeat it. This parental response is particularly reinforcing if the parent gives in only on random occasions (see earlier discussion on reinforcement schedule and extinction). Even when a parent stops giving in, the child is likely to increase the behavior temporarily in what is known as an **extinction burst** before the extinction phase begins. On the other hand, children who are rewarded randomly for good behavior will have their behavior shaped in a more positive direction.

Some innate behaviors are **developmentally fixed** and are extremely resistant to shaping strategies. A classic example of this is the "monkeys and M&Ms" study. In this study, researchers placed two amounts of M&M candies, one larger and one smaller, in a dish. They attempted to teach the monkeys that if they chose the smaller of the two amounts, they would receive the larger amount. In other words, the researchers attempted to shape the monkeys' behavior in direct opposition to the innate trait to pick the larger pile of candy. Despite multiple trials, and the monkeys' evident distress every time they picked the larger pile (and watched it go instead to the researcher), the monkeys had extreme difficulty going against their innate behavior. From this, the researchers concluded that some behaviors are so innate and fixed that reshaping them by conditioning is extremely difficult or impossible. Even when such behaviors are changed, the subject will often drift back to the innate behavior—a process the researchers called **instinctive drift**.

Another biological factor that is very difficult to shape is **conditioned taste aversion**. This condition occurs when a single negative food or drink experience creates a very long-term wish to avoid that food. For example, if a person eats spaghetti and later that evening comes down with a severe stomach flu, that person may experience a conditioned taste aversion to spaghetti and may never eat it again. This developmentally fixed avoidance behavior is likely self-protective; the body influences the taste buds to avoid foods linked to danger.

Even after a behavior is learned, it is not static and can be modified by ongoing experiences. Those subsequent experiences may either reinforce or extinguish the originally learned behavior, or alter the parameters of that behavior (e.g., when or where the behavior occurs). This is true across both human and animal behaviors. There are also a number of inherent cognitive processes that increase the likelihood of associative learning. Between life experiences and the human cognitive processes that try to find reasons for a particular outcome, specific behaviors can be reinforced. For example, if a person wears bright red socks to a test and gets an A, that person might attribute the A to the red socks. He or she would continue to wear the red socks to every test and gain test-taking confidence, which may lead to ongoing success and reinforce the idea of the "lucky" socks. This individual has associated the outcome (the A) with the action (wearing red socks) and seeks to repeat the outcome by repeating the action. This process is called identifying **contingencies** in the environment. Identifying contingencies begins to explain the interaction between cognitive processes and life experiences in the process of associative learning.

OBSERVATIONAL LEARNING

In contrast to associative learning/operant conditioning, in which the individual learns about stimuli-response from his or her own actions in the environment, **observational learning** is based on the individual watching how others interact with the environment.

Albert Bandura is the classic researcher associated with observational learning and modeling behavior. In Bandura's model of observational learning, there are four basic processes:

- **Attention** requires that the learner actively observes the model's behavior and the consequences of that behavior.
- **Retention** requires that the learner has the capacity to mentally store and recall those observations, perhaps even long after the initial observation.
- **Reproduction** is the learner's ability to transform the mental representations of that memory and to physically reproduce the observed behavior in the appropriate setting (which may be difficult; watching someone else play baseball doesn't help you pitch a fastball).
- Finally, the **motivation** (e.g., reinforcer) to engage in reproducing the response must be present.

Latent learning, pioneered by the American psychologist Edward Tolman, occurs when an individual is not intending to learn something but gains information passively. For example, children who are driven around in the car every day eventually learn to navigate their neighborhood even though they are not explicitly taught. Information gained in latent learning may never be used, or it may be used at some distant point in time.

Observational learning can be observed in both animals and humans. Children often observe and model the behavior of adults around them. In Bandura's famous "Bobo doll experiment," children between the ages of 3 and 5 observed how an adult interacted with a 5-foot-tall doll and then were given an opportunity to play with the doll. Children who observed adults punching or kicking the doll were much more likely to act aggressively and violently toward the doll compared to children who observed the adult acting gently and kindly toward the doll. The gender of the child or adult did not matter, but the type of behavior the adult displayed (violent versus kind) had a strong influence on the child's later behavior. These results are potentially relevant to physical abuse; psychological and sociological studies show that children who are physically abused are more likely to become physical abusers as adults.

It is critical to understand that the acquisition of a specific behavioral response may be very different from the performance of that response, and this is a crucial difference between operant/associational and observational learning. Skinner (operant conditioning) and Bandura (observational learning) both agree that motivation and reinforcement are critical to the development of behavior. But Skinner believed that reinforcement is critical to the **acquisition** of a behavior, whereas Bandura believed that learning from observing occurs regardless of reinforcement, though the **production** of the behavior relies on reinforcement.

The brain appears to be hardwired to engage in observational learning. In terms of evolution, humans are almost unique in the animal kingdom in that they explicitly teach their young. By comparison, most young animals simply acquire adult behaviors by observation. Even so, young humans still acquire many of their behaviors from observing adult models. **Mirror neurons**, located in the premotor cortex, the somatosensory cortex, and the inferior parietal cortex, are critical in the process of observational learning. These mirror neurons fire when the observed behavior and the action of the observer match. These mirror neurons are also implicated in mirroring facial expressions and emotions in others (e.g., an adult smiles at a 1-year-old infant and the infant smiles back). It is believed that this is why people share emotions with persons whom they do not know (e.g., feeling sad when a character in a film dies and the film characters are sad). It is also suspected that dysfunction of mirror neurons may at least partially account for the symptoms of autism spectrum disorders.

Examples of observational learning in human and animal behavior abound. For instance, birds learn to open sugar packets from outdoor coffee stands, children reproduce curse words from observing their older siblings, and young athletes review experts' techniques to improve their own performance. Children learn procrastination or timeliness from watching their parents. Even among adults, observing a friend making healthy food choices can influence an individual to make healthier choices.

THEORIES OF ATTITUDES AND BEHAVIOR CHANGE

Altering attitudes and behaviors can be a difficult and complex process. The elaboration likelihood model, developed by John Cacioppo and Richard Petty, is an empirically supported model that explains how attitude change can occur. Cacioppo and Petty identified two "routes" to processing information that is designed to create attitude change. The two routes differ by the level of cognitive elaboration or processing that is done by the individual. The first is the **central route**, which is focused on more cognitive and logical arguments that the individual ponders carefully. Persuasive tactics that take this route place more cognitive load (high elaboration) on the individual, but result in more long-lasting attitude change and better predict behavior. The second is the **peripheral route**, which is more focused on nonlogical environmental persuasion tactics (e.g., loud music, attractive models, simple slogans) that place less cognitive load (minimal elaboration) on the individual. The peripheral route can create attitude change, but it is less long-lasting and less predictive of behavior.

Albert Bandura's **social cognitive theory** is another way to explain attitude change. Bandura identified the role of **reciprocal determinism** (the "two-way street") in how individuals learn to interact with their environment. In this view, behavior, environment, and cognitive factors all interact with each other to determine which behaviors are reinforced (and are more likely to be repeated in the future). For example, suppose the environment includes an advertisement for a designer briefcase. A man who sees the advertisement thinks that the briefcase will help him look more professional and get a promotion, so he purchases the briefcase. If his boss offers the man a job before seeing the briefcase, the man might think, "That was a waste of money, I'll never do that again." Or he might think, "Perfect, the briefcase will look great in my big new office." So the cognitions interact with the environment to determine if the behavior of purchasing expensive clothing is likely to be repeated. The environment of the persuasive statement interacts with the cognitions of the individual to determine the effect on the outcome (behavior).

A number of specific intrapersonal factors can also alter how a persuasive message is received. The **source** of the message is one such factor. The individual's perception of the source's expertise, credibility, and likability affects how the message is received. Other factors relate to the message itself. These factors include whether the argument presented is one-sided or two-sided (and if a two-sided argument involves straw-man arguments), the level of logic versus emotion in the message, and any appeals to emotions (e.g., fear or hope). Finally the characteristics of the **receiver** can affect how the message is heard. The receiver's resistance to change, strong preexisting attitudes, and access to counterarguments can all decrease the likelihood of persuasion. It should also be noted that the "likability" of the source can be affected by the receiver's biases regarding race, gender, or other demographic and social factors. While altering attitudes and behaviors is extremely challenging, there has been a great deal of research in this area by social psychologists, health psychologists, and public health specialists who hope to use these techniques to encourage healthy behavior (e.g., smoking cessation). In addition, advertisers and politicians have studied persuasion techniques for business and political purposes.

Unit II Minitest

16 Questions **30 Minutes**

This minitest is designed to assess your mastery of the content in Chapters 4 through 6 of this volume. The questions have been designed to simulate actual MCAT questions in terms of format and degree of difficulty. They are based on the content categories associated with the foundational concept that is the theme of this unit. They are also designed to test the scientific inquiry and reasoning skills that the test makers have identified as essential for success in medical school.

In this test, most of the questions are based on short passages that typically describe a research study or some similar process. There are also some questions that are not based on passages.

Use this test to measure your readiness for the actual MCAT. Try to answer all of the questions within the specified time limit. If you run out of time, you will know that you need to work on improving your pacing.

Complete answer explanations are provided at the end of the minitest. Pay particular attention to the answers for questions you got wrong or skipped. If necessary, go back and review the corresponding chapters or text sections in this unit.

Now turn the page and begin the Unit II Minitest.

Directions: *Choose the best answer to each of the following questions. Question 1 is not based on a passage.*

1. Which personality theory characterizes personality as comprised by the interaction between three factors: the id, the ego, and the superego?
   A. psychoanalytic theory
   B. social-cognitive theory
   C. humanistic theory
   D. behaviorism

Questions 2–5 are based on the following passage.

Passage I

Research evaluating human performance under conditions of sleep deprivation has generally found that impaired functioning is observed during specific time intervals.

One such study used surveys to determine the characteristics of car accidents to evaluate the relationship between time of day and incidence of car accidents.

The following graph shows the number of accidents on the *y*-axis and the time of day on the *x*-axis.

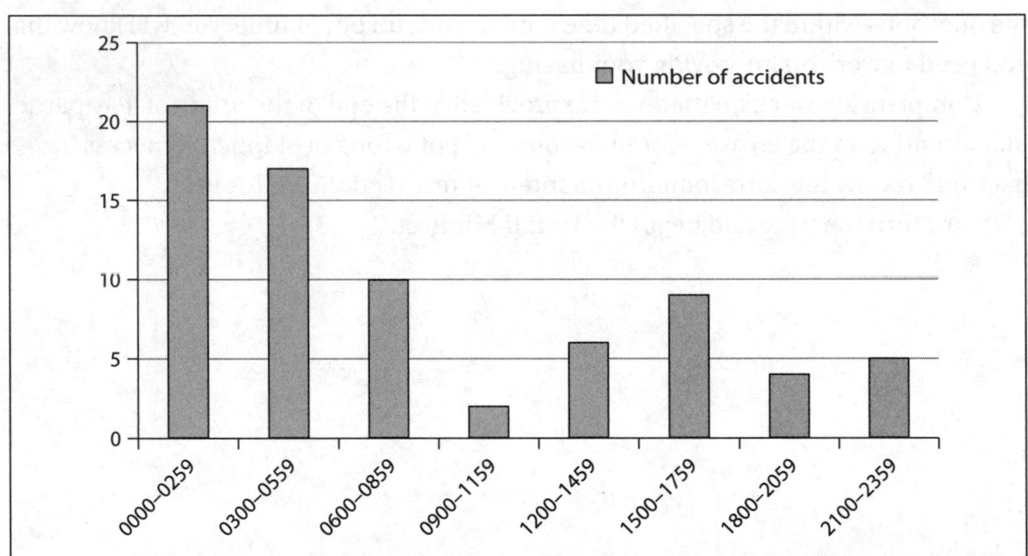

Number of accidents by time of day. *Source*: Adapted from Horne, J. A., & Reyner, L. A. (1995). "Sleep-related vehicle accidents." *British Medical Journal,* 310(6979), 565–567.

2. Based on the graph, which of the following is the MOST accurate statement?
   A. Time of day is not related to the number of accidents.
   B. Sleep deprivation has more impact during the day than at night.
   C. Accidents were more likely during the early morning.
   D. Accidents were more likely in the evening than at midday.

3. What would happen to performance results over time if a similar study was conducted in an artificial environment and in the absence of circadian cues such as light?
   A. The accident peaks would drift to the left on the graph with a slightly shorter circadian cycle.
   B. The accident peaks would drift to the right on the graph with a slightly longer circadian cycle.
   C. There would be no change in the cycle, and the increased risk of accident would occur at the roughly the same time.
   D. There would be a breakdown in the cycle, and accidents would be equally likely to occur in any time frame.

4. Why might you expect the results to this study to remain consistent even for people who are time-shifted and consistently work during the early morning hours?
   A. Circadian timing is fixed and therefore cannot be shifted outside normal daytime hours.
   B. Circadian timing is flexible but highly dependent on darkness, which will pressure the circadian cycle toward the nighttime hours.
   C. Circadian timing is flexible but highly dependent on social interaction. The reason the data would remain the same is because people working at night have limited social interaction.
   D. Circadian timing is flexible but highly dependent on light, which will push the circadian cycle toward the daylight hours.

5. Light exposure readjusts the circadian rhythm by acting on which brain structure?
   A. thalamus—lateral geniculate nucleus
   B. midbrain—superior colliculus
   C. brain stem—reticular formation
   D. hypothalamus—suprachiasmatic nucleus

Question 6 is not based on a passage.

6. Which of the following is TRUE about somatoform disorders?
   A. Individuals can experience an exacerbation of symptoms of existing medical conditions.
   B. Individuals are often faking symptoms of existing medical conditions.
   C. Individuals will often explicitly cause harm to themselves to create medical conditions.
   D. Pain can easily be identified as somatoform or real.

Questions 7–10 are based on the following passage.

Passage II

In a famous series of experiments, the social psychologist Stanley Milgram captured important observations about human compliance. Participants in the experiments were told to play the role of "teachers" and ask "learners" to answer questions. They were not told that the learners were actually actors. Every time a learner gave an incorrect answer, a confederate posing as an authority figure instructed the teacher to administer an electric shock to the learner. The learner would then pretend to suffer pain, even though the "shock" delivered via a realistic-looking apparatus was actually harmless. If a learner continued to provide incorrect answers, the authority figure told the teacher to increase the intensity of the "shock" all the way up to what was said to be a lethal level.

The results from the experiment are depicted in the following graph.

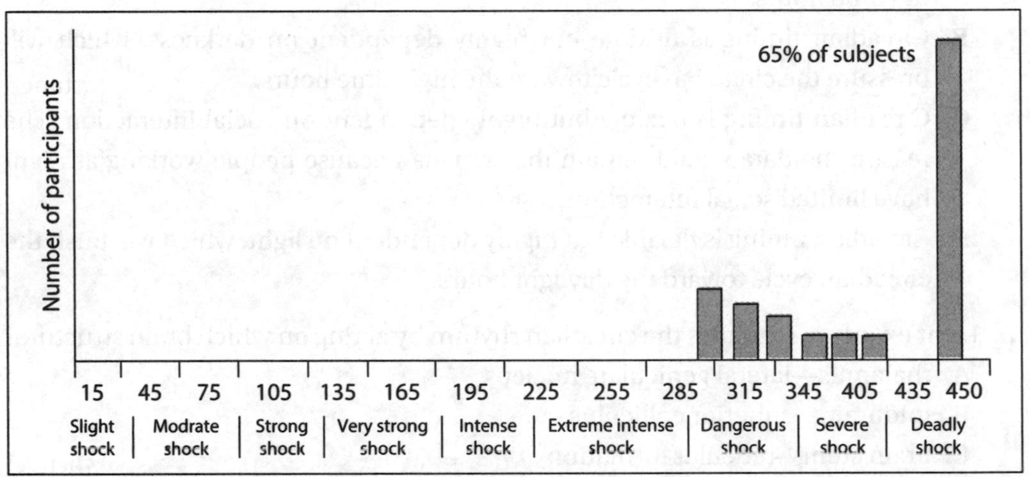

The Milgram experiment. Pretended shock intensity is listed on the x-axis and the number of participants is listed on the y-axis. *Source*: Adapted from Milgram, S. (1963). "Behavioral study of obedience." *The Journal of Abnormal and Social Psychology*, 67(4), 371.

7. Based on the results from this study, which of the following is TRUE?
   A. The majority of participants administered what they believed was a potentially lethal shock.
   B. The majority of participants refused to administer what they believed were lethal shocks.
   C. The data can be interpreted to show that the teachers inadvertently administered what they believed were lethal shocks.
   D. The data can be interpreted to show that the learners inadvertently answered questions that resulted in teachers administering what they believed were lethal shocks.

8. In the Milgram experiment the participant teacher would typically
   A. obey the authority figure despite the discomfort or pain exhibited by the learner
   B. resist the authority figure because of the discomfort or pain exhibited by the learner
   C. obey the learner despite protests from the authority figure
   D. obey the learner even when the learner exhibited discomfort or pain

9. The Milgram experiment has been repeated in a number of cultures and with a number of design changes. Based on your knowledge of social psychology, what was shown to reduce the likelihood of the participant teacher administering a perceived lethal shock?
   A. The experiment was completed in a formal lab where the teacher was alone with the authority figure.
   B. The authority figure was dressed in a lab coat and stood close to the teacher when giving the commands.
   C. The participant teachers were recruited from an older population.
   D. The participant teachers took part in a group discussion about the importance of ethics immediately prior to the teaching portion of the experiment.

10. In social psychology research, what does the term *obedience* represent?
   A. compliance to direct commands
   B. compliance to requests from a group of people
   C. compliance to implied pressure from social norms
   D. compliance with internal morals and beliefs

Question 11 is not based on a passage.

11. Jack's roommate has offered to pay him 1 dollar per week for doing the dishes. Jack is reluctant because he doesn't like this chore, but he accepts. After a few days Jack decides that the chore is somewhat enjoyable. This reaction is consistent with which theory?
   A. group think theory
   B. the bystander effect
   C. cognitive dissonance
   D. self-perception theory

Questions 12–15 are based on the following passage.

Passage III

Classical conditioning is a long-studied and well-documented scientific concept. The Russian physiologist Ivan Pavlov is most associated with this concept and described the conditions necessary for conditioning to occur. Subsequent studies from both comparative and human psychology have supported these initial findings and expanded upon them.

The following graph shows a hypothetical example of conditioning trials for one of Pavlov's dogs over a number of days. During these trials a bell has been paired with the presentation of food. Trial numbers are displayed on the x-axis and the number of drops of the dog's saliva is displayed on the y-axis.

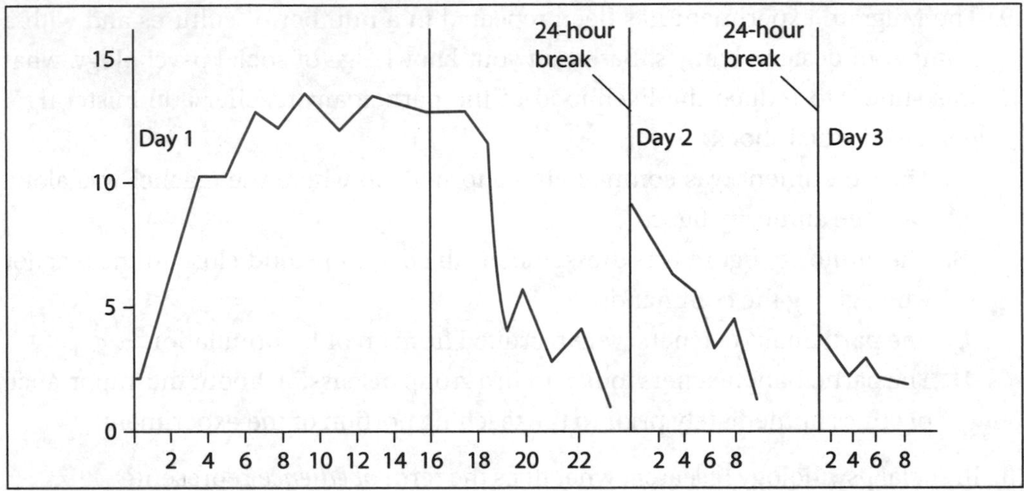

Classical conditioning. The number of drops of a dog's saliva is shown on the y-axis. The number of trials is shown on the x-axis.

12. Based on the saliva responses to stimuli shown in the graph, where would you expect the unconditioned stimulus to be present?
    - **A.** The unconditioned stimulus would be paired with the conditioned stimulus in initial trials on day 2.
    - **B.** The unconditioned stimulus would be paired with the conditioned stimulus in initial trials on day 3.
    - **C.** The unconditioned stimulus would be paired with the conditioned stimulus in initial trials on day 1.
    - **D.** The unconditioned stimulus would be paired with the conditioned stimulus on initial trials over the course of all three days.

13. Based on the saliva responses to stimuli shown in the graph, where would you expect the conditioned stimulus to be presented?
    - **A.** The conditioned stimulus would be present only on day 1.
    - **B.** The conditioned stimulus would be present only on day 2.
    - **C.** The conditioned stimulus would be present only on day 3.
    - **D.** The conditioned stimulus would be present on trials over the course of all three days.

14. In the study described in the passage, what is the major difference between the conditioned stimulus and the unconditioned stimulus?
   A. During conditioning trials the amount of saliva increases in response to the bell but decreases in response to the food.
   B. During extinction the amount of saliva decreases in response to the food and in response to the bell.
   C. Only the food elicits a response during conditioning.
   D. Only the food elicits a response prior to conditioning.

15. The increase in response to the bell on the initial trials on days 2 and 3 is consistent with which concept?
   A. spontaneous recovery
   B. the presence of the UCS
   C. acquisition
   D. extinction response

Question 16 is not based on a passage.

16. Anna misbehaves at school. The teacher places her in a 5-minute time-out during which she must sit quietly in a corner of the room. This is an example of which type of operant conditioning?
   A. positive reinforcement
   B. positive punishment
   C. negative reinforcement
   D. negative punishment

This is the end of the Unit II Minitest.

Unit II Minitest Answers and Explanations

1. **The correct answer is A.** The psychoanalytic theory is characterized by the interaction between the id (basic needs and wants), the ego (based on realistic expectations), and the superego (mediator of both the id and the ego).
2. **The correct answer is C.** Accidents were more likely during the early morning. The data collected show two peaks. The first is in the early morning hours. The second, smaller peak is during the late afternoon. However, the early morning peak is the most substantial peak.
3. **The correct answer is B.** The accident peaks would drift to the right on the graph with a slightly longer circadian cycle. In the absence of circadian cues, sleep research has shown that the human circadian cycle has been shown to drift toward 25 hours rather than 24. In this artificial case the main accident peak would continue to occur at the trough of the cycle and so would shift along with it.
4. **The correct answer is D.** Circadian timing is flexible but highly dependent on light, which will push the circadian cycle toward the daylight hours. Research suggests that exposure to light moves the circadian cycle toward the active daylight hours and is a cue that strongly influences behavior.
5. **The correct answer is D.** Hypothalamus—suprachiasmatic nucleus. The suprachiasmatic nucleus located in the hypothalamus is the brain structure that seems to readjust the biological clock based on light exposure. Because some retinal pathways bypass the occipital lobe and project light information directly to the suprachiasmatic nucleus, it is possible for some individuals who are blind but still have this pathway intact to have normal circadian rhythms that respond to light.
6. **The correct answer is A.** Individuals can experience an exacerbation of symptoms of existing medical conditions. Somatoform disorders are characterized by the experience of a medical condition that is exacerbated or alleviated by psychological conditions. They are often mistaken for factitious disorders, in which symptoms are intentionally created, or malingering, in which symptoms are reported but not experienced by the individual. True somatoform disorders are not intentional. Pain has multiple psychosocial factors that affect the pain experience, and all pain has a psychosomatic component to it.
7. **The correct answer is A.** The majority of participants (65%) obeyed the authority figure to the point that they administered what they believed were lethal shocks.
8. **The correct answer is A.** The participant teacher would obey the authority figure despite discomfort or pain exhibited by the learner. Most participants continued to administer shocks at the insistence of the authority figure until the shocks appeared to be potentially lethal.

9. **The correct answer is D.** The group discussion makes ethics more salient to the participant teachers, and the influence of the group is likely to polarize the individual toward increasing the importance of ethics through group think phenomena.
10. **The correct answer is A.** In social psychology research, obedience represents compliance to direct commands from an authority figure.
11. **The correct answer is C.** For such a small amount of money, Jack could not justify that he was doing the dishes for the money; therefore, cognitive dissonance theory indicates he will change his attitude about the chore. Cognitive dissonance results when there is a disconnect between an individual's actions and beliefs. When these are at odds, the individual will often change his or her attitudes or beliefs to bring them into line with his or her actions.
12. **The correct answer is C.** The unconditioned stimulus would be paired with the conditioned stimulus in initial trials on day 1. The unconditioned stimulus is paired with the conditioned stimulus during learning trials. In the graph, the saliva is shown to increase only during trials in which the pairing is present (day 1; trials 2–16). The increase between days is typical of spontaneous recovery.
13. **The correct answer is D.** The conditioned stimulus would be present on trials over the course of all three days. The conditioned stimulus would be paired with the unconditioned stimulus on initial trials on day 1 (during pairing/learning). It would also be present during the extinction and spontaneous recovery trials on the remaining day 1 trials as well as the trials over the next two days.
14. **The correct answer is D.** Only the food elicits a response prior to conditioning. The food is the unconditioned stimulus and will elicit the saliva response without any conditioning. During trials, the bell is paired with the food and will elicit the conditioned response by itself in absence of the unconditioned stimulus. However, the response to the conditioned stimulus will drop over time without any new UCS-CS pairings.
15. **The correct answer is A.** The increase is consistent with the concept of spontaneous recovery. This phenomenon has been noted in certain classical conditioning paradigms. It is characterized by the reappearance of an extinguished response after a period of nonexposure to the conditioned stimulus.
16. **The correct answer is D.** Negative punishment is characterized by the removal of stimulus to reduce a behavior. In this case the misbehavior is being punished by the removal of social interaction.

UNIT III

Self and Others

Foundational Concept: Biological, psychological, and sociocultural factors influence how we think about ourselves and others.

CHAPTER 7

Self-Identity

Read This Chapter to Learn About

- ➤ Self-Concept and Self-Esteem
- ➤ Identity Formation
- ➤ Early Attachment and Socialization

SELF-CONCEPT AND SELF-ESTEEM

The **self-concept** is the collection of internal evaluative schemas that a person holds about her- or himself. These individual **schemas** (e.g., "I am a good driver," "I am bad at math") collectively make up a person's self-concept. Unlike the self-concept, an individual's **social identity** comprises solely external characteristics, such as group memberships (e.g., gender, ethnicity, and religious faith), occupational role, and family role, and the value that the individual places on belonging to each of those roles or groups. But it is important to note that there are actually many different types of **identities** that define an individual. Some of the most obvious are demographic identities (gender, race, ethnicity, age, sexual orientation), but there are also identities of choice such as social relations (friend, acquaintance, enemy), family relations (parent, spouse), geographic location (resident of northeastern United States, Italy, Mexico), and occupation. The sum total of all of these is an individual's **self-identity**, which is an integration of internal evaluations (e.g., self-concept, beliefs about one's traits and characteristics) and external characteristics (e.g., relationships, roles, group memberships).

The self-concept drives a person's **self-esteem**, or feelings of value to the world and to those with whom the person interacts. Because a person's schemas include how effective he or she is at maneuvering in the world, these schemas are usually learned from the interactions with the surrounding world. A person who has high levels of **self-efficacy** (belief in the ability to achieve goals successfully) and an **internal locus of control** (the feeling of being in control of current life and future goals) is more likely to have better self-esteem. A person who has low self-efficacy beliefs (e.g., "I couldn't succeed even if I tried, so why bother?") and an external locus of control (e.g., "Even if I do everything right, my car will probably break down and I'll miss my test appointment anyway") is more likely to have low self-esteem and a self-concept that is rooted in feelings of failure.

High self-esteem may not always be fully appropriate. If a child is continually given easy tests and never needs to work for a goal, he or she may develop an overabundance of self-esteem. This could lead to an **identity crisis** (a mismatch between internal self-concept and external signals) when the child enters a difficult academic or work setting that challenges his or her success schemas (e.g., "I'm so smart and don't have to work for it").

IDENTITY FORMATION

In the process of developing an identity and a self-concept, an individual progresses through certain stages on the way to creating an adult identity. According to the Soviet Belarusian psychologist Lev Vygotsky, the road of child development is not a smooth path. He believed that there are long periods of stability, punctuated with crises that spur development. Vygotsky's **zone of proximal development (ZPD)** describes how children learn by observing adults. In Figure 7-1, the internal circle is what a child can complete on his or her own, the middle circle is what the child can do with assistance (ZPD), and the external circle is too far beyond the child's understanding. The zones are constantly changing as the child grows and increases cognitive and

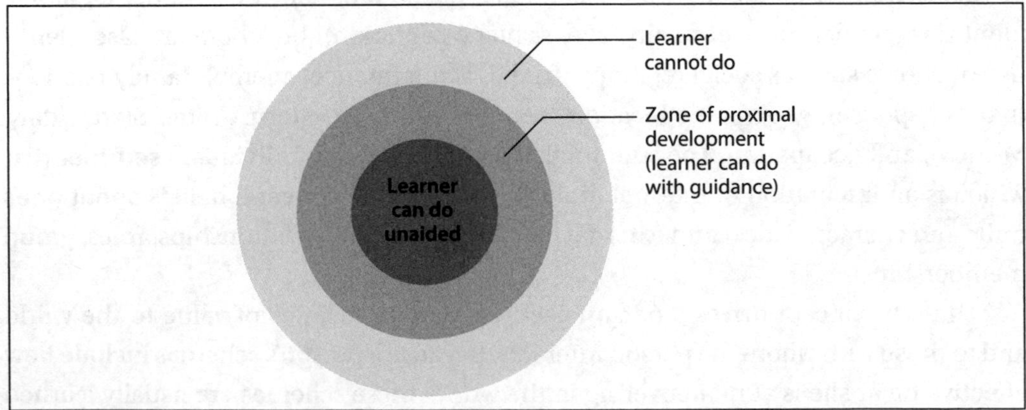

FIGURE 7-1 Vygotsky's zone of proximal development.

physical skills. Upon becoming an adolescent, he or she gains the ability to understand abstract concepts and is better able to contemplate different identities and alternative future roles.

The German-born American developmental psychologist Erik Erikson was one of the first to recognize that identity formation does not end when a person reaches adulthood, but continues throughout the person's lifetime. Erikson's research suggests that if a person reaches each identity milestone at the appropriate time, he or she will generally be content (see the following table). But when there is a disconnection between age and stage of development, there can be internal conflicts that cause psychological difficulties.

Erikson's Stages of Psychosocial Development

Stage	Age	Primary Life Event	If Successful
Trust vs. mistrust	Birth–18 months	Feeding	Form a loving, trusting relationship with caregiver
Autonomy vs. shame/doubt	2–3 years	Toilet training	Develop a sense of control over the body and a sense of independence
Initiative vs. guilt	3–5 years	Independence	Develop self-efficacy in the environment and a sense of purpose
Industry vs. inferiority	6–12 years	School	Integrate into a larger social network and develop competence in academics
Identity vs. role confusion	12–18 years	Social relationships	Develop personal identity and a sense of self and values
Intimacy vs. isolation	19–40 years	Close relationships	Develop intimate, strong, supportive relationships
Generativity vs. stagnation	40–65 years	Work, parenthood, mentorship	Develop things or ideas that are a lasting positive contribution to the world
Ego integrity vs. despair	65 years to death	Reflection on life	Feel a sense of fulfillment and completeness to life's work

The American psychologist Lawrence Kohlberg recognized that along with the development of identity, the development of moral reasoning and values is also critical. Kohlberg identified 6 stages in three levels of moral development (see the following table). He determined the level of moral reasoning by asking a complex ethical question. The level or stage is determined not by the answer to a moral question, but by the reasoning that a person uses to produce that answer. It is important to note only 20–25% of adults ever achieve Stage 5, and only a handful of individuals have reached Stage 6.

Kohlberg's Stages of Moral Development			
Level 1		Preconventional Morality	Base moral decisions on the likelihood of receiving a reward or punishment
	Stage 1	Obedience and punishment	
	Stage 2	Egocentric	
Level 2		Conventional Morality	Base moral decisions on societal rules and social norms
	Stage 3	Good child	
	Stage 4	Authority and social order	
Level 3		Postconventional Morality	Base moral decisions on personal values and principles
	Stage 5	Contractual-legalistic	
	Stage 6	Conscience	

EARLY ATTACHMENT AND SOCIALIZATION

The individuals who surround a growing child will naturally influence that child's identity formation. If children are raised by actively involved parents, rather than by uninvolved or highly critical parents, they tend to be more comfortable developing independent identities. At a young age, children will initially take on "play" roles that mimic the adults around them. They will imitate the roles they see in their family as part of practicing different identities in preparation for adulthood.

The impact of early attachment on identify formation also holds true in the animal world. The American psychologist Harry Harlow performed a famous series of studies on the formation of mother-infant attachment in rhesus monkeys. He created two artificial monkey "mothers," one made of bare wire and the other made of soft terry cloth. The wire mother provided milk for the baby monkeys, but the terry-cloth mother provided no food. Harlow placed the two mothers in cages with baby rhesus monkeys to see whether mother-infant attachment would take place. He theorized (incorrectly) that based on evolutionary principles, the baby monkeys should prefer the food-bearing wire mother over the terry-cloth mother, even if the soft terry-cloth version were more emotionally comforting than the bare wire version. Harlow was surprised when the baby monkeys repeatedly attached to the comforting terry-cloth mother, even though it provided no food to them. This study helped developmental psychologists understand that attachment to caregivers depends on more than simply providing food and that emotional comfort is the primary motivator for infants in attachment.

Early socialization has a direct effect on identity formation. According to studies by Canadian-American developmental psychologist Mary Ainsworth, the type of attachment that a child feels at an early age toward caregivers can have a lifelong influence on attachment characteristics (see the following table). A **securely** attached child feels free to explore the environment but will return to the caregiver periodically for comfort and connection. A child who has an **anxious/ambivalent** attachment will often avoid leaving the caregiver for fear the caregiver will leave or pay no attention. A child with an **avoidant/rejecting** attachment style will not connect with the caregiver at all, only exploring the environment but not interpreting the caregiver as a safe place in times of fear. These styles of childhood attachment are carried into adulthood. They affect a person's interactions with friends and romantic partners. They can also affect how a person grows and develops an identity and the level of security the person feels in "trying on" different self-concepts with the onset of adolescence.

Caregiver and Attachment Styles

Caregiver Style	Infant Attachment	Adult Attachment
Responsive: good relationship between the caregiver and the child	*Securely attached*: willing to explore a new environment but returns to the caregiver periodically for security	*Secure*: comfortable with establishing close relationships
Rejecting: not responsive to the child's needs; distant and cold	*Avoidant*: insecure bond with caregiver; tends to ignore the caregiver; no separation anxiety	*Avoidant*: avoids emotionally close relationships; may ask more of romantic partners than is willing to give emotionally
Ambivalent: inconsistent "hot and cold" caregiving style dependent on the caregiver's mood at the moment	*Anxious/ambivalent*: insecure bond with caregiver; may not explore a new environment due to strong separation anxiety	*Anxious/ambivalent*: strong desire for close relationships but also strong fear of abandonment; may rush into intimate relationships

As children grow and enter school age, they encounter a larger social network. At this age, children become more influenced by **groups**. These include both the group that the children most closely identify with (**reference group**) and those around them. The reference group will be important to the individual's identity for the rest of his or her life, either because of maintaining a connection to that original group or intentionally separating from it. The role of the in-group/out-group relationship (e.g., What is "me"? What is "not me"?) and the value that the person places on different groups can change the direction of identity formation. If a person is part of a peer group that is comfortable with its identify formation and provides positive support, he or she is less likely to feel inferior to peers, regardless of the societal judgment of that peer group (e.g., "jocks," "nerds," "geeks"). In positive identity development, the exact "type" of group is less important than whether or not the individual feels comfortable in that peer group and the stability of that peer group.

Culture will strongly influence identity formation because of the influence of culture on the schemas that a person develops as part of his or her self-concept. For example, the individual's role in a culture may be valued differently based on gender (girls versus boys), the understanding of sexual orientation (accepting versus shaming), age (youth versus adult), even the individual's skills (academic ability versus athletic prowess). The values of society can strongly influence how individuals view themselves, their self-concept, and their self-esteem.

CHAPTER 8

Social Thinking

Read This Chapter to Learn About

- Attribution Theory
- Prejudice, Bias, and Discrimination
- Stereotypes and Ethnocentrism

ATTRIBUTION THEORY

Attribution theory examines how individuals explain their own behavior and the behavior of those around them. When a person attributes behavior based on individual abilities, traits, and characteristics, that behavior is said to be due to **internal attributions**. By contrast, when a person attributes behavior to external causes such as a particular situation or social environment, the behavior is said to be due to **external attributions**. However, people often have biases when explaining the behavior of themselves and others.

The **fundamental attribution error** describes the common human tendency to overattribute the behavior of others to stable internal causes (e.g., someone cuts you off in traffic, and your immediate thought is, "He is a jerk," rather than, "He didn't see me."). The social psychologist Bernard Weiner increased people's understanding of the attribution error by discovering that people ascribe internal and external attributions to behavior differently depending on whether they are judging themselves or others. When judging their own behavior, people are more likely to ascribe bad outcomes to external attributions (e.g., "I was cranky because I was tired after work today."). But they are more likely to ascribe good outcomes to internal attributions (e.g., "I did well on that presentation because I am a good public speaker."). This can also be called the **self-serving bias**. When judging the behavior of others, this pattern is reversed: people are more likely to ascribe bad outcomes to internal attributions and good outcomes to external attributions (see the following table).

	Internal Attribution	External Attribution
Self	Good outcomes	Bad outcomes
Others	Bad outcomes	Good outcomes

Individuals' perceptions of themselves can alter how they perceive others. If they have the self-schema of a victim, they are more likely to perceive others as trying to take advantage of them. People who are extremely self-critical may flip the self-serving bias and ascribe bad outcomes for themselves to their own internal attributes and good outcomes for others to those others' internal attributes.

People's culture can affect the extent to which the self-serving bias affects their judgment about the actions of themselves and others. People from individualistic societies are more likely to use the self-serving bias and fall prey to the fundamental attribution error. People from more collectivist cultures are more likely to use a **self-effacing bias** that minimizes their own input to successful projects and overemphasizes their input to failures.

People's worldviews may also affect how they perceive those around them. A person with a just-world belief is more likely to provide defensive attributions to protect that worldview. For example, such a person may see another individual experiencing difficulties (e.g., homelessness, crime) and attribute those difficulties to the other person's internal characteristics.

PREJUDICE, BIAS, AND DISCRIMINATION

Unfortunately, attributions can expand to attribute behaviors and characteristics to entire groups of people rather than just an individual. When that occurs, prejudice, bias, and stereotypes emerge. **Prejudice** is the negative evaluation of a group of people. People with prejudices often support them with inaccurate beliefs that they consider to be "facts" that allow them to engage in negative stereotyping. Prejudice (a *cognitive* process) against a certain group often leads to the *behavior* of **discrimination** against members of that group.

Individual discrimination refers to the behavior of individuals and the actions that they take against some specific group due to the group members' gender, race, ethnicity, or some other characteristic. Institutional discrimination is different. The term **institutional discrimination** identifies rules, laws, and policies that are intentionally put in place to create a harmful effect upon a specific group. Institutional discrimination can both produce or be a product of individual discrimination.

Jane Elliot, a schoolteacher, famously performed a controversial "exercise" with grade school children in the late 1960s to demonstrate that prejudice is not inborn, but socially learned. She divided the children into those with brown eyes and those with blue eyes. For one day she made discriminatory comments about the two groups (e.g., praising blue-eyed children's correct responses and emphasizing mistakes made by brown-eyed children) and arranged classroom privileges (e.g., who was first in line to go out to recess) for the benefit of the blue-eyed children (institutional discrimination). Blue-eyed children were encouraged to interact only with other blue-eyed children. Soon blue-eyed children began to make derogatory remarks about brown-eyed children (individual discrimination), and the brown-eyed children appeared to internalize those negative remarks. During that single day, the blue-eyed children's academic scores and self-esteem improved, and they became arrogant and acted superior to their brown-eyed classmates. At the same time, the brown-eyed children's scores and self-esteem declined, and they became passive and subservient. On the following day, the teacher reversed the pattern and began treating the brown-eyed children as superior. Once the teacher—the authority figure—reversed her support, almost immediately the two groups of children swapped personality characteristics. This experiment showed how quickly prejudicial ideas—an increase in the power and unearned benefits of one group—will result in discrimination behaviors by children. Children quickly learn the prejudicial thought processes, take the unearned benefits as their entitlement, and begin to act in a discriminatory manner, especially when those thought processes have the support of an authority figure (e.g., a teacher, parents, or national figures).

Thus prejudice is quickly learned, and discriminatory actions can occur even more quickly when prejudice arises in the context of fear. Prejudice can develop along a number of different lines (power, prestige, class, gender), but it is more likely to develop when there is competition for some type of resource (a tangible resource or an intangible one such as prestige). A person who fears a loss of resources is more likely to engage in prejudicial thoughts and discriminatory actions. Further, when a person is fatigued, stressed, rushed, or not getting enough sleep (sleep debt), the brain is more likely to engage in cognitive processes that take less energy. The use of stereotyping and pigeonholing leading to prejudicial thinking requires a much lower cognitive load. A person whose brain is already overfatigued is more likely to use these forms of judgments about others rather than using complex thought processes.

Cognitive processes can also play a role in prejudice and discrimination. Some of these processes are conscious, but some may not be. The brain automatically classifies individuals into in-groups and out-groups. An **in-group** is the group that an individual feels that he or she belongs to, associates with, and identifies with. An **out-group** is made up of "others." Evolutionary psychologists believe that this process of identifying in/out groups increased group cohesiveness for small tribes of humans. Biologically, it is suspected that the hormone oxytocin is at least partially responsible for in-group cohesion. In-group members often use positive schemas and stereotypes to describe their own group and negative stereotypes to describe out-group members. This can especially be seen in wartime. For example, US military recruitment posters from World War I presenting Germans as "Huns" and similar posters from World War II presenting caricatures of Japanese soldiers are vivid illustrations of the negative stereotypes used to dehumanize a wartime enemy.

Appearance can play a role in how an individual is perceived. Viewing a person's appearance is often the first step in **pigeonholing** that person into a specific social schema. **Social schemas** are categories that the brain uses to process interactions with others more efficiently. For example, if you see a person wearing tie-dyed clothing made of organic hemp fibers, you might quickly assume that the person is an environmental activist and possibly a vegan. In this way, your brain has quickly created a framework to engage with that other person. However, such speedy assumptions often occur at the expense of accuracy.

STEREOTYPES AND ETHNOCENTRISM

Stereotypes are a special subtype of schema. Whereas schemas are more personalized, stereotypes are widely held beliefs that an individual has certain characteristics because he or she belongs to a certain group. Stereotypes can be positive (e.g., "Asians are good at math.") or negative (e.g., "Women are overly emotional."). Stereotypes can affect academic performance and personality both positively and negatively. Research shows that individuals who are subjected to stereotyping often find that these are **self-fulfilling prophecies** that can predict life outcomes (e.g., a girl who is told that she will be bad at math because of her gender is much more likely to be a poor math student than a girl who is supported in her math goals). Unfortunately, stereotypes can be easily reinforced due to **illusory correlations** that occur when examples that reinforce a stereotype are more easily recalled than examples contrary to a stereotype (e.g., a local news story about a Latino man committing a crime is recalled, reinforcing a negative stereotype, while Latino men who are community leaders are forgotten).

Individuals who are subjected to stereotyping may also experience stereotype threat. A **stereotype threat** is the fear that an individual has of reinforcing a negative stereotype because of his or her own behaviors or characteristics. The fear may be conscious or unconscious. A famous series of studies by Claude Steele and Joshua Aronson showed that African-American college students performed more poorly on tests than their white classmates when race and racial stereotypes were repeatedly emphasized throughout the testing protocol. In contrast, when race was not emphasized, African-American and white students had similar test scores. Thus students who perceived a stereotype threat in regard to themselves were less able to fully live up to their academic abilities.

One of the difficulties is the fundamental role played by **ethnocentrism**, or judging another culture based solely on the beliefs and values of one's own culture of origin. Anthropologists studying other cultures often have to be careful in their descriptions of other cultures to ensure that they are not imposing judgments because of their own cultural of origin. Anthropologists use the tool of cultural relativism to attempt to maintain objectivity in describing other cultures. **Cultural relativism** attempts to overcome the assumption that ideas from the culture of origin (usually Western culture) are obvious and self-sustaining, and instead view each culture as a collection of unique beliefs, values, and behaviors that developed independently and should be studied independently from the biases of other cultures.

CHAPTER 9

Social Interactions

Read This Chapter to Learn About

- Expressing and Detecting Emotion
- Impression Management
- Romantic Attraction
- Aggression/Altruism
- Social Behavior Among Strangers

EXPRESSING AND DETECTING EMOTION

There is evidence to suggest that the expression and detection of emotions is at least partially genetically driven. The social psychologist Paul Ekman identified six **universal emotions** that could be recognized by facial expressions across cultures: anger, sadness, fear, disgust, happiness, and surprise. The universal recognition of these emotions allows for nonverbal cross-cultural communication. More recently, Ekman expanded his research to include eleven additional universal emotions: amusement, pride in achievement, contentment, relief, excitement, satisfaction, sensory pleasure, contempt, embarrassment, guilt, and shame. While not all of these emotions are easily recognizable cross culturally, Ekman found that these emotions occur in every culture. However, even though these various emotions are universally experienced, culture still determines how, when, where, with whom, and how intensely they are displayed.

Margaret Mead performed groundbreaking anthropological work in the 1920s in her studies of preliterate cultures. While her early work on gender roles across societies is somewhat controversial, she provided evidence that there are many cross-cultural differences regarding how the genders interact with each other, and how they express emotion. Mead thus argued for nurture over nature in emotional expression and intergender communication. In some cultures in which the female gender role is seen as passive, women are more likely to express emotion privately and in same-sex-only interactions, and women's public expression may be very limited. In other cultures in which women have a more active gender role, female public expression is more accepted. Additionally, cultures that have a complex structure and numerous social rules may place restrictions on the emotional expression of both men and women.

Cultural roles regarding hierarchy, age, and gender roles have a major influence on the exchange of information. Who speaks first? How is important content delivered? How far away do two speakers stand from each other when engaging in communication? What is the appropriate length of pause between questions and answers? Even before any verbal information is communicated, social rules communicate how a conversation should proceed.

Message content and context may differ across cultures, but interpersonal communication is fundamental to a functioning society. **Communication** can occur in multiple forms, but there are two primary types: focused interactions and unfocused interactions. **Focused interactions** occur when there is intentional or direct contact between two individuals (e.g., saying "hello" in a hallway). **Unfocused interactions** occur when people are in the same location but not directly engaging with each other (e.g., two strangers sitting next to each other in a library).

There are also four levels of communication:

1. **Verbal** communication includes any active communication that provides an explicit message that is transmitted in word form (there is controversy as to whether the hand movements in sign languages are verbal or nonverbal language).
2. **Paraverbal** communications are those vocal messages that are communicated in the context with the verbal communication (e.g., tone, volume, speed, prosody). The same words (verbal) can be received very differently based on the paraverbals that accompany the words.
3. **Nonverbal** communication is body language that can either accompany verbal communication or transmit a message on its own (e.g., frowning at someone transmits a message even without words). Nonverbal communication may also include external displays that signify rank (e.g., military uniforms), wealth (e.g., designer clothing, jewelry), sexual availability (e.g., wedding rings, marital shawls), and status (e.g., a nun's habit) within a community. Written communication (both artistic and word-based) is a form of nonverbal communication.
4. **Hormonal** communication involves chemical signaling using pheromones.

Research suggests that approximately 55 percent of face-to-face communication occurs using nonverbal communication and 38 percent of face-to-face communication occurs with paraverbals. Therefore, these important language augmenters that humans use to convey and understand meaning are lost when the level of communication changes from face-to-face to telephone communication (loss of nonverbals, and hormones) and are reduced even more in written communication (additional loss of paraverbals).

Humans are somewhat limited in their ability to control **pheromone** communication, whereas some animals, particularly insects, appear to use this as their primary form of communication. Animals also use the same levels of communication (verbal, nonverbal, paraverbal, and hormonal). While animals use a less word-focused form of language (to the best of scientific knowledge), there are multiple examples of each type of language in the animal world. Verbal language such as whale songs, paraverbals such as the volume of verbalizations, nonverbals such as threatening stances to scare away competitors, and hormone-based information exchange as seen in ant interactions are common examples of animal communication.

IMPRESSION MANAGEMENT

The Canadian sociologist Erving Goffman proposed the **dramaturgical approach** to social interactions, in which the individual is always playing some type of role. According to this theory, the **front-stage self** is the face that a person presents to the world (there may be many of these depending on situational demand and goals). The person (or "actor") needs to present him- or herself (front-stage self) in a certain way to achieve specific goals. Using **impression management**, the actor identifies the characteristics of the "audience" and the type of presentation needed to achieve those goals (e.g., persuading the audience, making them laugh or cry, and so on). The actor self-monitors for the front stage, maintaining **self-awareness** that he or she is presenting the desired image. This **self-verification** involves making sure that the chosen audience consists of people who will validate the actor's self-view. Thus according to this theory, a person's identity is not stable, but rather an ever-shifting experience that adjusts to the environment, the audience, and the person's goals. The person's **backstage** self (or those actions and thoughts that cannot be seen by others) may be slightly more stable. The individual is still engrossed in the social presentation role, but can take a step back for processing. For example, during a job interview, a person who is being very careful about impression management might also be carrying on an internal dialogue in phrases such as "Take deep breaths," "You can do this," and the like. In this scenario, people are not truly themselves until they are **off-stage** and alone, and even then a person may still engage in activities to improve impression management in preparation for subsequent social situations. For example, an employee may read a book recommended by a boss in order to be knowledgeable about a topic during a subsequent conversation.

The sociologist Harold Garfinkel developed **ethnomethodology** to study how people make sense of everyday interactions. According to Garfinkel, individuals use

background expectancies, or culturally based scripts, to socially interact with those around them. Most of these expectancies are things that individuals do by habit. The scripts of action are ingrained in the individual and using them requires less cognitive processing during routine interactions (e.g., in much of Western culture when two people pass in a hallway, one person says, "Hi, how are you?" and the other replies, "Fine," whether or not that is the case). Garfinkel used a technique called **breaching experiments** to watch how people react when an experimenter breaks cultural norms (e.g., walking into an elevator and facing the back wall rather than the door). He noted negative reactions by the observed group (e.g., people in the elevator became uncomfortable when the experimenter broke the innocuous taboo of facing the wrong way), and negative emotional reactions by the experimenters themselves (usually graduate students) who were asked to break established social norms.

ROMANTIC ATTRACTION

Attraction to romantic partners can be due to a number of different factors. Most research on this topic has been done with heterosexual couples; there has been only limited research on same-sex partners. Physical attractiveness is often the first step. While there are cultural differences in what constitutes attractiveness, some aspects of attractiveness appear to be genetically linked and cross-cultural. Facial symmetry has been shown to be important in cross-cultural ratings of attractiveness. Additionally, some research suggests that across cultures, if woman's waist-to-hip ratio is approximately 0.7, she will be more attractive regardless of the overall size of her body. Evolutionary psychologists suggest that this is due to fertility factors that men subconsciously find attractive. The **matching hypothesis** is based on data indicating that individuals are more likely to select romantic partners who are similar to them in attractiveness, and that relationships between similarly attractive people are more likely to be harmonious.

Environmental factors can alter judgments about attractiveness. In the classic "swinging bridge" study by Donald Dutton and Arthur Aron, some individuals were asked to place themselves upon a low, stable bridge and others upon a high, swinging bridge. The swinging bridge was so unstable that the people who were on it experienced fear-based rushes of adrenaline. Each group was then asked to rate the attractiveness of an opposite-sex research assistant. The same assistant was rated as more attractive by the people on the swinging bridge than by the people on the stable bridge. The people on the swinging bridge consistently misattributed their fear-induced adrenaline rushes as stronger attraction to the research assistant rather than the environmental factor of a dangerous situation.

Another environmental factor that influences romantic attraction is the placement of children in a sibling relationship. Humans are socially (and likely genetically) encouraged to avoid mating with siblings. Studies of children raised on kibbutzim in

Israel (collective living situations) showed that few of those children married within their own kibbutz. Even though these children were not genetically related, the environmental factor of growing up among sibling-like peers decreased the likelihood of romantic partnerships. A similar rarity of romantic partnerships is found in studies of adopted children and their nongenetically related siblings.

Even biological-hormonal factors may influence whom men and women want to associate with at different stages of their hormonal cycle. In the "white T-shirt" study series by Claus Wedekind, researchers asked women to wear white T-shirts during different phases of their menstrual cycle (to pick up pheromone scents). They also asked men to wear white T-shirts. They then asked people of the opposite gender to rate the attractiveness of the scent of each T-shirt. Men gave the highest rating to T-shirts worn by women at mid-cycle (highest fertility). Women who were at mid-cycle during the test gave the highest rating to T-shirts worn by men who were genetically dissimilar, but women in phases of lower fertility were more likely to prefer genetically similar (family member) scents. Interestingly, hormonal birth control appears to significantly alter attraction and attractiveness, which may have significant implications for human mating behavior.

Research studies into animal mating behavior suggest that similar biological factors, including facial and body symmetry and pheromones, affect mating choice. Environmentally, in areas of few resources polyandry (mating with multiple male partners) is more common among animals. For females in resource-poor areas, mating with more males is a way of accessing the resources needed to ensure the survival of any offspring (even though with multiple male sexual partners, there is decreased likelihood that the offspring belongs to any one male). In resource-rich areas, polygyny (mating with multiple female partners) is more common. In these areas, males can have multiple female sexual partners without a commitment to raise their genetic offspring, yet are relatively assured of the survival of those offspring. Female animals in resource-rich areas seek mates that are most likely to provide the genetic characteristics that ensure their offspring's survival.

In addition to physical attraction, humans are more likely to form partnerships with individuals who share **attitude similarity**. Over time, most couples merge their attitudes further in a process called **attitude alignment**. And the stability of a relationship is often contingent on the process of **emotional reciprocity**. Humans are more likely to love those who demonstrate that they love them back.

AGGRESSION/ALTRUISM

Aggression occurs when there is fear of a loss of resources (e.g., food, sexual partners) or a loss of some secondary means to access resources (e.g., money, prestige). Because physical aggression may also cause a loss of resources (e.g., injury to body, damage to important items, loss of esteem), nonviolent aggression (e.g., loud vocalizations, physical displays of prowess) is also frequently seen among both animals and humans.

At the other end of the spectrum is altruism. **Altruism** means helping someone else with no expectation of any recompense. However, there is some research that suggests that true altruism is rare. In human communities, helping others occurs more frequently among family members or within limited social networks where the help given is more likely to be reciprocated at some future date. The fact that assistance is more likely to be given where it is more likely to be reciprocated is an argument against the existence of true altruism. Additionally, help is more likely to be given to those that the giver identifies as fellow "in-group" members. "In-group" may be defined by geographic location (e.g., live in the same town), nationality (e.g., US citizen), ethnicity (e.g., Latino), socioeconomic status (e.g., middle class), family, or other individually defined social network. However, research suggests that the larger the in-group with which a person identifies, the better is that person's psychological health. By identifying with a larger in-group, a person experiences more social support and the more opportunities to obtain instrumental support (e.g., food and shelter) in times of need. Thus, pro-social behaviors may occur in small ways or large ways, but are more likely to occur among those who are within the same group. Additionally, one of the most commonly discussed threats to the idea of altruism is the positive feeling that someone gets when performing a pro-social act. The positive impact on self-identity, self-esteem, and mood may make a person feel better about him- or herself, and therefore the "altruistic act" is not truly without a benefit to the individual.

True altruism seems to be rare in the animal kingdom as well. However, this does not mean there are not instances of self-risk among animals. This phenomenon is often explained using Richard Dawkins' **selfish gene theory**, according to which animals are more likely to risk themselves on behalf of those to whom they are genetically related if that risk means the continuation of their genes. For example, a gopher pack that is foraging will often have one or two "lookouts" that will screech if they see a hawk in the area, warning the pack to dive for cover. Standing guard is risky for the gopher. Making noise during an alarm draws the hawk's attention to them, plus they are not able to forage for food while on guard. This type of animal self-risk behavior is more likely to occur in closely related packs in which the risk-to-benefit ratio means the survival of genes in siblings, children, cousins, nieces, and nephews. A similar idea is the concept of **inclusive fitness** whereby an animal's survival success is judged not only by how many offspring it has, but rather by how many of those offspring survive, find mates, and reproduce. Social behavior of animals, including shared risk and resources, may enhance an animal's inclusive fitness by increasing the survival rate of offspring.

For all animals, survival depends on the ability to forage for food. The **optimal foraging model** identifies how animals find the optimal cost-benefit ratio for foraging. Each animal has to balance the level of resources available in the area, how much energy will be expended in accessing those resources (e.g., food, mating partners), and dangers in accessing those resources (e.g., predators). This may be a complex analysis. For example, suppose that a prairie dog finds a berry patch food source. It shares those resources with members of its family. In this scenario, the prairie dog may lose part of the food for its individual benefit, but foraging in a group is safer because there are more lookouts for predators, and there is the expectation of reciprocity when another member of the prairie dog family finds another food source in the future. In this scenario, animals balance the loss of immediate resources against group protection during foraging and the prospect of increased resources in the future.

SOCIAL BEHAVIOR AMONG STRANGERS

It is not possible always to be surrounded by those who are genetically similar. Therefore, humans and animals need a method to determine if an unrelated individual is worthy of trust and sharing of resources. When unrelated individuals interact, game theory comes into play. **Game theory** is strategic decision making in social interactions; it is observed among both humans and animals. While games based on similar premises had been played for years, modern game theory was developed academically by John van Neumann and later updated in the 1950s by John Nash (the main character in the movie *A Beautiful Mind*). In one of the most popular forms of game theory (also called the "prisoner's dilemma" game), players need to decide whether to trust the opponent or to betray him. Game theory boils down to a simple question: "Do you trust or not trust?" In the first interaction between individuals ("players"), each one must decide whether or not to trust the other, without knowing which option the opponent chose. Then in the second interaction, each player must decide how to respond based on whether the other player chose to trust or betray in the first interaction. While the final decision is simply between trusting or not trusting the opponent (human or computer), making that decision requires complex calculations about the opponent's behavior in an attempt to predict the opponent's future responses.

Multiple games and even an international series of contests have been developed based on game theory. As an example, suppose the parameters of a game have been laid out in the following chart. The chart shows possible outcomes for the initial interaction between players, with point values assigned to each outcome. Games like this may go on for as many as 100 rounds.

		Player 1	
		Trust	**Betray**
Player 2	**Trust**	+10 points to both	+20 points to Player 1
	Betray	+20 points to Player 2	0 points to both

While this may change slightly depending on how the parameters of the game are set up, the most frequently successful model in game theory appears to be to trust first, and afterward to respond in kind. Betrayal results in one win and then a series of losses; therefore, it is in the best interest of the players to not focus only on the higher payout, but to trust and cooperate rather than betray. Game theory is easily applied to social interactions. Generally among strangers, humans have to choose how they are going to interact. When a stranger approaches, you do not know if he or she will help you or steal from you. Based on the mathematical model, the best option is to trust first and then, if betrayed, betray as well until the other person "evens the score" by trusting you, after which you may trust again.

Unit III Minitest

16 Questions **30 Minutes**

This minitest is designed to assess your mastery of the content in Chapters 7 through 9 of this volume. The questions have been designed to simulate actual MCAT questions in terms of format and degree of difficulty. They are based on the content categories associated with the foundational concept that is the theme of this unit. They are also designed to test the scientific inquiry and reasoning skills that the test makers have identified as essential for success in medical school.

In this test, most of the questions are based on short passages that typically describe a research study or some similar process. There are also some questions that are not based on passages.

Use this test to measure your readiness for the actual MCAT. Try to answer all of the questions within the specified time limit. If you run out of time, you will know that you need to work on improving your pacing.

Complete answer explanations are provided at the end of the minitest. Pay particular attention to the answers for questions you got wrong or skipped. If necessary, go back and review the corresponding chapters or text sections in this unit.

Now turn the page and begin the Unit III Minitest.

Directions: *Choose the best answer to each of the following questions. Question 1 is not based on a passage.*

1. Which of Erik Erikson's stages occurs immediately after an individual is successful at integrating into larger social networks and achieving competence in academics?
   A. identity versus role confusion
   B. industry versus inferiority
   C. ego integrity versus despair
   D. generativity versus stagnation

Questions 2–5 are based on the following passage.

Passage I

The psychologist Harry Harlow conducted a series of famous experiments investigating maternal attachment in monkeys with multiple derivations on his classic study comparing infant attachment to nutrients versus comforting inanimate objects. This research is often referenced to show the development of early attachment and is an example of comparative psychology. The results of Harlow's research present some compelling evidence for the criticality of infant relationships.

The graphs that follow show one of Harlow's later experiments in infant monkey attachment with hypothetical data representing the behavior captured by Harlow in that study. This data set represents the amount of time (hours per day) that infant monkeys spent with surrogate (artificial) representations of their mothers. The surrogates were either made of wood covered in cloth or made of bare wire. Both the cloth

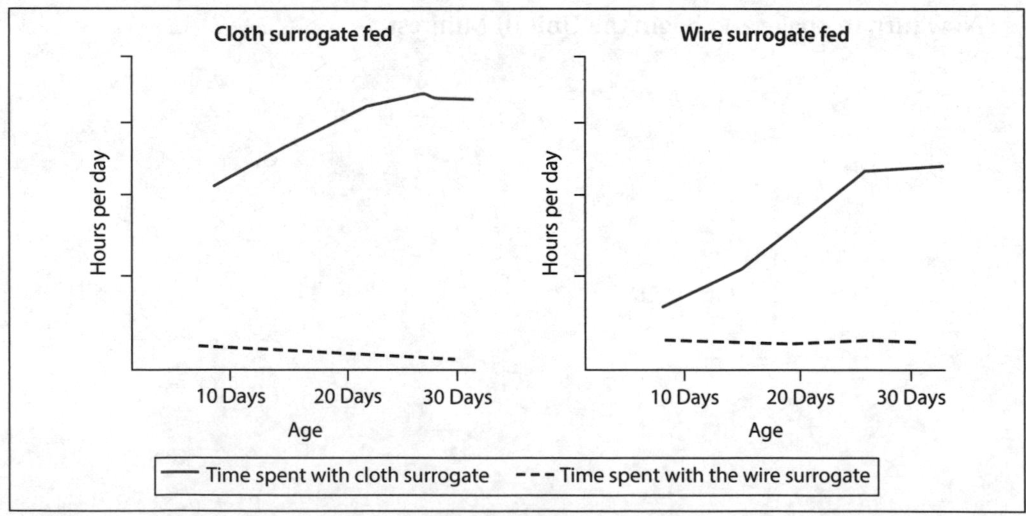

Two graphs representing two different artificial surrogate mothers, both equipped for feeding, and the hours per day that infant monkeys spent with them. *Source*: Data from Harlow, H. F., and Zimmerman, R. R. (1958). "The development of affectional responses in infant monkeys," *Proceedings of the American Philosophical Society*, 102(5), 501–509.

surrogate and the wire surrogate were provided with a rubber nipple that allowed for feeding. Both surrogates were present for all monkeys. The aim of the study was to determine which of the two surrogates the infant monkeys would choose to spend time with. The graph on the left shows the data collected from the group of infant monkeys who took food from the cloth surrogate. The graph on the right shows the data collected from the group of infant monkeys who took food from the wire surrogate. The time spent with the cloth surrogate is represented by the heavy blue line. The time spent with the wire surrogate is represented by the dotted line.

2. Which of the following statements is TRUE?
   A. The infant monkeys preferred to spend more time with the surrogate from which they took food.
   B. The infant monkeys preferred to spend more time with the surrogate that they did not use for feeding.
   C. The infant monkeys preferred to spend more time with the cloth surrogate regardless of whether they took food from the cloth surrogate or the wire surrogate.
   D. The infant monkeys preferred to spend more time with the wire surrogate regardless of whether they took food from the cloth surrogate or the wire surrogate.

3. Which of the following statements BEST describes Harlow's findings?
   A. Infant monkeys prefer whichever surrogate they took food from because a nutritive surrogate is of more evolutionary value.
   B. Infant monkeys prefer the cloth surrogate because they were attached to the emotional comfort that the cloth provides.
   C. Infant monkeys do not prefer one surrogate over the other, because both attachment and nutrition are needed equally.
   D. Infant monkeys prefer wire surrogates only when they are being fed by them.

4. Based on Harlow's work and socialization research, which of the following would happen if the infant monkeys were presented with a stimulus (e.g., an unfamiliar object) that caused fear?
   A. The infant monkeys would seek comfort from the cloth surrogate regardless of which surrogate they took food from.
   B. The infant monkeys would seek comfort from the wire surrogate regardless of which surrogate they took food from.
   C. The infant monkeys would seek comfort from whichever surrogate they took food from.
   D. The infant monkeys would not seek comfort from either surrogate, because they have already been associated with specific needs.

5. What additional experiment would BEST examine attachment in infant monkeys?
   A. Continue the experiment until the monkeys were more developed in order to test whether they would value nutrition more during a later developmental stage.
   B. Use two wire surrogates and no cloth surrogates to see whether the infant monkeys would attach to the wire surrogate through which they were fed.
   C. Feed adult monkeys from cloth surrogates to see if they develop attachment.
   D. Feed infant monkeys from both the cloth and wire surrogates at the same time.

Question 6 is not based on a passage.

6. Based on self-concept and identity, which of the following is TRUE about low self-esteem?
   A. It results from high self-efficacy and an internal locus of control.
   B. It results from low self-efficacy and an external locus of control.
   C. It results from high self-efficacy and an external locus of control.
   D. It results from low self-efficacy and an internal locus of control.

Questions 7–10 are based on the following passage.

Passage II

Attribution theory seeks to explain how individuals think about themselves and how they behave toward individuals around them. This theory also examines how an individual views internal and external traits, how he or she acts upon them, and how those views influence self-identity.

The following graphs show hypothetical data regarding last year's academic competition between students from two rival schools. The competition consists of three rounds of quizzes. Last year's competition ended in a tie since each side scored the same number of points.

The first graph shows the percent of questions each team answered correctly in each of the three quiz rounds.

The second graph shows the results from a survey of students who participated in the competition. The survey asked contestants what factors they thought helped them and their opponents pick correct answers. Specifically, they were asked what percent of the correct answers their own team picked and what percent the other team picked were attributable to each of the following two factors:

➤ study and preparation

➤ whether the test questions favored one team over the other

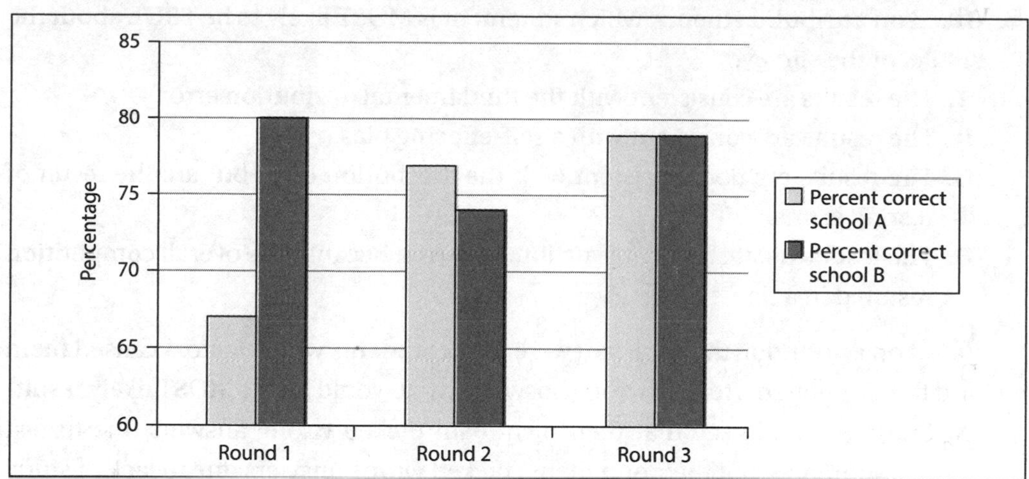

Percent of questions answered correctly by each school team by round.

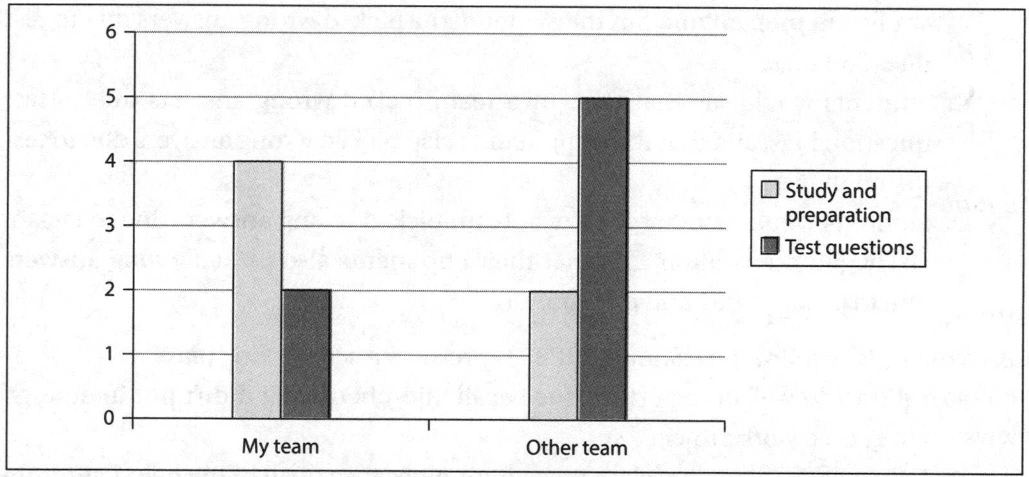

Survey results showing which factor students believed most helped contestants pick correct answers.

7. Based on the passage, which is the following is TRUE about the data set in the second figure?
   A. Students were more likely to attribute correct scores to study and preparation regardless of whether judging their own team or their opponents.
   B. Students were more likely to attribute correct scores to bias in the test questions regardless of whether judging their own team or their opponents.
   C. Students were more likely to judge their own team's correct scores as resulting from study and preparation and their opponents' correct scores as resulting from test question bias.
   D. Students were more likely to judge their own team's correct scores as resulting from test question bias and their opponents' correct scores as resulting from test question bias.

8. Based on attribution theory, which statement is MOST likely to be TRUE about the results of the survey?
   A. The results are consistent with the fundamental attribution error.
   B. The results are consistent with a self-effacing bias.
   C. The results are not consistent with the attribution error but are the result of testing errors.
   D. The results do not show any attribution error, because the overall competition resulted in a tie.

9. Based on attribution theory, if you were to ask students which factors caused them and their opponents to pick wrong answers, what would be the MOST likely result?
   A. Students would say that their own team picked wrong answers due to test question bias, but their opponents picked wrong answers due to lack of study and preparation.
   B. Students would say that their own team picked wrong answers due to lack of study and preparation, but their opponents picked wrong answers due to test question bias.
   C. Students would say that their own team picked wrong answers due to test question bias, and that their opponents also picked wrong answers due to test question bias.
   D. Students would say that their own team picked wrong answers due to lack of study and preparation, and that their opponents also picked wrong answers due to lack of study and preparation.

10. Which of the following examples BEST represents a self-serving bias?
   A. I didn't do well on a performance evaluation because I didn't put in enough effort on a work project.
   B. I did a great job on my class presentation because of all of the help I got from my classmates.
   C. The sound system was great, but my speech really wasn't very good.
   D. I got a terrible performance evaluation because those evaluations never measure actual skill.

Question 11 is not based on a passage.

11. Which of the following BEST describes Margaret Mead's findings?
   A. They indicated that biology was more important in determining gender roles than culture.
   B. They indicated that nature rather than nurture should be considered when determining gender roles.
   C. They indicated that gender roles were stable across multiple cultures.
   D. They indicated that in some cultures female public expression of opinions, thoughts, and feelings is more accepted.

Questions 12–15 are based on the following passage.

Passage III

Research studying people's ability to identify emotions from facial expressions has been carried out by a number of researchers. One such study by Paul Ekman and Wallace Friesen looked at agreement in judging facial expression in a number of countries. In a series of studies, Ekman and Friesen showed pictures to individuals from a number of cultures and asked them to categorize the facial expression. A sample of their findings is displayed as follows.

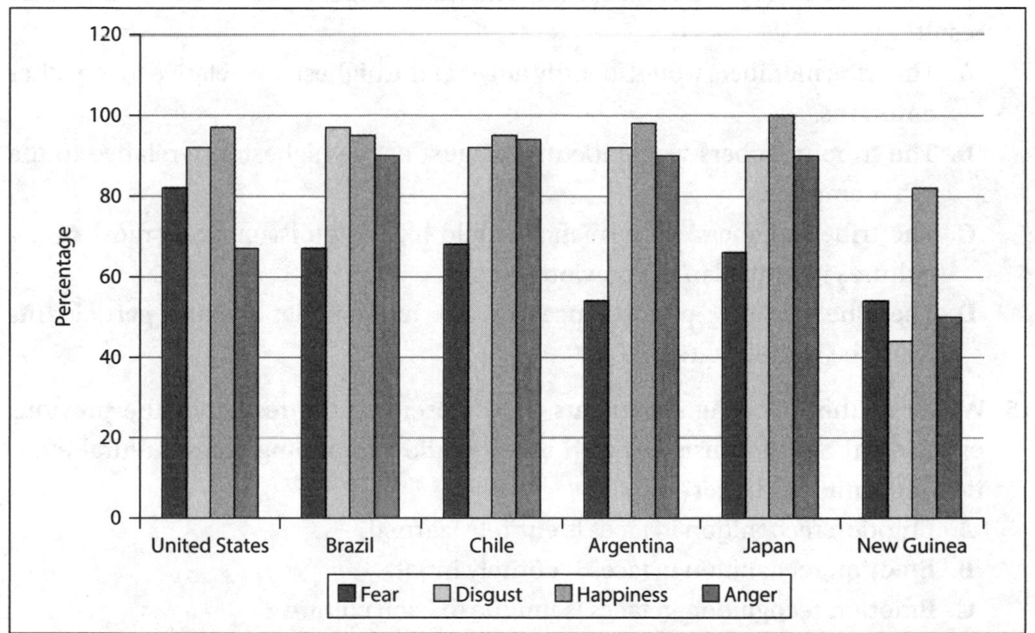

Facial expression agreement by country. *Source*: Data from Ekman, P., & Friesen, W. V. *Unmasking the Face: A Guide to Recognizing Emotions from Facial Clues.* Malor Books, 2003.

12. Which of the following statements is TRUE about the preceding data set?
    - **A.** Between-culture agreement was highest for the facial expression for fear.
    - **B.** Between-culture agreement was highest for the facial expression for anger.
    - **C.** Between-culture agreement was highest for the facial expression for happiness.
    - **D.** There were no differences between cultures regarding facial expressions.

13. Based on the data, which of the following statements is MOST accurate?
    A. Facial expressions are innately linked to emotion and therefore universal across cultures.
    B. The level of agreement between cultures for facial expression is fairly high, but there are important differences.
    C. The level of agreement between cultures for facial expression is low.
    D. The agreement rate for facial expressions is fairly high between the cultures except for New Guinea, which means they must have different genetic components for recognizing facial expressions compared to the other groups.

14. If you were to conduct a similar study recruiting participants from an extremely isolated tribe in the South American rainforest, what would be the MOST likely result?
    A. The tribe members would identify anger at the highest rate relative to the other emotions.
    B. The tribe members would identify disgust at the highest rate relative to the other emotions.
    C. The tribe members' performance would likely be dissimilar to most of the cultures identified in the previous graph.
    D. The tribe members' performance would be most similar to that of participants from the United States.

15. Which of the following statements BEST describes the results of the previous experiment and is consistent with other studies examining cross-cultural emotion recognition in faces?
    A. Emotion recognition in faces is entirely learned.
    B. Emotion recognition in faces is entirely innate.
    C. Emotion recognition in faces is unique to each culture.
    D. Emotion recognition in faces has a strong genetic influence but is also influenced by cultural differences.

Question 16 is not based on a passage.

16. Jason was attempting to tell his parents that he was doing well in school. His parents became somewhat suspicious of his assertion when the intensity and speed of his voice dramatically changed when talking about his geology class. What type of communication are Jason's parents responding to?
    A. verbal communication
    B. paraverbal communication
    C. nonverbal communication
    D. body language

This is the end of the Unit III Minitest.

Unit III Minitest Answers and Explanations

1. **The correct answer is A.** During the industry versus inferiority stage, an individual must successfully integrate into larger social networks and become competent in academics. Once this conflict is resolved, the individual then progresses to the identity versus role confusion stage.
2. **The correct answer is C.** The infant monkeys preferred to spend more time with the cloth surrogate regardless of whether they took food from the cloth surrogate or the wire surrogate. The data indicate that monkeys fed by either surrogate (cloth or wire) spent more time with the cloth surrogate.
3. **The correct answer is B.** Infant monkeys prefer the cloth surrogate because they were more attached to the emotional comfort that the cloth provides. The data show that regardless of which surrogate fed the infant monkeys, they preferred spending time with the more comforting cloth surrogate.
4. **The correct answer is A.** The infant monkeys would seek comfort from the cloth surrogate regardless of which surrogate they took food from. The monkeys would seek comfort from the cloth surrogate because they had become emotionally attached to the cloth surrogate. They would prefer the surrogate with which they had formed an attachment if presented with a stimulus eliciting fear.
5. **The correct answer is B.** This potential design would allow you to see whether attachment could be formed to the wire surrogate if given the right conditions. Using adult monkeys would not help you learn more about attachment in infant monkeys. Feeding monkeys from both surrogate types at the same time would most likely not result in any differences, since the infant monkeys already have shown their preference for the comforting (cloth) surrogate over the wire surrogate.
6. **The correct answer is B.** Low self-esteem results from low self-efficacy and an external locus of control. Low self-efficacy beliefs such as feeling that you cannot succeed and an external locus of control such as feeling that events are outside of your control are associated with low self-esteem.
7. **The correct answer is C.** Based on the data shown in the second figure, students were more likely to judge their own team's correct scores as resulting from study and preparation and their opponents' correct scores as resulting from test question bias.
8. **The correct answer is A.** Participants in the survey believed that correct scores for their team were the result of study and preparation (internal factor) and that correct scores for the other team were the result of test question bias.
9. **The correct answer is A.** Students would say that their own team picked wrong answers due to test question bias, but their opponents picked wrong answers due to lack of study and preparation. This is consistent with attribution theory, which posits that one's own personal successes are attributed to internal characteristics,

but others' successes are due to external factors. Conversely, one's own failures (wrong answers) are attributed to external factors (test question bias), while others' failures are attributed to internal factors (lack of study and preparation).

10. **The correct answer is D.** Self-serving bias is the tendency to attribute personal successes to personal traits/characteristics and personal failures to external causes. This answer is consistent with self-serving bias.
11. **The correct answer is D.** Mead examined gender roles across societies. One of her findings is that in some cultures female public expression is more accepted. As a result, women in those cultures are more active in social situations. This trend favors nurture over nature for emotional expression and intergender communication.
12. **The correct answer is C.** Between-culture agreement was highest for the facial expression for happiness. In all the countries studied except Brazil, the facial expression for happiness was the one that the most participants recognized, and even in Brazil, 95 percent of participants recognized the happiness expression. Further, the total average is highest for happiness relative to fear, disgust, and anger.
13. **The correct answer is B.** The rate of between-culture agreement for facial expression is fairly high between cultures, but there are important differences. The data in the graph indicate that the overlap is high despite cultural differences. However, for the most disparate culture studied (New Guinea), the overlap is much less robust. People in New Guinea do identify the facial expressions at better than by chance, but there is not as much overlap as with other cultures.
14. **The correct answer is C.** The tribe members' performance would likely be dissimilar to most of the other cultures in the graph. One criticism of Ekman and Friesen's research was that the cultures studied had a history of contact with one another and also had been exposed to culturally specific media (images, movies, etc.) of other cultures. Due to this criticism, Ekman and Friesen tested participants in New Guinea who had limited contact with the rest of the world. The isolated South American tribe would not have contact with the other major cultures in the graph and therefore would interpret facial cues solely on the basis of their own culture. The responses from the isolated participants described in the question would be the most similar to the participants from New Guinea, although the completely isolated tribe members' performance may be even lower than those from New Guinea.
15. **The correct answer is D.** Emotion recognition in faces has a strong genetic basis but is also influenced by cultural differences. The results of this study show a strong overlap between similar and disparate cultures. This is evidence for a genetic influence. However, the results also show that the agreement is not absolute and that

more disparate cultures differ the most, suggesting that there is also a cultural and learned influence.

16. **The correct answer is B.** Paraverbal communication is characterized by aspects of the verbal communication such as tone, volume, speed, and prosody. As such, the same words can be received very differently depending on the paraverbal aspects accompanying the words.

UNIT IV

Social Structure

Foundational Concept: Social and cultural differences influence well-being.

CHAPTER 10

Understanding Social Structure

Read This Chapter to Learn About

- ➤ Social Structure and Development
- ➤ Social Institutions
- ➤ Culture

SOCIAL STRUCTURE AND DEVELOPMENT

There are two divergent forces that create social structure:

- ➤ **Agency** is the ability of a person (an **agent**) to act independently and individually. The agent typically seeks to maximize the efficacy of his or her actions.
- ➤ **Institution** provides the structure of the society within which the agent acts.

The two forces are in constant interaction and at times conflict with one another. The agent attempts to act individually, and the structure of institutions resists individual action. Some thinkers, such as the famous French sociologist Émile Durkheim, have believed that individual agency is definable only within the limits of the institution in which the agent lives. Others, such as the noted German sociologist Max Weber, have believed that the institution is built only through the actions of individual agents.

Theories of Social Structure

There are different viewpoints on the structure and function of society.

- ➤ **Functionalism** is a theoretical paradigm based on the idea that the parts of the society are separate but interrelated. Émile Durkheim likened society to the human body, each component acting separately, but critical to the functioning of the whole. A disruption in one area can disrupt the entire system. This view of society supports the status quo and attempts to avoid any disruptions in the system.

- **Conflict theory** is a contrasting view to functionalism. According to this theory, developed by the radical German philosopher Karl Marx, society is fundamentally in conflict because there is an uneven distribution of resources. Differences in prestige and resources create fundamental power struggles between groups of people. The divisiveness extends across gender, race, and socioeconomic status.
- **Symbolic interactionism** is yet another view of society. This theory focuses on how individuals interact with each other using symbols of social structure. The pioneering social psychologist George Mead (not to be confused with the anthropologist Margaret Mead) proposed that an individual's identity is developed through social interactions. These social interactions are refined by symbols that are defined by a society (e.g., Is long hair on men a norm or an anomaly? Is wearing white a symbol of a wedding or mourning? Are downcast eyes a sign of respect or lying?). These symbols set the stage for the interactions that create the individual.
- **Social constructionism** is a theory that attempts to address the fact that an individual needs to understand the world to act as an agent within it. Developed by the Canadian philosopher Ian Hacking, this theory holds that the understanding of the world is constructed not by the individual, but rather by the collection of all individuals who make up the society. The mechanism of this construction is the shared language among a society that creates a model for reality. The individual absorbs this construct of reality by living in the society and adopts this construction of reality for him- or herself.
- **Globalization** is a theory regarding the spread of culture that has gained increasing currency since the 1980s. As the world becomes increasingly interconnected across the areas of economics, communications, and travel, many sociologists have come to believe that individual cultural differences are falling away in favor of a single global world culture. Globalization has become an increasingly active field of study in sociology.

SOCIAL INSTITUTIONS

Each society develops its own institutions and determines how those institutions interact with its culture.

Education

The structure of **education** is societally determined. Not only does a society determine who receives the education (only the wealthy? only males? only children up to a certain age?), but also the appropriate content of that education (rote memorization versus abstract problem solving, ancient versus modern languages, mathematics versus literature). Even the methodology of transmitting information is socially determined (e.g., books, online lectures, self-directed study versus directed course of study). The role of education may be viewed differently depending on the theoretical paradigm adopted. For functionalists, education may be seen as a way to reinforce the status quo. For conflict theorists, education may be viewed as a means either to reinforce inequalities or to distribute knowledge and begin to equalize differences among groups.

Family

Family is a social institution that is partly private but that also has a very public and political component. Identifying who is "family" and who is not depends on whether the family is primarily limited to the **nuclear family** or if it is defined to also include a broad network of genetically (and/or maritally) related individuals. Also, whether family is traced using matrilineal or patrilineal bloodlines is socially determined. Once it has been defined who is in the family, the roles of family members can be defined by society. Who can be married, how many individuals constitute a marriage, and what is the function of marriage (e.g., procreation, social or political connections, convergence of economic wealth) are very much political and public discussions. Each society's answer to these questions also determines the status of offspring from sexual connections and how those offspring fit (or do not fit) into that society's definition of family. Across almost every culture, family is one of the fundamental building blocks of society. However, who is included in that building block may vary greatly across cultures.

Religion

Religion and religious institutions can have a powerful effect on society. The impact can be on the structure of a society (e.g., prayer times, holidays, charity donations) and on a society's worldview, traditions, and values via religious beliefs. Depending on the sociological viewpoint, religious institutions may enhance or degrade the cohesion of the society. According to conflict theorists, religion acts to maintain the inequalities inherent in society. Functionalists believe that religion enhances social cohesion by creating a sense of belonging as part of a collective consciousness.

Economic Institutions

Every society creates economic systems and institutions to perform and control the allocation of resources. Within each economic system there are three levels of production. **Primary production** includes producing or extracting raw goods and materials (e.g., farming and mining). **Secondary production** is the conversion of those raw goods into manufactured products for use or sale (e.g., turning trees into lumber for construction). **Tertiary production** (also called the service sector) is the share of the economy that is focused on providing services such as health care to other members of the community. The institutions that perform and regulate economic activity at each level can include business corporations of every size and function, banks, stock exchanges, and innumerable other institutions.

Government

There are also three primary types of government recognized by sociologists:

1. **Authoritarian** government is a system in which a ruling class of individuals controls the government with little input from the population.
2. **Totalitarian** government is a highly developed authoritarian system that controls society down to the minutiae of individuals' lives. The general population has little or no input into how government functions. Often this type of government is headed by a single individual whose power is virtually unlimited and who is supported by a cult of personality.
3. **Democratic** government is a system in which the general population actively participates by electing government officials.

There are variations on these themes in governments across the world, but these are the primary forms.

As the globalization paradigm suggests, government and economic institutions are becoming increasingly interconnected across the world. Despite the increasing globalization of these institutions, there is still a great deal of societal differences about level of individual participation in government and level of financial disparity in a society. Most global societies use some form of national government and also currency as part of the exchange for goods and services. However, smaller societies may still use community level government for the establishment of social rules and use the barter system to arrange for the distribution of materials, goods, and resources.

CULTURE

Culture is a complex phenomenon that describes the beliefs, customs, language, and institutions that make up a community.

- **Material culture** describes the tangible objects that individuals use to describe or transmit their culture. Material culture objects may also have symbolic cultural meaning (generic jeans versus designer jeans). Material objects may be a mechanism for communication to others about the symbolic value of themselves or others.

- **Symbolic culture** comprises the intangible aspects of a culture. **Beliefs** are the assumptions that a culture collectively holds about the surrounding world (e.g., people are fundamentally good). Beliefs give rise to a culture's **values** that determine the worth of ideas (e.g., it is important that people who commit crimes be treated for mental disorders). Collective actions of the society then arise from those values (e.g., an increase in mental health treatment availability). The symbolic culture also includes the cultural norms and the rituals that a culture uses to create group cohesion. The **norms** of a culture describe the daily rules of behavior that circumscribe the actions of members of a society and the rules of role expectation for individuals. **Rituals**, on the other hand, are unique behaviors that are not an ordinary part of everyday life. Rituals can be used to increase group cohesion and promote a sense of unity among group members.

Culture Versus Social Groups

An individual may belong to multiple social groups, but social groups are not necessarily equivalent to cultures. **Social groups** may be based on shared traits such as gender socioeconomic status or other common factors such as shared belief systems. Such groups are intrinsically social constructs that are based on the culture from which they stem. While individuals in these groups share similar experiences and shared group experiences are a critical component of culture, some sociologists would argue that those shared experiences are not enough to be called a culture. **Cultures** must include not only shared social groupings, but also shared language, world construct, ideological beliefs, social norms, and values.

Humans are by nature pack animals. While individuality may be highly valued in some cultures, all cultures support positive interaction with other human beings. Humans evolved to engage in frequent social interactions and to rely on other members of the species. Humans across the world have created structures in their social interactions to increase ease of communication and interaction. Environmental and individual pressures altered the development of social cultures to develop the unique configurations of society and culture seen in the world today. It is the nature of culture to become increasingly complex over time.

CHAPTER 11

Demographic Characteristics and Processes

Read This Chapter to Learn About

➤ Elements of Social Interactions

➤ The Demographic Structure of Society

ELEMENTS OF SOCIAL INTERACTIONS

Social interactions are affected by status, as well as by social and cultural roles. How, where, and with whom the interactions occur can communicate culturally based information before any verbal information is exchanged.

Status

An individual's **status** within a culture may affect multiple aspects of social interaction. There are three types of status:

1. **Ascribed status** is the status that is placed upon a person by society (e.g., being born into a royal family).
2. **Achieved status** is status that is conferred because of a person's accomplishments (e.g., receiving a doctorate degree).

3. **Master status** is the overarching status that a person may exercise in society. This kind of status may establish rules about who initiates a conversation. It can affect body language during a conversation (e.g., standing versus sitting).

In many cultures, status is expressed through clothing or body display and therefore does not need to be explicitly stated. But in cross-cultural interactions, status may not be as evident. This can create difficulties when individuals work from scripts based on their own cultures but those scripts conflict. Cross-cultural status issues can be particularly difficult for younger medical professionals. In some cultures, medical professionals are given the elevated status of "experts" and patient participation in care is expected to be minimal. However, this may conflict with the cultural expectation that a younger person should acquiesce to the direction of older individuals. The result may be status conflicts that young medical professionals should be aware of when working with cross-cultural populations.

Social and Cultural Roles

Culturally delineated roles can have an important influence on social interactions. Some cultures have more rigid role boundaries, while others have more flexible role boundaries (e.g., can a medical professional have the roles of both "physician" and "friend," or are those roles kept distinct?). Flexible boundaries may create **role strain**, which occurs when the two roles a person plays are in tension (e.g., sitting with a sick person for a long time may be the role of a friend, but a physician has multiple patients in need of treatment). There may also be **role conflict**, when two roles are diametrically opposed to each other (e.g., listening to someone talk about personal problems may be the role of a friend, but a physician cannot share a litany of personal problems with his/her patient and then expect the patient to have confidence that the physician is providing quality treatment).

Gender roles also play a significant part in social interactions, but these vary in importance across cultures. For example, touching members of the opposite sex (including shaking hands with them) or being in a room alone with a member of the opposite sex may adversely affect social interactions with individuals from conservative Christian, Muslim, or Hasidic Jewish groups. Gender roles may also affect what is determined to be a comfortable speaking distance between two individuals.

Group membership may also influence culturally defined roles. Group membership can include those social groups that are selected by the individual (e.g., religious affiliation, professional career), those that are biologically based (e.g., sex, age), and those who are variable depending on life status (e.g., socioeconomic status, geographic location). Group membership may affect both the roles that an individual plays in social interactions as well as the individual's status within a culture.

Group membership will also define an individual's **social network**. However, the level of obligation that is entailed by involvement in a social network may change from culture to culture. For example, in Chinese culture, *guanxi* is a social network relationship that implies a strong mutual obligation that overrides social status. In other cultures, a social network may be more of a loose group of acquaintances with limited or no obligations implied.

THE DEMOGRAPHIC STRUCTURE OF SOCIETY

Various factors create the demographic structure of society, such as age, gender and sex, race and ethnicity, and regional subgroups. Most of these demographic factors are emphasized by culturally defined dress and behavior patterns.

Age

Age is a critical factor in determining how someone is treated in a society. In some societies, infants are coddled and closely nurtured until school age. In others, children are largely benevolently ignored until they reach adulthood. The age at which an individual is considered to have reached adulthood differs from society to society. A person may be called an adult upon reaching a certain age (e.g., 18 or 21 years) or only following a demographic transition such as marriage. However, even within a culture this may change. In the United States, some sociologists have proposed a new "transitional age youth" category that ranges from 15 to 30 years old, blurring the transition to adulthood. In some cultures, people are thought to reach a post-adult "age of wisdom" somewhere between 40 and 60 years old; an example of this attitude is the Jewish proscription against studying Kabbalah before the age of 40. Elderly persons may be revered, as in Japanese culture, or less so, as in much of American culture—attitudes that carry over into patient care. An age structure chart is often used in sociology to identify the age demographics of a society. This (usually) pyramid-shaped chart identifies how many individuals in each age category live in the society. (See Figure 11-1.)

Gender and Sex

Gender is different from biological sex. **Sex** is a biological construct that is genetically determined. Most humans are either XX-female or XY-male, though there are genetic anomalies that result in XXY or XYY sex genotypes. **Gender**, on the other hand. is a sociological construct that is often reflected in the phenotype of sexual organs (though this is not universal). Gender identity tends to occur at a fairly young age, though

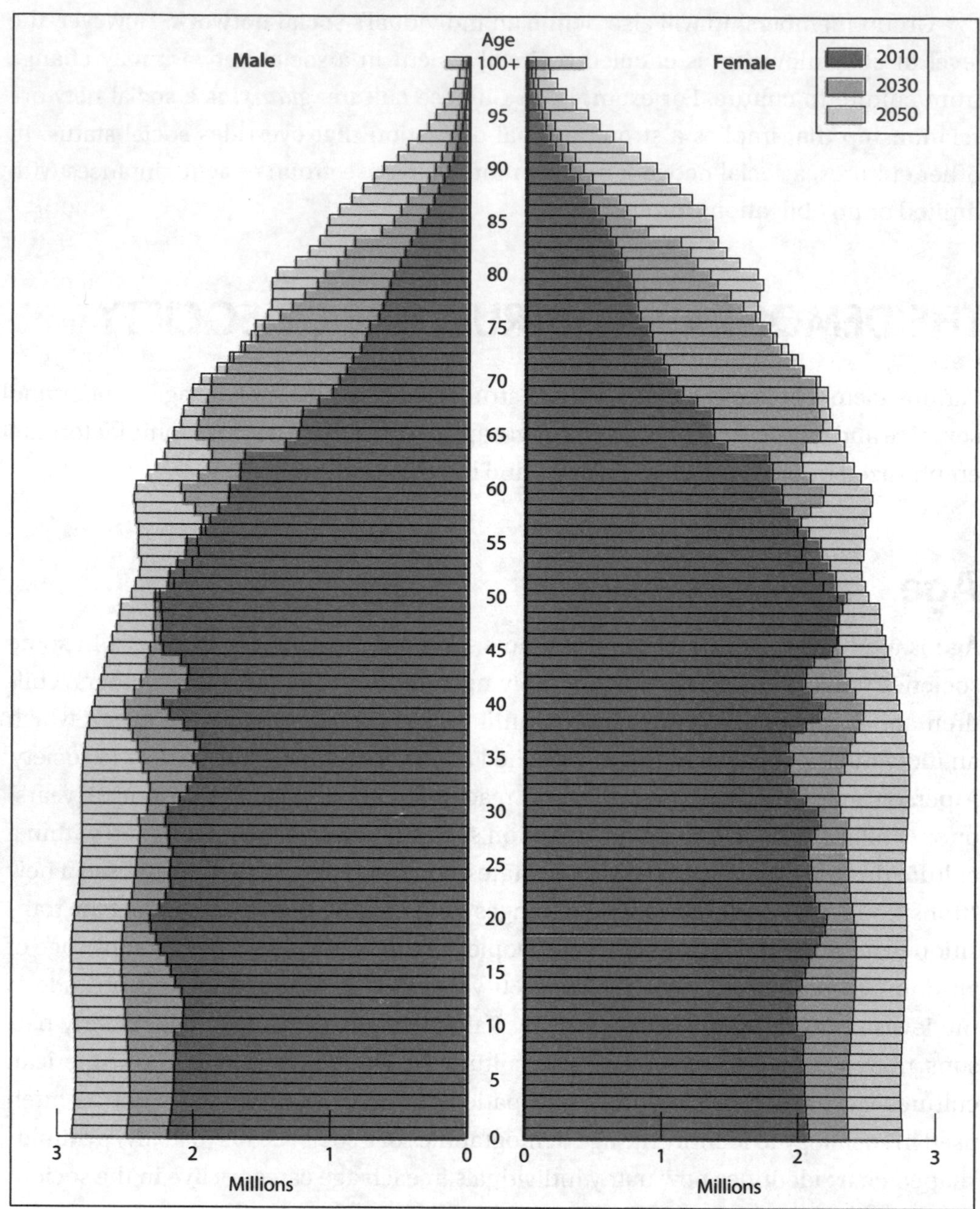

FIGURE 11-1 Age structure chart of the US population. *Source*: US Census Bureau, 2008.

estimates range from age 2 to age 10. Gender in Western culture is primarily reflected in the terms *man* and *woman*. Sandra Bem introduced the idea of gender schema theory to describe how gender is developed in Western society. In her research she identified four gender categories:

1. sex-typed (in which gender matches biological sex)
2. cross-sex typed (gender is aligned with the opposite sex)
3. androgynous (gender identity includes both sexes)
4. undifferentiated (limited processing of sex-typed information on gender)

Other cultures may include multiple genders such as the third gender in Indian culture, the "Hijras." One sociologist (Gopi Shankar) has identified up to 20 different categories of gender. His work highlighted the importance of language and culture in gender identification and gender identity.

Sexual orientation describes an individual's preferred sexual partner. Sexual orientation may not be identified until the individual reaches puberty or early adolescence. Gender identity in the context of culture is tied to sexual orientation (fewer recognized gender identities in a culture may result in fewer options of sexual orientation). In Western culture sexual orientation is most widely categorized as a tri-part structure (heterosexual, homosexual, bisexual), though these three categories may not capture the full diversity of sexual orientation. Sociologist Shankar has identified 10 different sexual orientations, again highlighting the role of culture and language in the social process of defining sexual orientation (though not necessarily orientation itself).

Race and Ethnicity

Similar to sex and gender, race and ethnicity are different. **Race** is determined by biological, genetic factors, though these are obviously even more complex than sex. An individual's skin tone, bone structure, eye color, and hair color are phenotypes of genetic racial characteristics. Some phenotypic differences exist between the races, though both the genetic and phenotypic lines differentiating the groups may not be clear. **Ethnicity** is a social construct that includes cultural factors. While race may be one aspect of ethnicity, it is not the defining factor. For example, an individual's race may be Caucasian, but ethnicity could include French, English, or Nordic.

Regional Subgroups

Geographic location is also an artificial construct that is frequently used to describe cultural or socioeconomic status similarities. In the United States, terms such as "Appalachian region," "Plains states," or "Deep South" are frequently used to identify subgroups. However, as the population becomes increasingly mobile, the geographic groups are less likely to be coherent uniform groups and may provide less reliable information.

Unit IV Minitest

15 Questions **30 Minutes**

This minitest is designed to assess your mastery of the content in Chapters 10 and 11 of this volume. The questions have been designed to simulate actual MCAT questions in terms of format and degree of difficulty. They are based on the content categories associated with the foundational concept that is the theme of this unit. They are also designed to test the scientific inquiry and reasoning skills that the test makers have identified as essential for success in medical school.

In this test, most of the questions are based on short passages that typically describe a research study or some similar process. There are also some questions that are not based on passages.

Use this test to measure your readiness for the actual MCAT. Try to answer all of the questions within the specified time limit. If you run out of time, you will know that you need to work on improving your pacing.

Complete answer explanations are provided at the end of the minitest. Pay particular attention to the answers for questions you got wrong or skipped. If necessary, go back and review the corresponding chapters or text sections in this unit.

Now turn the page and begin the Unit IV Minitest.

Directions: *Choose the best answer to each of the following questions. Questions 1–2 are not based on a passage.*

1. Mental health hospitals and prisons are forms of
   A. agencies
   B. institutions
   C. functionalism
   D. social cohesion

2. Separate the following into ascribed and achieved status.
   1. woman
   2. Olympic athlete
   3. mayor
   4. parent
   5. Christian
   6. rabbi
   7. 45 years old
   8. physician
   A. Ascribed: 1, 2, 3, 4; Achieved: 5, 6, 7, 8
   B. Ascribed: 1, 4, 5, 7; Achieved: 2, 3, 6, 8
   C. Ascribed: 4, 5, 6, 8; Achieved: 1, 2, 3, 7
   D. Ascribed: 1, 3, 7, 8; Achieved: 2, 4, 5, 6

Questions 3–6 are based on the following passage.

Passage I

Significant changes took place in the United States over the past century regarding how and when US citizens were institutionalized. The accompanying graph tracks the rate of adults' institutionalization in mental hospitals and prisons in the period 1928–2000.

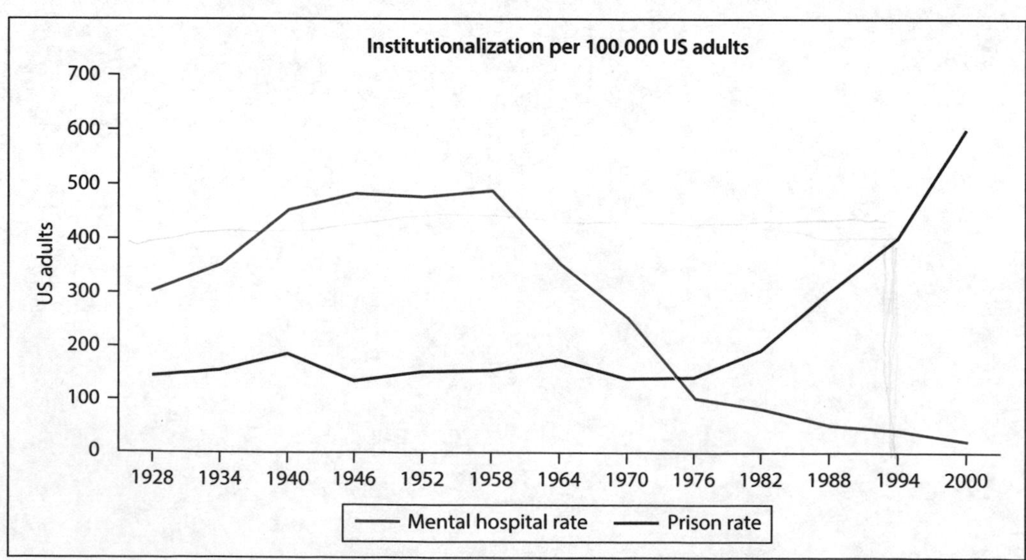

Source: Based on statistics from the federal Census Bureau, Department of Health and Human Services, and Bureau of Justice Statistics.

3. What was the rate of institutionalization in mental hospitals and prisons for US adults in 1994?
   A. 0.4% in mental hospitals; 0.2% in prison
   B. 0.04% in mental hospitals; 0.02% in prison
   C. 0.02% in mental hospitals; 0.04% in prison
   D. 0.2% in mental hospitals; 0.4% in prison

4. Which of the following can you conclude from the graph?
   A. The rate of mental health hospitalization decreased in the period during which the imprisonment rate increased.
   B. The decrease in the mental health hospitalization rate caused the increase in the imprisonment rate.
   C. There is a relationship between the number of individuals in prison and the number of individuals in mental health institutions.
   D. The increase in the imprisonment rate caused a decrease in the mental health hospitalization rate.

5. What possible hypothesis might be extrapolated from this graph?
   A. Some individuals with severe mental illness need to be institutionalized in prison or mental health hospitals.
   B. Prisons provide good mental health treatment similar to mental health hospitals.
   C. Without sufficient treatment in mental health hospitals, some severely mentally ill people may commit crime and face imprisonment.
   D. Prisons are cheaper than mental health hospitals and can treat people more efficiently.

6. Which of the following options is the BEST way to test the hypothesis suggested by the data in the graph?
   A. by comparing which provided the best treatment option, imprisonment or mental health hospitalization
   B. by tracking individuals released from mental health institutions to assess their imprisonment status longitudinally
   C. by identifying the percentage of prison inmates who have mental health needs
   D. by comparing recidivism rates between prison and mental health hospitals

Questions 7–8 are not based on a passage.

7. Health care is an example of which level of economic production?
   A. primary
   B. secondary
   C. tertiary
   D. quaternary

8. What is the difference between race and ethnicity?
   A. Race is primarily genetically determined; ethnicity is primarily determined by social characteristics.
   B. Race is identified by skin color; ethnicity is identified by geographic region.
   C. Race determines sexual orientation; ethnicity determines the term used to describe sexual orientation.
   D. Race determines family; ethnicity determines marriage relationships.

Questions 9–12 are based on the following passage.

Passage II

Every year, the US Department of Education records how many degrees are awarded based on demographic factors. The following chart shows bachelor's degrees awarded to US students during the school year 2009–2010, categorized by race, ethnicity, and gender.

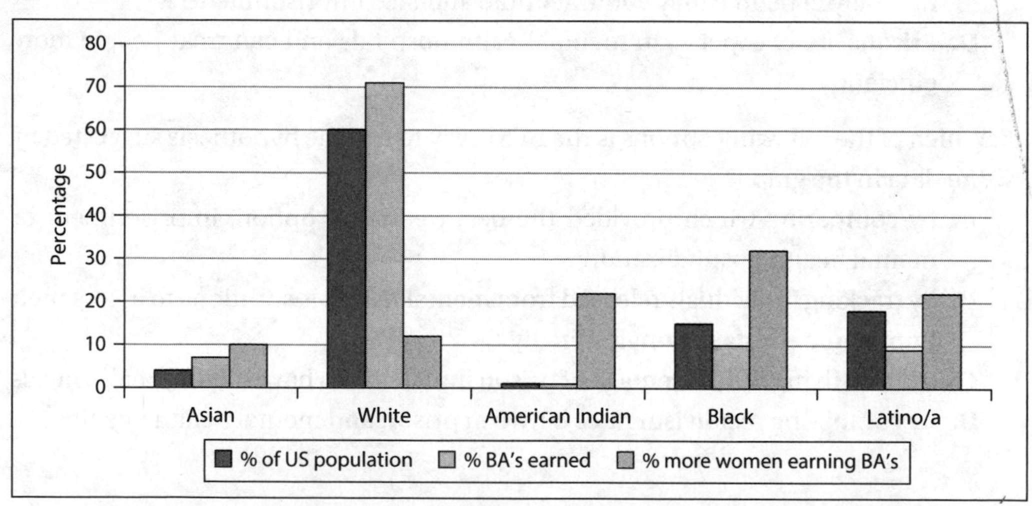

US bachelor's degrees awarded by race/ethnicity and gender. *Source*: Adapted from US Dept. of Education, National Education Statistics 2011.

9. According to the chart, in 2009–2010 which racial/ethnic group(s) earned a higher percentage of bachelor's degrees than their percentage in the US population?
   A. black, Latino/a
   B. American Indian, black
   C. white, Asian
   D. only whites

10. According to the chart, during 2009–2010 in which ethnic or racial group(s) did women earn more bachelor's degrees than men?
   A. none of the racial or ethnic groups
   B. every racial or ethnic group except whites
   C. only whites
   D. every racial or ethnic group

11. What can be concluded from the data in the chart?
   A. Women are more interested than men in pursuing higher educational opportunities.
   B. Financial aid is being offered to greater numbers of women to pursue their education.
   C. Women are completing bachelor's degrees more often than men.
   D. More women than men are pursuing higher-paid careers.

12. Despite their increased education levels, women earn less money than their male counterparts. What sociological phenomenon might explain this?
   A. In the United States, ascribed statuses influence women's master status more strongly than achieved statuses.
   B. Women are more likely to experience sociological role strain because they have more flexible boundaries, which negatively affect their intelligence.
   C. Social functionalism explains the difference because the careers chosen by women tend to be less critical to the functioning of society compared to the careers chosen by men.
   D. More women live in geographic locations that offer lower pay (e.g., rural areas), whereas men tend to live in geographic areas that offer higher pay (e.g., cities).

Questions 13–15 are not based on a passage.

13. Which of the following is characteristic of a totalitarian government?
    A. active participation in government by the population being governed and periodic election of officials
    B. a government headed by a single executive whose powers are limited by a written or unwritten constitution
    C. a government dominated by an elite who obtain membership in the ruling class based on birth, property ownership, or some other criterion
    D. a government that exercises power arbitrarily and without limits and that seeks to control every sphere of activity including citizens' actions and even thoughts

14. Which of the following is NOT necessarily an aspect of culture?
    A. shared language
    B. shared customs
    C. shared race
    D. shared institutions

15. Which of the following statements is TRUE about gender?
    A. Gender is a sociological concept.
    B. All cultures subdivide into two genders.
    C. Gender identity in the context of culture is tied to sexual orientation.
    D. Gender is biologically determined.

This is the end of the Unit IV Minitest.

Unit IV Minitest Answers and Explanations

1. **The correct answer is B.** Both mental health hospitals and prisons are institutions.
2. **The correct answer is B.** Labels (1) woman, (4) parent, (5) Christian, and (7) 45 years old are given to a person based on the person's demographic information or group membership. By contrast, labels (2) Olympic athlete, (3) mayor, (6) rabbi, and (8) physician describe achieved statuses that require specific study, effort, or directed energy to obtain.
3. **The correct answer is D.** According to the graph, in 1994, 200 out of every 100,000 US adults were in mental hospitals (0.2%), and 400 out of every 100,000 US adults were in prison (0.4%).
4. **The correct answer is A.** This graph does not provide sufficient information to imply a causal or any other type of relationship between the two rates of institutionalization. While other research has expanded people's understanding of this relationship, the only definitive statement about these two rates that can be made based on the graph is choice A.
5. **The correct answer is C.** According to the graph, there was an initial decrease in the rate of mental health hospitalizations, followed (after a lag of a few years) by an increase in the rate of imprisonment. This data could suggest that some individuals who were prematurely discharged from mental health hospitals due to a policy change later committed crimes that required imprisonment.
6. **The correct answer is B.** The hypothesis is that some individuals who were prematurely discharged from mental health hospitals due to a policy change later committed crimes that required imprisonment. By tracking individuals released from mental health hospitals, a researcher might be able to see if individuals who were prematurely released later committed crimes requiring imprisonment. This would be one of the few ways to establish this kind of cause-effect relationship for the data in the graph. Choice C would not be the best answer, because not all mental health needs require hospital-level care.
7. **The correct answer is C.** Health care is part of the service sector, which is the tertiary level of production in an economy.
8. **The correct answer is A.** Race is determined by genetic characteristics that may have similar phenotypes, but not necessarily (e.g., an individual who is of African heritage but has albinism may appear white but still be genetically African/black). Ethnicity, by contrast, is determined by social characteristics such as language, religion, and cultural values.
9. **The correct answer is C.** Within each group of three vertical bars, the bar on the left represents the percentage of the US population that identifies as that racial/ethnic group, and the bar in the middle represents the percentage of bachelor's degrees earned by that racial or ethnic group. The bar in the middle is higher than the bar on the left only for the Asian and white populations.

10. **The correct answer is D.** In the chart, the third vertical bar in each group represents the percentage of women earning more BAs than men within that racial or ethnic group. In every case, the presence of the bar indicates that women earn more than 50 percent of the BAs. If the women in a group were earning fewer BAs than men, there would be no vertical bar in that position.
11. **The correct answer is C.** While choices A, B, and D may be true, interest levels, financial aid, or career choice cannot be extrapolated from this chart. The only conclusion is that women are more successful than men at completing bachelor's degrees.
12. **The correct answer is A.** Research suggests that a woman's ascribed status (mother, wife) may have a greater influence on her overall status in US society than her personal and educational accomplishments. Women's ascribed statuses may also have greater role demands than men's (e.g., for a woman in the United States, being a "parent" and "wife" usually still requires assuming more than 50 percent of child care and household responsibilities, as compared to a man's role demands as a "parent" and "husband").
13. **The correct answer is D.** A totalitarian government is one that exercises power arbitrarily and without limits and that seeks to control every sphere of activity, including citizen's actions and even thoughts. The term was applied to both the Nazi and the Soviet governments in the mid-20th century.
14. **The correct answer is C.** Culture is a complex phenomenon that includes beliefs, customs, language, and the institutions that make up a community. While race overlaps this concept, it is not necessary for race to be homogenous across a culture.
15. **The correct answer is A.** Gender is a sociological construct. By contrast, sex is a biological construct that is genetically determined. Gender is often reflected in the genetic phenotype of sexual organs, but this categorization is not universal. Some cultures divide gender into multiple types of identities, and gender is not necessarily linked to sexual orientation.

UNIT V

Social Strata

Foundational Concept: Social stratification affects access to resources and well-being.

CHAPTER 12

Social Inequality

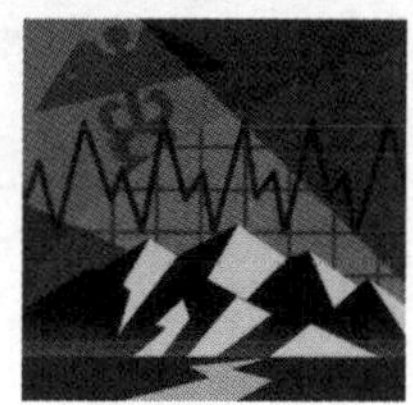

Read This Chapter to Learn About

- Social Class
- Theories of Stratification
- Poverty
- Health Care Disparities

SOCIAL CLASS

Social class has been defined by sociologists, economists, and others in numerous ways. In one common and basic definition, a social class is a group of people who share similar material wealth, influence, and status in society. Sociologists often designate class with the label socioeconomic status (SES). In the United States, sociologists generally recognize anywhere from three to five primary SES groups. One of the most widely used definitions, proposed in 2005 by William Thompson and Joseph Hickey, recognizes five primary SES categories. The graph in Figure 12-1 shows the following class categories in the United States.

Measured in economic terms, the **upper class** comprises the top 1 percent of Americans. People in this group earn more than $350,000 per year and hold approximately 25 percent of total US wealth. Approximately half of the individuals who fall into this category were born into this class, while half rose into it from lower classes.

The **middle class** is the largest single class and is commonly divided into the upper middle class and lower middle class. The difference between the upper middle class and lower middle class is not solely based on income level. It also includes values, education levels, lifestyle, and occupation. Generally, individuals in the **upper middle class** comprise approximately 15 percent of the US population. Upper middle class households have above-average incomes of more than $100,000 per year. People in this category also tend to value education, and many hold graduate degrees and

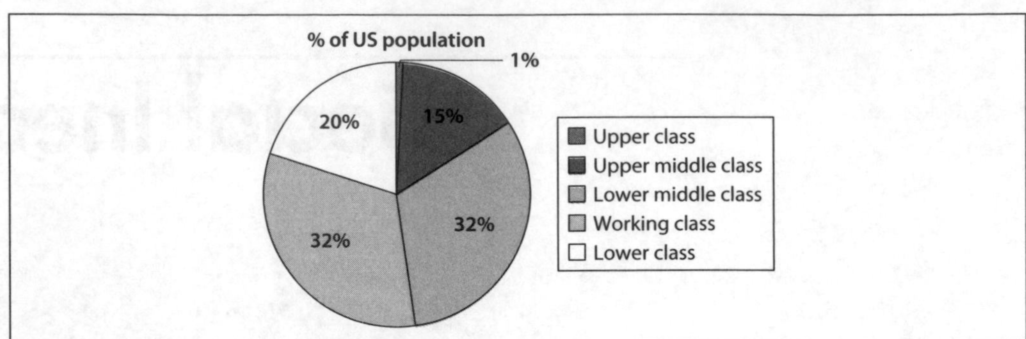

FIGURE 12-1 Percentage of US population in each class category.

jobs that allow for greater flexibility in the workplace. **Lower middle class** individuals comprise approximately 32 percent of the US population. Individuals in this category usually have some education beyond high school and often work in lower-level "white collar" administrative positions with household incomes ranging from $35,000 to $75,000 per year.

Working class households make up approximately 32 percent of the US population. Individuals in this category usually have completed high school and work in "blue collar," or basic clerical, positions that often have low job security. Household incomes in this category usually range from $16,000 to $30,000 per year.

Lower class households make up approximately 20 percent of the US population. Individuals in this category may not have finished high school and rely on unreliable and low-paid positions. They may also rely on government funds to meet their basic needs.

THEORIES OF STRATIFICATION

There are multiple ways that a society may stratify its population, and these often revolve around class, status, or power. From a **functionalist** sociology approach, stratification serves to preserve the functioning of society. Rewards are given to individuals who occupy positions that are more critical to the functioning of society; those individuals are rewarded with increased resources. Those rewards then serve to attract the "best and brightest" to the positions that are most critical to the functioning of the society. This ties closely to the idea of **meritocracy**, a society in which individuals with significant achievements are rewarded with power and prestige. Ancient China was one of the first governments to make use of the idea of meritocracy. Men who performed well on increasingly difficult civil service exams could be appointed to increasingly higher levels of government. However, in a true meritocracy, everyone would have equal access to educational opportunities.

In contrast to the functionalists, **social conflict** theorists believe that a functionalist system may be viable only at a certain point in the development of a given society.

However, once social stratification becomes entrenched, it then becomes a means for those with the most power and resources to maintain their dominant position. Because everyone does not have access to the same opportunities (e.g., education, safety), stratification acts to maintain the existing social hierarchy.

Social mobility refers to the ability of an individual to move up or down through the social strata. The opposite of social mobility is **social reproduction**, which is a term for those institutions and behaviors that transmit social inequality from generation to generation. Where social mobility is available, many parents will use their own social or cultural capital to help their children maintain or improve their social standing. **Nepotism** is the practice by higher-status persons of providing privileges to younger or lower-status family members as a way of expanding those family members' wealth and prestige. It is an example of how families use social capital to entrench their own social status.

Social reproduction is transmitted through four interrelated types of capital:

- **Financial capital** is the monetary wealth and goods of an individual.
- **Cultural capital** involves the world outlook and beliefs that are passed from parents to children (e.g., "Education will make you successful.").
- **Human capital** involves the education or skills that an individual acquires in preparation for his or her future (e.g., should you end schooling at high school or sacrifice current time and resources to achieve a college degree?). The cultural capital that a child receives from parents can influence that child's degree of and decisions about human capital.
- **Social capital** describes the network that an individual develops. This network can affect a future career (e.g., going to college, you can meet other college grads who might be able to hire you for a job in the future).

These types of capital are highly interdependent to the point of becoming circular as human capital influences social capital, and social capital can then directly affect an individual's financial capital. Because this capital system is circular, it encourages social reproduction: these types of capital are passed across generations, affecting social mobility (or social status rigidity).

Cultural capital can have the greatest impact on intergenerational social mobility. Even in the context of low financial capital, strong cultural capital transmission that emphasizes human capital values is most likely to contribute to the family's upward mobility. This process can be seen in immigrant families who come to the United States with low financial capital but transmit values (cultural capital) such as obedience to the law and pursuit of education to promote their children's upward mobility.

Unfortunately, there is also downward mobility. Illness, injury, job loss, or a series of poor choices can contribute to downward mobility. The fewer available resources that people have, the less chance they have of overcoming setbacks and other negative experiences. There is some evidence that all individuals within a specific social stratum have similar opportunities to succeed or fail. However, a single poor choice can have a more pronounced effect on the life trajectory of lower social strata individuals compared to those at higher levels. For example, having a baby at age 15 may result in dropping out of school and lifelong poverty for a woman from a lower social stratum, but a woman with more resources who can afford child care may be able to continue her education and maintain her social position.

Fertility is particularly pertinent in women's economics and social mobility. Earlier age at first childbirth and more children are statistically associated with less upward mobility for women. This is not necessarily true for men. Cross-culturally, according to the World Health Organization, early fertility is a major risk factor to women's ability to move out of poverty. In addition to hampering upward mobility, frequent childbirth becomes a significant health risk for women in poverty due to the physical toll and the increased nutritional demands of pregnancy that women in poverty have difficulty meeting.

POVERTY

Two types of poverty are recognized by the World Health Organization. **Relative poverty** indicates that very basic needs are met, but compared to other members in society the individual has significantly less financial capital, material goods, and access to services (e.g., health care). **Absolute poverty** indicates that the individual has difficulty meeting even the most basic needs of housing, food, and clean water.

Some have argued that there is a "culture of poverty." According to the **culture of poverty** theory, individuals who are in poverty will likely remain in poverty because of an overwhelming "cultural" momentum resulting in less adaptive choices by lower SES individuals. These choices include not pursuing education, engaging in early sexual activity, and engaging in frequent drug use. This theory has now been largely discredited in favor of social reproduction theory and research identifying the more pronounced effect of a single poor life choice among those in a lower SES bracket. Additionally, a greater understanding of how prejudice and discrimination may lead to social exclusion and reduced educational opportunities has further discredited the culture of poverty theory. However, the theory still has some proponents.

HEALTH CARE DISPARITIES

There are well-validated disparities in health care based on social strata. In areas where people have fewer financial resources, there are fewer medical care facilities and fewer mental and physical health care providers. In the United States, individuals from non-white racial backgrounds also tend to have less access to treatment and may have less effective treatment when they do receive care. This leads to greater morbidity and mortality, along with poorer health-related quality of life. Unfortunately, this is a trend across much of the world where poverty, racial differences, and class may alter the quality and quantity of health care that an individual receives.

In the United States, the Centers for Disease Control and Prevention (CDC) has found that lower SES communities have less access to healthier food choices (e.g., fresh fruit and vegetables). Many inner-city areas have been labeled "grocery wastelands," meaning that grocery stores are lacking and that people purchase food mainly in the small grocery sections in convenience stores, which tend to stock primarily processed foods and have extremely limited fresh fruit and vegetable choices. As a result, healthy food choices are difficult, if not impossible, to obtain. Many of the same neighborhoods that are labeled "grocery wastelands" also have fewer parks and green spaces for exercise, and more environmental health hazards. Each of these factors has contributed to greater health risks in areas where health care resources are already inadequate.

Health care disparities are noted in the United States among poorer individuals and among non-white groups. Future health practitioners need to be aware of these disparities. African-Americans and Latino-Americans are two times more likely to be diagnosed with obesity and obesity-related diseases such as hypertension, cardiovascular disease, and type II diabetes. Many are also underdiagnosed and undertreated for other obesity-related disorders such as obstructive sleep apnea. African-Americans are also much more likely to be diagnosed with HIV/AIDS and have a 10 percent greater risk of cancer compared to individuals of European descent.

Health care disparities mainly arise due to three kinds of barriers to obtaining health care: **socioeconomic**, **environmental**, and **personal**.

Socioeconomic Barriers

Socioeconomic barriers to obtaining health care include those that are financial or racially driven. These may include **financial barriers** to purchasing insurance coverage, seeing a health care provider, receiving wellness counseling, and obtaining prescription medications. In the United States, the Affordable Care Act may have a positive impact in reducing these kinds of barriers.

Beyond financial barriers, **social barriers** may also create health disparities. **Language differences** with physicians for individuals who are not fluent in English may interfere with timely or effective provider-patient communication. Further, even among individuals who are fluent in English, lower education levels can also impact **health care literacy**, which includes the patient's ability to understand how the health care system works (e.g., specialty physicians may not be able to treat other problems). Health care literacy can also interfere with how someone understands health care information (e.g., the danger of having a blood pressure of 200/110 and the need to treat it even if the patient does not feel sick at that moment). These may negatively impact a patient's ability to follow through with recommendations by providers. Communication of critical information may be improved when the provider and patient are from the same ethnic background. However, with only 4 percent of US physicians from an African-American background and only 5 percent from a Latino background, it is difficult for patients from these ethnic groups to find a provider who matches their background. Further, there is some evidence that even providers from minority backgrounds may hold ethnic stereotypes that influence their treatment recommendations and prescribing practices when treating individuals from the same background.

Environmental Barriers

Environmental barriers to obtaining health care include those that are structurally related to the surroundings of the patient. **Spatial inequality** can be a significant barrier to maintaining good health. This phenomenon is related to the differential in living locations that is due to social stratification. Residential segregation is a longstanding sociological phenomenon in Western culture. Historically, homes that were closer to amenities (e.g., water access) were more valuable, while those farther from positive amenities or closer to negative amenities (e.g., butchers, leather tanners) were less valuable. In modern times negative amenities may include power plants, mines, industrial areas, noisy high-traffic areas, and airports. When these differences in value exist, people tend to congregate in areas based on those areas' relative affordability. This is segregation by financial stratification. Spatial inequality can also be due to racial or ethnic stratification, in which those who are racially or ethnically stratified to lower levels of society reside in a specific location (by choice or by assignment).

Unfortunately, spatial inequality and living near negative amenities may have negative health consequences. Environmental hazards may include noise pollution, leading to disrupted sleep and poor concentration. There may also be air or water pollution in heavily industrial areas. Spatial inequality may also include older housing that has health risks due to lead paint and asbestos.

Additionally, there are environmental barriers to accessing health care once there is an illness or injury. These barriers include a **scarcity of health care providers** located in inner city and rural areas, resulting in long wait times and few available appointments. There is significant research detailing the lack of both primary care and specialty providers available in certain areas of the country. The scarcity of nearby providers may be exacerbated by environmental **transportation difficulties** that may impede a person traveling to a medical center and limit when that person is able to arrive for appointments. Limited public transportation options and relying on friends or family for transportation may be a barrier to arriving for appointments.

Personal Barriers

Finally, the role of **education levels** and **age** cannot be dismissed when considering health care disparities. Older Americans often share many of the same difficulties seen among minority populations. They may live on a fixed income with few financial resources to seek treatment, they may have limited transportation options if they do not drive, they may have lower health literacy levels, and they may have less access to technology and the Internet to improve their health literacy. Further, research suggests that some individuals may not report serious symptoms, because they believe that it is just a part of getting older. But if left untreated, these symptoms may significantly impact quality of life. A recent study showed that older individuals often underreport pain, which then led to decreased activity levels, diminished social engagement, and depression. However, when pain and depression were actively addressed through medical and psychological treatment, the same individuals were able to resume normal daily functioning and improve their quality of life. Further, individuals with lower education levels may have difficulty with literacy generally, and specifically health literacy, which can negatively impact accessing preventive care and receiving treatment for health concerns.

Other reasons for health care disparities and health care discrimination may include reasons based on individual characteristics that cut across ethnicity or economic status. Significant factors that may negatively impact access to health care and cause people to be discriminated against in treatment include **sexual preference** (e.g., lesbian, gay, bisexual, transgender) and **sexual status** (e.g., being pregnant while unmarried). Additionally, the **stigma associated with a diagnosis** can alter how an individual is approached by health care providers (e.g., HIV+, addiction, schizophrenia) and affect access to treatment and treatment options (beyond those changes required by disease status).

Addressing Health Care Disparities

Health care providers, systems, and payers are attempting to address some of these disparities by creating an expanded and more dynamic definition of health care providers to include psychologists, social workers, nutritionists, physical/occupational therapists, and other allied health providers. Access to interpreters who can reduce language barriers, social workers who can assist with transportation and financial issues, community health workers or parish nurses who can offer wellness education based on the immediate environment of patients, and health psychologists who can address the mental health needs of patients and the psychosocial barriers to medical health are all crucial health professionals who are actively working to reduce health care disparities.

In addition, it is vital to expand training for health professionals to increase their cultural competency regarding the role of family in treatment, traditional healers, and cultural values. This training is occurring not only at the level of direct-care providers, but also at administrative levels to improve recruitment and retention of providers from a variety of SES and to create a medical system that appreciates and values diversity in its employees.

By developing a responsive health system that addresses socioeconomic, environmental, and personal factors, efforts are being made toward reducing barriers to adequate health care and alleviating health care disparities.

Unit V Minitest

8 Questions **15 Minutes**

This minitest is designed to assess your mastery of the content in Chapter 5 of this volume. The questions have been designed to simulate actual MCAT questions in terms of format and degree of difficulty. They are based on the content categories associated with the foundational concept that is the theme of this unit. They are also designed to test the scientific inquiry and reasoning skills that the test makers have identified as essential for success in medical school.

In this test, most of the questions are based on short passages that typically describe a research study or some similar process. There are also some questions that are not based on passages.

Use this test to measure your readiness for the actual MCAT. Try to answer all of the questions within the specified time limit. If you run out of time, you will know that you need to work on improving your pacing.

Complete answer explanations are provided at the end of the minitest. Pay particular attention to the answers for questions you got wrong or skipped. If necessary, go back and review the corresponding chapters or text sections in this unit.

Now turn the page and begin the Unit V Minitest.

Directions: *Choose the best answer to each of the following questions.*
Questions 1–4 are not based on a passage.

1. Going to college directly increases what type of capital?
   A. financial
   B. human
   C. cultural
   D. environmental

2. Which of the following does NOT explain why the culture of poverty theory has been denounced?
   A. Culture of poverty theory uses blame-the-victim techniques that help higher SES individuals reinforce a just world theory viewpoint.
   B. Social reinforcement better explains the maintenance of societal economic stratification.
   C. Individuals from a lower SES do not have the intellectual ability to merit receiving sufficient financial capital to move out of poverty.
   D. Research has shown that individuals from a lower SES make an equal number of bad choices about their life opportunities compared to individuals from a higher SES.

3. Sandra's family is from a lower socioeconomic stratum. Despite encouragement by her parents, she struggled in her inner-city grade school and did not enjoy learning. A new job required her parents to move to a new town that has better schools. In her new school Sandra was able to improve her grades and consider additional educational opportunities beyond high school. She received a scholarship to attend college. Upon graduating she was offered a position that paid $50,000/year. This scenario is an example of
   A. social mobility
   B. nepotism
   C. social reproduction
   D. social stratification

4. ____________ theory indicates that stratification preserves society's ability to reward those who occupy positions most critical to society.
   A. functionalist
   B. meritocracy
   C. social conflict
   D. nepotism

Questions 5–8 are based on the following passage.

Passage I

Greater sleep coherency with fewer awakenings and more consistent sleep is associated with better quality sleep. However, sleep measurements often require complex

EEG sensors that require specific placement and are messy to attach to the head. This makes EEG sleep measurements difficult to perform in a home environment. One distal method to measure sleep coherency is using actigraphy. Lightweight cloth bands (e.g., sweat bands) with sensors in them are placed on the wrists and ankles to measure nighttime movements. More activity can indicate less coherent sleep patterns.

A researcher interested in the effect of noise pollution on those living near the negative amenity of an active airport recruits 100 people to wear actigraphs for one week while they are in bed. The results are shown on the following graph.

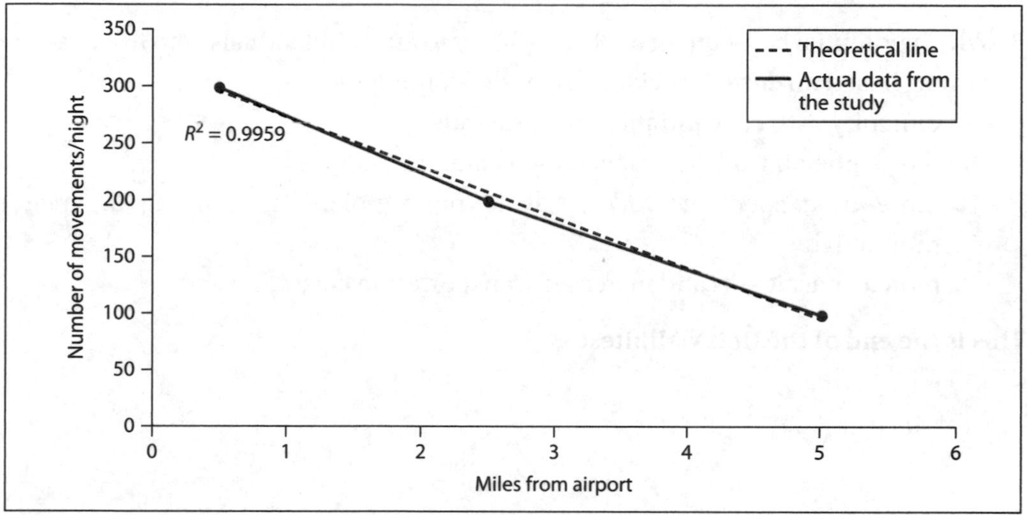

Nighttime actigraphy levels by distance from the airport

5. What does this graph show?
   A. Living close to an airport has a significant impact on sleep coherency.
   B. There is an inverse correlation between proximity to the airport and sleep quality.
   C. Sleep and nighttime activity are not correlated.
   D. Living close to an airport is related to increased nighttime movements, which suggest poorer sleep quality.

6. Given your knowledge about neighborhoods near negative amenities, what other conditions might be TRUE?
   A. Individuals who work at the airport probably live near the airport and probably have to get up at night to go into work.
   B. Individuals who live near noisy environments eventually adapt, so the people in this study who live close to the airport and have high nighttime activity levels must be new to the area.
   C. The closer a neighborhood is to negative amenities, the cheaper the home prices and the more likely that the neighborhood qualifies as a lower SES.
   D. Lower SES individuals tend to make poor housing choices and therefore are more likely to experience disrupted sleep.

7. The next logical step to study this phenomenon would MOST likely be
   A. a laboratory-based study with EEGs in an environment that mimics airport noise
   B. comparing IQ ratings for people who live 0.5 miles, 2.5 miles, and 5 miles away from the airport
   C. asking people how long they have lived in those neighborhoods and why they live near the airport
   D. identifying racial or ethnic characteristics of the neighborhood that may account for night movement

8. Which potential consequence is LEAST likely to affect individuals who live near the airport based on current sociological understanding?
   A. difficulty with concentration; poorer grades
   B. more time off work due to increased colds and flus
   C. more time spent at work to avoid noise pollution, resulting in greater productivity
   D. more car accidents and increased transportation costs

This is the end of the Unit V Minitest.

Unit V Minitest Answers and Explanations

1. **The correct answer is B.** Human capital reflects an individual's effort to gain new skills or learn new knowledge to increase the likelihood of achieving a higher SES. Financial and cultural capital may benefit the individual, but the individual has minimal control over these forms of capital. Environmental capital does not exist.
2. **The correct answer is C.** Intelligence does not differ among SES groups. However, opportunities that allow a person to take advantage of his or her intelligence are rarer among lower SES groups. Individuals who hold a just world theory commonly use blame-the-victim techniques (e.g., claiming that someone is in poverty because he or she deserves it) to explain why they do not experience a negative event (e.g., "I am not in poverty, because I work harder."). Social reinforcement is a better explanation of decreased social mobility among established societies. Lower SES individuals encounter greater environmental health risks, fewer economic opportunities, and fewer educational opportunities, all of which maintain the status quo SES. Research has shown that lower and higher SES individuals do not differ in their ability to make good choices about their opportunities. However, individuals from lower SES have fewer opportunities, and any poor decisions that they make have a greater impact on their SES trajectory.
3. **The correct answer is A.** Sandra moved from lower SES to middle SES due to an improvement of her educational opportunities and an increase in her human capital. She avoided the social reproduction of maintaining her parents' lower SES. Social stratification does exist in this scenario, but the scenario shows movement across social strata, so social mobility is a better answer. Nepotism does not apply, because Sandra's family members were not in a position to provide her with a higher paying position upon graduation.
4. **The correct answer is A.** Functionalist theory supports societal stratification as a way to reward the best qualified individuals and lure them into the positions that are the most critical to the functioning of that society.
5. **The correct answer is D.** The graph can tell you *only* the relationship between distance from the airport and nighttime activity. You have to make the cognitive leap that nighttime movements can be a distal measure of sleep coherency. There is a likely association, but since actigraphy is not the most proximal measure of sleep coherency, you cannot make a definitive statement.
6. **The correct answer is C.** Negative amenities tend to decrease housing costs in the affected area, which means that individuals with lower financial resources can afford to live in that area. It is important to note that individuals will report that they "adapt" to noisy environments, but in reality psychology studies show that they continue to have the same level of physiological activation in response to noise disruption and there is no physiological adaptation.

7. **The correct answer is A.** Since actigraphy is a good measure of movement, but is only a distal measure of sleep coherency, the logical next step would be to make sure that sleep coherency is really affected by airport noise using the more proximal measure of direct EEG measurements of sleep.
8. **The correct answer is C.** All of the other answers are known outcomes from living near negative amenities with high levels of noise pollution, but improved productivity is not. Individuals living near airports are more likely to experience disrupted sleep leading to increased illness (due to inefficient immune systems), poorer grades (due to difficulty concentrating and sleep deprivation), and more car accidents (for the same reason as poorer grades).

PART 2

CRITICAL ANALYSIS AND REASONING SKILLS

What Is Tested in Critical Analysis and Reasoning Skills
How the Section Is Scored
Preparing for Critical Analysis and Reasoning Skills
Practicing Critical Analysis and Reasoning Skills
Critical Analysis and Reasoning Skills Minitest

Critical Analysis and Reasoning Skills

Read This Part to Learn About

- ➤ What Is Tested in Critical Analysis and Reasoning Skills
- ➤ How the Section Is Scored
- ➤ Preparing for the Critical Analysis and Reasoning Skills Section
- ➤ Practicing Critical Analysis and Reasoning Skills

WHAT IS TESTED IN CRITICAL ANALYSIS AND REASONING SKILLS

In contrast to the sections on Physical and Biological Sciences, the Critical Analysis and Reasoning Skills section of the MCAT does not test specific knowledge. Instead, it assesses your ability to comprehend, evaluate, apply, and synthesize information from an unfamiliar written text. Its format is familiar to anyone who has attended school in the United States. Most reading comprehension tests look just like it.

The MCAT Critical Analysis and Reasoning Skills section consists of 5 or 6 passages of about 500 to 600 words, each of which is followed by a set of multiple-choice questions. There are 60 questions in all. The passages are nonfiction and may be on topics from the humanities, from social sciences, or from those areas of the natural sciences that are not routinely tested elsewhere in the exam. The expectation is that you are not familiar with the content of a given passage, or that if you are familiar with it, you are not an expert.

For this reason, it is not possible to **study** for the Critical Analysis and Reasoning Skills section of the MCAT. That being said, however, there are some things you may do to **prepare** for it.

HOW THE SECTION IS SCORED

As with all the multiple-choice sections of the MCAT, you receive 1 point for each correct answer on the Critical Analysis and Reasoning Skills section, with no penalty for incorrect answers (which makes it okay to guess!). After that, the numeric score is scaled on a 15-point scale, with extra weight given to the more difficult questions, and less weight given to the easier questions. Your score for this section appears as a number from 0 to 15.

PREPARING FOR THE CRITICAL ANALYSIS AND REASONING SKILLS SECTION

By this stage in your educational career, you should have a pretty good sense of your test-taking skills. If you have achieved solid scores on reading comprehension tests in the past, the MCAT Critical Analysis and Reasoning Skills section should be no problem at all. If your comprehension skills are not quite as good as they should be, if you freeze when faced with difficult reading passages, if you read very slowly, or if English is not your first language, you should take the time to work through this section of the book.

Read

The best way to learn to read better is to read more. If you read only materials in your chosen discipline, you are limiting yourself in a way that may show up on your MCAT score. Reading broadly in subject areas that do not, at first glance, hold much appeal for you trains you to focus your attention on what you are reading. Pick up a journal in a field you are not familiar with. Read an article. Summarize the key ideas. Decide whether the author's argument makes sense to you. Think about where the author might go next with his or her argument. Finally, consider how the content of the article relates to your life or to the lives of people you know.

All of this sounds like a chore, but it is the key to making yourself read actively. An active reader interacts with a text rather than bouncing off it. Success on the MCAT Critical Analysis and Reasoning Skills section requires active reading.

You can use any of the following strategies to focus your attention on your reading. You may use many of them already, quite automatically. Others may be just what you need to shift your reading comprehension into high gear.

ACTIVE READING STRATEGIES

- **Monitor your understanding.** When faced with a difficult text, it's all too easy to zone out and skip through challenging passages. You do not have that luxury when the text you are reading is only 500 words long and is followed by 8 questions that require your understanding. Pay attention to how you are feeling about a text. Are you getting the author's main points? Is there something that makes little or no sense? Are there words that you do not know? Figuring out what makes a passage hard for you is the first step toward correcting the problem. Once you figure it out, you can use one of the following strategies to improve your connection to the text.
- **Predict.** Your ability to make predictions is surprisingly important to your ability to read well. If a passage is well organized, you should be able to read the introductory paragraph and have a pretty good sense of where the author is going with the text. Practice this one starting with newspaper articles, where the main ideas are supposed to appear in the first paragraph. Move on to more difficult reading. See whether your expectation of a text holds up through the reading of the text. Making predictions about what you are about to read is an immediate way to engage with the text and keep you engaged throughout your reading.
- **Ask questions.** Keep a running dialogue with yourself as you read. You don't have to stop reading; just pause to consider, "What does this mean? Why did the author use this word? Where is he or she going with this argument? Why is this important?" This becomes second nature after a while. When you become acclimated to asking yourself questions as you read a test passage, you may discover that some of the questions you asked appear in different forms on the test itself.
- **Summarize.** You do this when you take notes in class or when you prepare an outline as you study for an exam. Try doing it as you read unfamiliar materials, but do it in your head. At the end of a particularly dense paragraph, try to reduce the author's verbiage to a single, cogent sentence that states the main idea. At the end of a longer passage, see whether you can restate the theme or message in a phrase or two.
- **Connect.** Every piece of writing is a communication between the author and the reader. You connect to a text first by bringing your prior knowledge to that text and last by applying what you learn from the text to some area of your life. Even if you know nothing at all about architecture or archaeology, your lifetime of experience in the world carries a lot of weight as you read an article about those topics. Connecting to a text can lead to "Aha!" moments as you say to yourself, "I knew that!" or even, "I never knew that!" If you barrel through a text passively, you do not give yourself time to connect. You might as well tape the passage and play it under your pillow as you sleep.

Pace Yourself

The Critical Analysis and Reasoning Skills section is timed. If you are a slow reader, you are at a decided disadvantage. You have 90 minutes to read 5 or 6 passages and answer 60 questions. That gives you about 10 minutes for each passage and question set. It would be a shame to lose points because you failed to complete a passage or two.

Studies have shown that people read 25 percent slower onscreen than they normally read. Because the MCAT is entirely computer-based, you may benefit from practicing reading longer passages onscreen. Try http://www.bartleby.com/. This website, which bills itself as "Great Books Online," contains a number of long classic works to be read onscreen. You can find fiction and nonfiction of all sorts with which to practice your onscreen reading skills.

You do not need to speed-read to perform well on the Critical Analysis and Reasoning Skills section, but you might benefit from some pointers that speed-readers use.

SPEED-READING STRATEGIES

- **Avoid subvocalizing.** It's unlikely that you move your lips while you read, but you may find yourself "saying" the text in your head. This slows you down significantly, because you are slowing down to speech speed instead of revving up to reading speed. You do not need to "say" the words; the connection between your eyes and your brain is perfectly able to bypass that step.
- **Don't regress.** If you don't understand something, you may run your eyes back and forth and back and forth over it. Speed-readers know this as "regression," and it's a big drag on reading speed. It's better to read once all the way through and then reread a section that caused you confusion.
- **Bundle ideas.** Read phrases rather than words. Remember, you are being tested on overall meaning, which is not derived from single words but rather from phrases, sentences, and paragraphs. If you read word by word, your eye stops constantly, and that slows you down. Read bundles of meaning, and your eyes flow over the page, improving both reading speed and comprehension.

Preview

When it comes to taking tests, knowing what to expect is half the battle. The MCAT's Critical Analysis and Reasoning Skills section assesses a variety of reading skills, from the most basic comprehension skills to the higher-level application and synthesis skills. Here is a breakdown of skills you should expect to see tested.

FOUR KINDS OF QUESTIONS

➤ **Comprehension.** These questions look at the author's main idea and support for his or her hypothesis. Expect questions on Finding the Main Idea, Locating Supporting Details or Evidence, Choosing Accurate Summaries or Paraphrases, Comparing and Contrasting, Interpreting Vocabulary, Identifying Hypotheses, and Asking Clarifying Questions.

SAMPLE QUESTION STEMS

In the context of the passage, the word X *means . . .*
The main argument of the passage is . . .
The central thesis of the passage is . . .
The discussion of X *shows primarily that . . .*
According to the passage, all of these are true EXCEPT . . .

➤ **Evaluation.** These questions deal with your understanding of the author's assumptions and viewpoints. Expect questions on Analyzing an Argument; Judging Credibility; Assessing Evidence; and Distinguishing Among Fact, Opinion, and Unsupported Assertions.

SAMPLE QUESTION STEMS

Which of the following statements is NOT presented as evidence . . .
The passage suggests that the author would most likely believe . . .
Which of the following assertions does the author support . . .
The author's claim that X *is supported by . . .*

➤ **Application.** These questions deal with the purpose and structure of the passage and may require you to apply concepts or hypotheses to real-life situations. Expect questions on Making Predictions, Solving Problems, Identifying Cause and Effect, Drawing Conclusions, and Making Generalizations.

SAMPLE QUESTION STEMS

According to the passage, why . . .
The passage implies that . . .
Based on the information in the passage, which of these outcomes . . .
The passage suggests that . . .
According to the passage, X *would best be described as . . .*

➤ **Incorporation of information.** These questions present some new information and ask you how it might affect your understanding of ideas in the passage. You may be asked if the new information supports the ideas in the passage, or if it contradicts them. You may also be asked about possible analogies between the new information and ideas in the passage. Expect questions on Combining Information.

SAMPLE QUESTION STEMS

Which of the following is MOST analogous to . . .
Which of the following is MOST similar to . . .
X *as described in the passage is MOST analogous to . . .*

Because the format of the test is a familiar one, you may not need to preview the format itself. However, you may benefit from these tips on taking reading comprehension tests.

Test-Taking Tips for Verbal Reasoning

1. **Preview** the passage. Read the first paragraph. Skim the passage.
2. **Skim** the question stems (the part of each question that does not include the answer choices). This gives you a quick idea of what to look for as you read.
3. **Read** the passage, using your active reading strategies.
4. **Answer** the questions. Questions on the Critical Analysis and Reasoning Skills section of the MCAT move from easiest to hardest within a question set, so answering them in order makes sense. However, if you are stumped on a given question, skip ahead and come back later.

PRACTICING CRITICAL ANALYSIS AND REASONING SKILLS

It is certainly true that the more you practice reading comprehension, the better you are likely to perform on the MCAT. Here are 10 practice passages followed by question sets and explanatory answers. Follow along and see how well your comprehension compares with the answers given. Remember that the easier questions come first in a question set. Notice whether you have trouble with those more basic questions or with the higher-level questions that follow. Try to use your active reading strategies as you read each passage. Can you make it through each passage and question set in 10 minutes or so?

SAMPLE PASSAGE I: SOCIAL SCIENCES

Fifty years ago, only New Yorkers lived in what is now termed a "megacity," an agglomeration of more than 10 million people living and working in an urban environment. In contrast, today there are more than 40 megacities, most in less developed countries, and more urban centers are expected to explode in population by the year 2015. Demographers and globalization experts are already referring to the 21st century as "the urban century."

Already, more people on our Earth live in cities than live in rural areas. This is an enormous change in population trends, and it skews the entire planet in ways we haven't begun to analyze.

Although some cities have seen immigration expand their borders, for most megacities, it is migration from within the country that has caused the city to grow. An example is China, where some 150 million rural inhabitants have migrated to cities in just the last ten years. In many cases, the cities house the only possibilities of employment in this global economy. That is what has grown Mumbai (Bombay), India, from a large city to a megacity of more than 18 million in just a few years. It's the cause of the explosion of population in Lagos, Nigeria; Karachi, Pakistan; Dhaka, Bangladesh; and Jakarta, Indonesia.

Whereas just a few years ago, most large cities were in developed nations, now the largest are suddenly in the less-developed countries of South America, Africa, and Asia. Imagine the pressure on the infrastructure of these already poor cities as the influx of workers pushes services to the breaking point. Slums and shantytowns spring up around the outskirts of the cities, and government is powerless to affect the disadvantaged workers, leaving them exposed to corrupt local officials or urban gangs. Imagine, too, what happens in the rural areas that these people have abandoned. China faces a desperate shortage of agricultural labor. So do other areas of Asia and Africa.

According to UN statistics, by the year 2030, more than 60 percent of the world population will be urban, up from 30 percent in 1950. Unlike the population growth in developed nations, the birth rate in less-developed nations is high, meaning that the cities continue to grow even as migration slows from the rural areas. Megacities such as New York have populations that have leveled off over time. Despite its location in a less-developed nation, even a megacity such as Mexico City has a slow rate of growth compared to Asian and African cities such as Mumbai or Lagos.

It is difficult to imagine what the growth of the megacities will mean to the world in the 21st century. Demographers foresee ecological overload, homelessness, uncontrolled traffic, and an infrastructure strained to the breaking point. Despite the notion that industrial jobs improve the lot of the workers, it is already possible to see that megacities are creating a new, even deeper division between rich and poor, as the poor concentrate in the outskirts of town and the rich barricade themselves behind walls and in towers.

1. The main argument of the passage is that
   A. megacities are more often found in less-developed nations but strain the resources of developed nations
   B. the growth in population and number of megacities means foreseeable changes, many of them negative
   C. the movement of population bases from rural to urban locations decimates the countryside and limits our ability to grow food
   D. we must begin to fight back against the growth of megacities in the less-developed nations of the world

2. The passage suggests that demographers
   A. have not been able to keep pace with the growth of cities
   B. focus primarily on population trends in the developing world
   C. are observing the growth of the world's cities with concern
   D. work hand in hand with the UN to plan for the future

3. The author's use of UN statistics helps
   A. strengthen her argument that urbanization is radically changing the world
   B. contradict demographers' claims about megacities and their effects
   C. indicate that the results of urbanization include poverty and crime
   D. complement her assertion that birth rate is the main reason for urban growth

4. According to this passage, why might skyscrapers be a sign of divisiveness?
   A. They cost too much to build.
   B. They are found only in developed nations.
   C. They separate rich from poor.
   D. They house businesses, not people.

5. Which new information, if true, might CHALLENGE the author's contention that cities will continue to grow despite a slowing of migration from the countryside?
   A. Scientists are creating new strains of rice and wheat that require far less in the way of hands-on care.
   B. The number of people living below the poverty level will climb in less-developed and developed nations.
   C. Inflationary trends in heating oil and gasoline prices will limit most people's discretionary spending.
   D. New methods of birth control will limit the population explosion in the developing world.

SAMPLE PASSAGE I: ANSWERS AND EXPLANATIONS

1. **The correct answer is B.** This is a **Comprehension** question on **Finding the Main Idea**. This kind of question does not require you to go beyond the boundaries of the passage. You should think, "What is the author trying to say?" In fact, the author never says choice A at all. Although the point is made that megacities are more often found in less-developed nations, the second half of that statement does not appear in the passage. Nor does the author discuss decimation of the countryside and limitations in our ability to grow food, as choice C would indicate. And although you might infer choice D, the author never makes any such assertion. The best answer, the one that best conforms simply to the words on the page, is choice B.

2. **The correct answer is C.** This **Comprehension** question has to do with **Supporting Details and Evidence**. You can answer it easily if you scan the passage for the word *demographer* and then see what information is directly presented. In paragraph 1, demographers "are referring to the 21st century as 'the urban century.'" In paragraph 6, "demographers foresee ecological overload, homelessness, uncontrolled traffic, infrastructure strained to the breaking point." Based on your quick scan of the passage, there is no evidence to support choices A, B, or D. The answer is clearly choice C.
3. **The correct answer is A.** This **Evaluation** question requires you to **Analyze an Argument**. Questions like this ask you to explain why an author included certain information. Scan the essay to locate the reference to UN statistics and you see that those statistics tell us, "by the year 2030, more than 60 percent of the world population will be urban, up from 30 percent in 1950." In other words, there has been a dramatic change in the look of the world, thanks to urbanization. This correlates to choice A. It does not contradict demographers' claims (choice B), nor does it say anything about poverty, crime, or birth rate (choices C and D). Notice that this kind of question asks you to think "outside" the passage a bit more than **Comprehension** questions 1 and 2 did.
4. **The correct answer is C.** This **Application** question looks at **Cause and Effect**, not as directly presented in the essay, but rather as implied by the essay. In fact, you may have been alarmed to see that the word *skyscraper* never appears in the passage at all, so scanning the passage does not help. Remember that questions get harder within a question set. This question, the fourth one in the set, is harder than the first three.

   The clue to the answer is in the last line of the essay. "Megacities," the author claims, "are creating a new, even deeper division between rich and poor, as the poor concentrate in the outskirts of town and the rich barricade themselves behind walls and in towers." Those "towers" are the high-rise apartment buildings in which the rich dwell, whereas the poor live in shanties on the cities' outskirts. The only answer supported by the text is choice C.
5. **The correct answer is D.** This **Incorporation of Information** question asks you to **Apply New Evidence** to an existing argument. This kind of question takes you furthest from the passage itself, in an effort to get you to recognize its real-world applications. You might begin by scanning to locate the part of the passage that deals with the contention mentioned: that cities will continue to grow despite a slowing of migration from the countryside. It appears in paragraph 5, and its causative link is the notion that "the birth rate in less-developed nations is high." If you take away this cause, as choice D would do, then the author's supposition that cities will continue to grow has no foundation. None of the other answer choices would collapse her argument, as well.

SAMPLE PASSAGE II: HUMANITIES

Muralism has long been a Mexican tradition, perhaps dating back to the Aztecs, who recorded their history on the walls of their pyramids. The covering of a white wall with political art made the careers of David Alfara Siqueiros, Jose Clemente Orozco, and the best-known of them all, Diego Rivera.

Siqueiros, born in Chihuahua, studied art from an early age. He organized a student strike at the age of 15 and later worked to unseat the Mexican dictator Huerta, attaining the rank of captain during the revolution that was taking place. He later brought his tactical knowledge to the world of organized labor, where his activism led to lengthy jail terms. That is where he created some of his finest artworks on canvas. During the 1930s, he went to Spain to join the anti-fascist forces. His life was that of a soldier–artist, and some considered him a dangerous, subversive gangster.

Orozco, too, studied art as a youth and was inspired by the Mexican Revolution. One of his famous murals depicts the Holy Trinity as a worker, a soldier, and a peasant. Later he turned his focus to the dehumanizing effect of large cities on the people who live there. When he wasn't painting vast murals, Orozco was drawing political cartoons.

Rivera, the third of these Mexican Social Realists, *los tres grandes*, remains the most famous through sheer force of personality. His storytelling, his love affairs, his radicalism, and his love–hate relationship with the land of his birth informed his life and his paintings. He incorporated Mexican folklore and cultural icons into his murals in an effort to educate working people in their own history.

In the Chicano neighborhoods of the southwestern United States, political muralism still explodes onto bare walls in the form of graffiti. Edward Seymour's 1949 invention of canned spray paint provided would-be artists with an easy mode of expression, and the graffiti mural took off as an art form in the 1960s and 1970s. It began as outlaw art, which surely would have appealed to an outlaw such as Siqueiros. Despite the new artists' lack of formal training, some members of the outlaw group managed to create something beautiful while making political statements about poverty, injustice, diversity, and racism.

One extraordinary thing about this kind of public art is that it is truly for everyone. You do not need to enter the halls of a museum to see it; it resides on the walls of your local bodega or school or health clinic; you bounce your ball off of it in the basketball or handball court; you cover it over with posters for your favorite band or flyers about your lost pet.

Certainly, many of the graffiti artists were reviled as nuisances, and their art was erased. For some, however, graffiti would prove a launching point into the world of fine art. Today, modern murals in Austin, San Antonio, Los Angeles, and Tucson, among others, attest to the power of the Mexican tradition of the muralist as purveyor of political thought.

6. In the context of the passage, the word *radicalism* means
   A. extremism
   B. intolerance
   C. discrimination
   D. fanaticism

7. The author probably mentions Orozco's political cartoons as a way of illustrating
   A. the lack of seriousness in Orozco's art
   B. how multitalented Orozco was
   C. Orozco's intertwining of politics and art
   D. why Orozco's work fell out of favor

8. The author's claim that Siqueiros might approve of Chicano graffiti is supported by
   A. details about Siqueiros's role in the Spanish Civil War
   B. the description of Siqueiros as an army captain
   C. the fact that Siqueirios moved from Mexico to Spain
   D. information about Siqueiros's gangster past

9. According to this passage, graffiti would BEST be described as
   A. an attractive way of making a political statement
   B. a pale imitation of the Mexican muralists' work
   C. a nuisance that must be tolerated by urbanites
   D. a way to educate the masses in their own history

10. In 1933, Diego Rivera was dismissed from his job painting a mural for Rockefeller Center and charged with willful propagandizing for including a portrait of Lenin in the center. How does this anecdote affect the author's contention that Rivera's goal was to educate the workers in their own history?
    A. It refutes it.
    B. It supports it.
    C. It supports the claim only if you believe that propaganda is educational.
    D. It refutes the claim only if you believe that Communism is part of Mexican history.

SAMPLE PASSAGE II: ANSWERS AND EXPLANATIONS

6. **The correct answer is A.** This **Comprehension** question has to do with **Interpreting Vocabulary**. The first thing to do is to scan the passage and search for the word **radicalism**. It appears in paragraph 4, in the context of qualities that informed Rivera's artwork. It is not used in a negative connotation, as choices B and C would indicate. Choice D is almost right, but again, it has a more negative connotation than the passage implies. Therefore, choice A is the best answer.

7. **The correct answer is C.** This **Evaluation** question asks you to **Analyze an Argument**. Authors rarely include information without a reason, and the MCAT often asks you to identify and assess the reasons behind the inclusion of a passage or phrase. Here, Orozco's art is discussed in its relation to politics, from his Trinity of workers to his political cartoons. Although choice B might be correct in a different context, choice C is the better answer.
8. **The correct answer is D.** This **Evaluation** question requires you to **Assess Evidence**. Ideally, a writer does not include a statement without adequate support. Here, the statement is that Siqueiros might approve of Chicano graffiti. If you scan to find the exact reference in paragraph 5, you see that the author states, "It began as outlaw art, which surely would have appealed to an outlaw such as Siqueiros." That is a clear giveaway that choice D is the best response; Chicano art was outlaw art, and Siqueiros was considered by many to be an outlaw, or gangster.
9. **The correct answer is A.** This **Application** question calls for **Making Generalizations** about a topic—in this case, graffiti. To do this correctly, you must put together the author's statements about the topic and draw a conclusion from the information you are given.

   Paragraphs on graffiti appear at the end of the passage. Although the author refers to it as "outlaw art" and mentions that some people considered it a nuisance, that is clearly not the author's own impression. Phrases such as "managed to create something beautiful while making political statements about poverty, injustice, diversity, and racism" and "public art . . . that . . . is truly for everyone" put a positive spin on the topic. The author does not believe that graffiti is a "pale imitation" (choice B); instead, she indicates that the graffiti artists are following in the muralists' tradition. Choice D appears as a description of Rivera's work and is not relevant to this discussion of graffiti. That makes choice A the most logical answer.
10. **The correct answer is B.** This **Incorporation of Information** question asks you to **Apply New Evidence** to an existing argument. It also requires you to have in your repertoire some background information that is not found in the passage itself. The inclusion of Lenin in a mural would tend to support the notion that Rivera's intention was to educate the workers, primarily because a large part of Lenin's philosophy has to do with the aims and needs of the working class. You do not need to believe that propaganda is educational (choice C) to understand the connection of Lenin to workers. Believing that Communism is a part of Mexican history would serve to support the claim, not to refute it (choice D). The best answer is choice B.

SAMPLE PASSAGE III: NATURAL SCIENCES

For years, anecdotal evidence from around the world indicated that amphibians were under siege. Finally, proof of this hypothesis is available, thanks to the concerted, Internet-based effort of scientists involved with the Global Amphibian Assessment.

Amphibians have a unique vulnerability to environmental changes thanks to their permeable skin and their need of specific habitats to allow their metamorphosis from larva to adult. Studies indicate that they are at risk due to global climactic change, reduction in the ozone layer leading to an increased exposure to ultraviolet rays, interference with migratory pathways, drainage of wetlands, pollution by pesticides, erosion and sedimentation, and exposure to unknown pathogens thanks to the introduction of non-native species. In other words, human progress is responsible for the losses this population is suffering.

The permeable skin of frogs, newts, and other amphibians provides easy entry for a variety of pollutants. Increases in ultraviolet radiation appear to have a deadly effect on eggs, causing mortality and deformities in the amphibians studied. Most amphibians need a clear pathway between land and water to complete their life cycle. Road building and swamp drainage for construction has eliminated many of the dispersal routes for amphibians worldwide. The same sensitivity that allows pollution to damage young amphibians makes them susceptible to fungal and other pathogens transmitted from species released by pet owners. One emerging infectious disease in particular has led to entire populations being wiped out in Australia and the Americas.

Scientists have long considered amphibians a barometer of environmental health. In areas where amphibians are declining precipitously, environmental degradation is thought to be a major cause. Amphibians are not adaptable. They must have clean water in which to lay their eggs. They must have clean air to breathe after they grow to adulthood. Their "double life" as aquatic and land-dwelling animals means that they are at risk of a double dose of pollutants and other hazards.

The Global Amphibian Assessment concluded that nearly one-third of the world's amphibian species are under immediate threat of extinction. Nearly half of all species are declining in population. The largest numbers of threatened species are in Colombia, Mexico, and Ecuador, but the highest percentages of threatened species are in the Caribbean. In Haiti, for example, nine out of ten species of amphibians are threatened. In Jamaica, it's eight out of ten, and in Puerto Rico, seven out of ten. Of all the species studied around the world, only 1 percent saw any kind of increase in population.

Certainly, this is a disaster for amphibians, but scientists rush to point out that it may be equally a disaster for the rest of us on Earth. Even recent pandemics among amphibians may be caused by global changes. True, amphibians are ultrasensitive to such changes, but can reptiles, fish, birds, and mammals be far behind? The threat to equatorial amphibians may be simply the first indication of a global catastrophe to come. The frogs and newts of our world are warning us that continued habitat destruction in the name of progress might ultimately destroy us all.

11. The central thesis of the passage is that
    A. the extinction of amphibians is due to global warming
    B. amphibians really are a barometer of environmental health
    C. only equatorial amphibians are currently under siege
    D. amphibians' "double life" on land and in water may end up saving them

12. The passage implies that the Global Amphibian Assessment has done science a favor by
    A. setting forth a hypothesis that connects the environment to species decline
    B. eliminating the need to study the connection between extinction and environment
    C. refuting a contention that had existed purely through anecdotal evidence
    D. collecting data to prove something that was previously just a hypothesis

13. Which of the following assertions does the author support with an example?
    I. The permeable skin of amphibians allows for the entry of pollutants.
    II. Amphibians are susceptible to unfamiliar pathogens.
    III. Most threatened species are in the Caribbean.
    A. I only
    B. III only
    C. I and II only
    D. II and III only

14. Which of the following predictors is MOST analogous to amphibians as described in the fourth paragraph?
    A. biomarkers in the blood predicting mental illness
    B. red sky at night predicting high pressure and dry air
    C. canaries in a coal mine predicting dangerous gases
    D. groundhog's shadow predicting longer winter

15. According to this passage, the continued degradation of the environment may well lead to
    A. global pandemics
    B. floods and droughts
    C. human deformities
    D. decline among insects

Format DOs and DON'Ts

The MCAT uses a special format for certain questions. It lists three choices headed with Roman numerals I, II, and III and asks you to decide which one—or which combination of two or three—is correct. DON'T assume that the answer will always be a combination. DO use logical thinking to eliminate choices and save time.

Suppose the answers are

A. I only
B. III only
C. I and II only
D. II and III only

If you know that I is NOT possible, then you have eliminated choices A and C as answers. If you know that II IS possible, then you are down to choices C and D.

SAMPLE PASSAGE III: ANSWERS AND EXPLANATIONS

11. **The correct answer is B.** This **Comprehension** question asks you to **Find the Main Idea**. It may be the most common question you find on MCAT Critical Analysis and Reasoning Skills, and it nearly always appears first in a question set. To find the main idea, you must read actively and summarize as you go. There are no titles on MCAT passages to give away the central thesis; it's up to you as a reader to derive it from the text.

    Review the answer choices. The author indicates that choice A is a possibility. Just because this detail is included does not make it the central thesis. Although the major threat is to equatorial amphibians (choice C), it is not true that "only" those species are in danger, nor is that the main idea. There is no support for choice D. The main idea, instead, revolves around choice B. The new study indicates that previous anecdotal evidence was correct: Amphibians really **are** a barometer of environmental health.

12. **The correct answer is D.** This **Application** question requires you to **Draw Conclusions** about an assertion that is not directly stated. The answer may be inferred from the opening paragraph, which thanks the scientists involved for offering "proof of this hypothesis" through their "concerted, Internet-based efforts." The Assessment did not set forth the hypothesis (choice A); that had already been done via anecdotal evidence. They certainly did not eliminate the need for more study (choice B); nor did they refute the contention (choice C). They proved it (choice D).

13. **The correct answer is D.** This is an **Evaluation** question that asks about **Unsupported Assertions**. It often appears in this particular format on the MCAT (see box). Unless you have a photographic memory, the only way to answer a question like this one is to return to the text and find the assertions listed, which are most likely not worded quite the way they are in the question. Assertion I appears in paragraph 3. The paragraph goes on to discuss other problems with permeability, but it never gives specific examples of pollutants harming amphibians. Because assertion I is unsupported, choices A and C are incorrect. Because choices B and D both include assertion III, you can assume that assertion III is supported in the text (as it is, with a list of countries). The only question you should have is about assertion II. This assertion is made toward the end of paragraph 3, and it is, in fact, supported by an example: "One emerging infectious disease in particular has led to entire populations being wiped out in Australia and the Americas." So the best answer is choice D.
14. **The correct answer is C.** This **Incorporation of Information** question requires **Combining Information**, applying what you know to what you have read. The passage refers to amphibians as "a barometer of environmental health," apparently because they are so sensitive. The closest correlation is to canaries in a coal mine, which traditionally were used as animal sentinels to warn miners about the presence of toxic gases. Because the birds were tiny and sensitive, they reacted to the gases long before humans would. Similarly, amphibian decline predicts hazards in the environment.
15. **The correct answer is A.** This **Application** question asks you to **Make Predictions**, which you must do based on the text rather than on any external knowledge of the topic you may have. The author never speaks of floods and droughts (choice B), so even though they may be an effect of environmental degradation, they cannot be the correct answer. Likewise, insects (choice D) are never mentioned, although "reptiles, fish, birds, and mammals" are. Choice C is a stretch, although it is possible. The final paragraph deals with an extrapolation of the information about amphibians to other species, and it mentions the idea that even the pandemics affecting amphibians now may be caused by global changes (which are, in turn, caused by environmental degradation). This makes choice A the best answer of the four.

Notice in this sample set that the most difficult question is not the one that requires highest-order thinking, or Incorporation of Information. Although in most cases, Comprehension questions will appear first and Incorporation of Information questions last, the MCAT order really depends on the difficulty of concepts rather than the hierarchy of thinking skills.

SAMPLE PASSAGE IV: HUMANITIES

The best-known poet in the history of Australian literature is a man who never existed. According to the story, Ernest Lalor Malley was born in 1918 and emigrated to Australia as a child. He worked as an insurance salesman and wrote poetry as a sideline and hobby, a fact discovered only after his death from Grave's disease at age 25. At that time, his sister Ethel, while going through Malley's meager possessions, discovered a sheaf of poems.

She sent the poems to a young editor named Max Harris, who ran a modernist magazine called *Angry Penguins*. The magazine had come under fire from many artistic conservatives, who considered the new modernist poetry humorless and nonsensical. Among these conservatives were the young poets Harold Stewart and James McAuley.

Harris adored Ern Malley's poems, which numbered 17 in all, and promptly produced a special edition of *Angry Penguins* that would contain them all. Immediately, controversy arose. Although many of Harris's colleagues found the poems fascinating, others began to question and even to ridicule the poems, claiming that they represented a hoax perpetrated on the literary scene by Max Harris.

The controversy found its way into the local newspapers, which made it their business to track down Ern Malley and put an end to the story one way or the other. It took only a few weeks for the Sydney *Sun* to determine that poets Harold Stewart and James McAuley had composed all 17 poems in a single afternoon, paraphrasing chunks of text from a dictionary of quotations, the works of Shakespeare, and whatever came into their minds. They had then invented the backstory for the hapless Ern Malley and submitted the whole to their least favorite editor, Max Harris.

The point, of course, was to prove that modernist poetry was indiscriminate and meaningless, and to some degree, that point prevailed. *Angry Penguins* closed up shop, and the modernist movement in Australia was completely derailed. Max Harris was actually tried and convicted for publishing obscene poetry. Perversely, he continued throughout his life to insist that hoax or not, Stewart and McAuley had managed to write real poetry, poetry that had meaning and substance. Surprisingly, others agreed. Although some critics who had leaped onto the Malley bandwagon when the poems first appeared now backpedaled furiously, others insisted that the poems had literary merit.

The poems continued to have a life of their own, and even today they are frequently reissued and anthologized. American poets John Ashbery and other members of the New York School of poetry, who championed a kind of surrealist, transcendental verse, became major devotees of the mythical Malley. According to Michael Heyward in *The Ern Malley Affair*, Ashbery would regularly print a legitimate poem next to a Malley poem for his creative writing class's final exam, and would ask students to identify the hoax. The results were usually about 50–50.

So, what is the moral of this cautionary tale? Certainly an editor should never be so trusting, and the provenance of all written works should be carefully researched. However, because Malley's work today remains better known than that of Stewart or McAuley under their real names, perhaps the lesson has to do with never taking oneself too seriously.

16. According to the passage, at the time of the hoax, McAuley and Stewart were all of these things EXCEPT
    A. Australian
    B. conservative
    C. youthful
    D. salesmen

17. Which of the following statements is NOT presented as evidence that the Ern Malley hoax had a profound influence on the direction of Australian poetry?
    A. *Angry Penguins* closed up shop.
    B. The New York School championed surrealist verse.
    C. The modernist movement was completely derailed.
    D. Some critics backpedaled furiously.

18. The passage implies that McAuley and Stewart were motivated by
    A. greed
    B. principle
    C. spite
    D. rage

19. Given the information in this passage, if you were given two unfamiliar poems, one by Ern Malley and the other by a distinguished poet, which of these outcomes would MOST likely occur?
    A. You would be as likely to praise the Ern Malley poem as the real poem.
    B. You would identify the Ern Malley poem as the legitimate work.
    C. You would be able to discern the true poem from the hoax.
    D. You would think both poems had equal merit.

20. Which of the following incidents BEST supports the author's belief that editors should never be as trusting as Max Harris was?
    A. For centuries, some scholars have insisted that either Bacon or Marlowe wrote works attributed to Shakespeare.
    B. Reporter Stephen Glass repeatedly falsified quotations in widely read stories for the *New Republic.*
    C. Investigative reporter Seymour Hersh first broke the story of the massacre of civilians at My Lai.
    D. Editor Harold Ross encouraged writers for the *New Yorker* to publish the truth always tinged with humor.

Format DOs and DON'Ts

Watch out for questions that require you to identify a negative. Questions that are worded in the following ways may trick you:

"All of these are true EXCEPT . . ."
"Which of these statements is NOT . . ."

DO look for the capitalized word in the question stem. The MCAT style is to capitalize the negative word. That's your clue that the answer requires identification of a negative. DON'T fall into the trap of choosing choice A because it's true when the question really asks you to find the statement that's false.

SAMPLE PASSAGE IV: ANSWERS AND EXPLANATIONS

16. **The correct answer is D.** This identifying-a-negative format (see box) occurs from time to time on the MCAT's Verbal section. This **Comprehension** question tests your ability to **Locate Supporting Details or Evidence**. In questions of this kind, everything you need to know is found directly in the text. The last line of paragraph 2 contains much of what you need: "Among these conservatives were the young poets Harold Stewart and James McAuley." The men were conservative (choice B) and youthful (choice C). Because everyone in the story is Australian save for the poets of the New York School mentioned at the end, it is safe to assume that choice A is true of McAuley and Stewart as well. Only Ern Malley is identified as a salesman (choice D); there is no indication that McAuley or Stewart is anything other than a poet.
17. **The correct answer is B.** This **Evaluation** question asks you to **Assess Evidence**. Look at questions like this one as you would mathematical proofs. The hypothesis is given in the question stem: The Ern Malley hoax had a profound influence on the direction of Australian poetry. You must then determine which of the answer choices supports that hypothesis and which one does not. The one that does not is the correct answer.

    Here, the fact that the literary magazine closed following the hoax (choice A) does support the hypothesis. The fact that the modernist movement was derailed (choice C) does support the hypothesis. The fact that some critics backpedaled (choice D) does support the hypothesis. The fact that the New York School championed surrealist verse (choice B) does not; the New York School is American, not Australian, and its love of surrealist verse has nothing to do with the effect of the hoax on Australian poetry.

18. **The correct answer is C.** This **Application** question asks you to **Draw Conclusions** about characters' motivations. It is a skill most often applied to fiction, but it works in this case for nonfiction as well. The word *implies* tells you that the answer is not directly stated. It is up to you to return to the passage and make inferences based on your own understanding of human nature. Although the author indicates that the two men wanted to prove the ridiculousness of modernist poetry, which might be a matter of principle (choice B), their use of the innocent Max Harris seems spiteful, making choice C the better answer. There is no support for either choice A or choice D. McAuley and Stewart have nothing to gain monetarily by the hoax, and they seem amused rather than irate.
19. **The correct answer is A.** This **Application** question requires you to **Make Predictions** about a hypothetical situation, based on the information that was laid out for you in the passage. The important clue is in paragraph 6, which mentions that John Ashbery used to perform just this experiment for his classes, with results that approximated 50–50. That information supports choice A, which calls for the same results. Because even professional critics were fooled, there is no reason to believe you would do any better or worse than Ashbery's students did.
20. **The correct answer is B.** This **Incorporation of Information** question requires you to **Combine Information** from the passage with new information to come up with a conclusion. The belief as stated is that "editors should never be as trusting as Max Harris was," and your job is to find the one answer choice that best supports this premise. Of the answers given, choices C and D pretty clearly do not support the premise, because they do not involve a question of trust between editor and writer. Choices A and B may involve trust, but in the case of choice A, it is more between editor and reader than editor and writer. Therefore choice B, in which a writer included false information in published materials, is the choice that best reflects the author's belief.

SAMPLE PASSAGE V: SOCIAL SCIENCES

"... for not an orphan in the wide world can
be so deserted as the child who is an outcast
from a living parent's love."

—Charles Dickens, *Dombey & Son*

Of course, in Dickens's day, and indeed, into more modern times, the child outcast from a living parent's love was likely to find him- or herself in the poorhouse or the workhouse or out on the streets. Today, in the United States, we deal with many such children—more than half a million at any one time—through the foster care system and the department of social services.

Certainly most of the children who find themselves in the foster care system are not really "outcast from a living parent's love," but most do have living parents. The goal of the foster care system is to reunite families that have been torn apart by circumstance.

The circumstances are many. According to the U.S. Department of Health and Human Services, about 60 percent of foster children come into the system for their own protection; in other words, as a result of abuse or neglect or both. Around 16 percent are there because their parents are "absent," perhaps in prison, perhaps simply vanished into the void of drug abuse, alcoholism, or mental illness. Another 14 percent or so are in the system due to their own criminal or delinquent behavior. A small minority, say 4 percent, are in foster care because their birth parent or parents cannot cope with their child's handicap.

Less than 1 percent of foster children are in the system because their parents have relinquished all rights to them. For the remaining 99 percent, then, the sponsoring agencies must try to create a plan by which the child and family can be reconciled. Sometimes this happens quickly; 20 percent of children remain in care for less than 6 months. Sometimes it happens slowly or not at all; 32 percent of children remain in care for more than 3 years.

In April 2005, the Casey Family Programs published a study they had performed in connection with several universities in which they looked at hundreds of former foster children in Washington and Oregon. Although each state differs in the rules for its foster care system, most withdraw care when a child turns 18. The Casey study looked at young adults between the ages of 20 and 33, and what they found was disturbing. Following their release from the system, around 25 percent of the young adults had been homeless for at least some period of time. At the point of the study, about 35 percent were living at or below the poverty level. More than 50 percent suffered from one or more mental health problems, from anxiety to depression to more serious issues.

Of the foster children studied, 56 percent had received a high school diploma, whereas 29 percent had received a GED instead. In the general population, 82 percent graduate from high school, and 5 percent receive a GED.

Other studies tend to corroborate the notion that foster care is not necessarily a positive step on the road to adulthood. According to the National Association of Social Workers, some 80 percent of prison inmates spent part of their childhood in the foster care system. And although that particular statistic might reveal more about the circumstances that led children to foster care than about the system itself, the National Center on Child Abuse and Neglect did find that children were 11 times more likely to be abused in state care than in their own homes. Could the Dickensian alternatives be worse?

21. In the context of the passage, the word *reconciled* means
    A. acquiescent
    B. resigned
    C. reunited
    D. resolved

22. The central thesis of the passage is that
    A. foster care has greatly improved since Dickens's day
    B. foster care is not as beneficial as it should be
    C. foster care relies on the kindness of strangers
    D. foster care's goal is the creation of a new, functional family

23. Based on the information in the passage, which of these outcomes is MOST likely when a young boy is placed in foster care?
    A. He will be reunited with his family within 3 years.
    B. He will spend part of his adulthood in prison.
    C. He will remain in the system due to delinquent behavior.
    D. He will be moved between two or three foster homes.

24. The passage implies that
    A. withdrawal of care at age 18 may be detrimental to foster children
    B. abuse and neglect are just as prevalent in foster homes as on the street
    C. handicapped children are twice as likely to end up in foster care
    D. a GED diploma is equivalent in value to a high school degree

25. Suppose a new study of former foster children found that those who were in foster care due to incorrigibility and delinquent behavior were those who later found themselves in prison for some part of their adulthood. This new information would most CHALLENGE the implication that
    A. foster care does not succeed in reuniting families
    B. state care alone increases the odds of future incarceration
    C. children are more likely to be abused in foster care
    D. many children enter foster care because of absent parents

SAMPLE PASSAGE V: ANSWERS AND EXPLANATIONS

21. **The correct answer is C.** This **Comprehension** question asks you to **Interpret Vocabulary**. The word in question appears in the fourth paragraph of the passage. The child and family are to be reconciled, which means that they are to be brought back together. Although choices A, B, and D are synonyms for *reconciled*, only choice C has this denotation of bringing back together.
22. **The correct answer is B.** To answer this **Comprehension** question on **Finding the Main Idea** correctly, ask yourself, "What point is the author trying to make?"

In quoting the largely negative Casey Family Programs study, it seems clear that the point is not choice A. If you have any doubt about that, the final sentence of the passage should clarify the author's stance. Choice C is never mentioned, and choice D is wrong—the goal of foster care, according to the passage, is "to create a plan by which the child and family can be reconciled." The best summary of the central thesis is choice B.

23. **The correct answer is A.** This is an **Application** question that asks you to **Make Predictions**. The key to this question is the phrase "MOST likely." Choice B has some likelihood. We do know that 80 percent of prisoners spent some time in foster care, but without having the numbers of prisoners compared to the number of foster children, we cannot calculate those odds. Choices C and D probably have some likelihood as well, but neither is mentioned in the passage. Statistics in paragraph 4 indicate that for 99 percent of foster children, the goal is reconciliation. Of those, 20 percent are reconciled within 6 months, and 68 percent are reconciled within 3 years. Choice A is correct.
24. **The correct answer is A.** You must **Draw Conclusions** to answer this **Application** question. To draw a conclusion, you must use information that actually exists in the passage. Abuse and neglect are clearly prevalent in foster homes (choice B), but whether they are as prevalent there as on the street is never implied. Only 4 percent of the children in foster care are there because of some handicap, and because we do not know total figures, we cannot draw the conclusion that is given in choice C. The implication in choice D is challenged by the author's statistics in paragraph 6. If a GED diploma were equivalent in value to a high school degree, it would hardly matter that foster children are much more likely to get GED diplomas than are children in the general population. The Casey study looked at young adults who were formerly in foster care and found that only a few years after their release from the system, many were doing poorly. The implication is that without the care, they often fail, so choice A is the best answer.
25. **The correct answer is B.** This **Incorporation of Information** question requires you to **Apply New Evidence**. The new study would indicate that the delinquency itself led to future incarceration, and that the foster care system was only incidental. That in turn would mean that foster care on its own was not the cause of future incarceration (choice B). The new study would not affect choices A, C, or D at all.

SAMPLE PASSAGE VI: NATURAL SCIENCES

A land bridge is land exposed when the sea recedes, connecting one expanse of land to another. One land bridge that still exists today is the Sinai Peninsula, which attaches the Middle East to North Africa. Central America is another land bridge, this one connecting North to South America.

Historical land bridges are many. There was a bridge connecting the British Isles to the European continent, and there was one between Spain and Morocco at what is now the Straits of Gibraltar. There were bridges connecting Japan to China and Korea. One of the most famous land bridges was the Bering Land Bridge, often known as Beringia, which connected Alaska to Siberia across what is now the Bering Strait.

The Bering Land Bridge was not terribly long. If it still existed today, you could drive it in your car in about an hour. It appeared during the Ice Age, when enormous sheets of ice covered much of Europe and America. The ice sheets contained huge amounts of water north of the Equator, and because of this, the sea level dropped precipitously, perhaps as much as 400 feet, revealing landmasses such as the Bering Land Bridge.

At this time, the ecology of the northern hemisphere was that of the Mammoth Steppe. It was a dry, frigid land filled with grasses, sedges, and tundra vegetation. It supported many large, grazing animals including reindeer, bison, and musk oxen, as well as the lions that fed on them. It also contained large camels, giant short-faced bears, and woolly mammoths.

The Bering Land Bridge may have been somewhat wetter than other areas of the Mammoth Steppe, because it was bordered north and south by ocean and fed by ocean breezes. Many of the animals of the Mammoth Steppe used the bridge to cross from east to west and back again. Eventually, their human hunters tracked them from Asia to North America.

Ethnologists and geologists generally believe that humans used the Bering Land Bridge to populate the Americas, which up until about 24,000 years ago had no sign of human life. Ethnologists use evidence such as shared religions, similar houses and tools, and unique methods of cleaning and preserving food to show the link between the people of coastal Siberia and the people of coastal Alaska.

There are those among the Native American population who dispute the land bridge theory. For one thing, it contradicts most native teachings on the origins of the people. For another, it seems to undermine the notion that they are truly "native" to the North American continent.

The waters returned about 12,000 years ago, and today global warming means that the sea level is rising steadily. It is difficult to stand on the shore of the Seward Peninsula today and picture walking across to Russia. It is easier to imagine if you look at a map. The borders are so close that the continents seem to kiss. Just a quick holding back of the waters, à la Moses in *The Ten Commandments*, and you can picture a Pleistocene hunter chasing a woolly mammoth across the land bridge to the untamed continent beyond.

26. According to this passage, the first people in North America lived

  A. in what is now Central America
  B. west of the Bering Strait
  C. below sea level
  D. in what is now Alaska

27. Based on information in the passage, about how long was the Bering Land Bridge?
    A. between 50 and 75 miles long
    B. between 90 and 120 miles long
    C. around 150 miles long
    D. around 200 miles long

28. According to the passage, which of these would be considered a land bridge?
    A. the Isthmus of Panama
    B. the Chesapeake Bay
    C. the Strait of Hormuz
    D. the Khyber Pass

29. Which of the following assertions does the author support with an example or examples?
    I. Ethnologists use evidence to show links between the people of Siberia and those of coastal Alaska.
    II. There are many historical land bridges.
    III. The Mammoth Steppe supported many large, grazing animals.
    A. I only
    B. III only
    C. I and II only
    D. I, II, and III

30. According to the passage, why does Beringia no longer exist?
    A. The Ice Age ended.
    B. Ozone depletion raised the sea levels.
    C. It was replaced with enormous sheets of ice.
    D. The continents drifted apart.

31. The author suggests that some contemporary Native Americans object to the land bridge theory because
    A. it equates them with Pleistocene man
    B. it challenges their history and status
    C. it relies on disputed science
    D. it belies the importance of southern tribes

32. Which of the following findings best supports the author's contention that Siberia was once connected to North America?
    A. Native American legends from the American Northwest feature enormous whales and large fish.
    B. People of coastal Siberia have features that distinguish them from people in the rest of Russia.
    C. Hunters in both Siberia and coastal Alaska continue to hunt seals, walrus, and sea lions.
    D. Large animal fossils found in both places prove that identical species once populated both regions.

33. Which new information, if true, would most CHALLENGE the claim that humans first moved to North America across the Bering Land Bridge?
   A. A new translation of an Inuit legend about Raven and a giant flood.
   B. New fossil records that place the Ice Age 1000 years earlier than believed.
   C. The discovery of human fossils in Kansas that predate the Ice Age.
   D. DNA proof that the musk ox of Siberia differed from the musk ox of Alaska.

SAMPLE PASSAGE VI: ANSWERS AND EXPLANATIONS

26. **The correct answer is D.** This straightforward **Comprehension** question asks you to **Locate Supporting Details**. The Bering Land Bridge is described as connecting Siberia to what is now Alaska. If humans walked across from Siberia, the first ones in North America would have emerged into Alaska.
27. **The correct answer is A.** This is a very simple **Application** question that requires you to **Solve a Problem** using details from the passage. According to the passage, you could drive across the bridge, if it still existed, in about an hour. Based on that information, you can infer that the bridge was about as long as a typical mileage per hour, which would put it at choice A, between 50 and 75 miles.
28. **The correct answer is A.** Again, this is an **Application** question, this time requiring you to **Make Generalizations**. A land bridge is a piece of land with water on either side that connects two larger pieces of land. That makes it equivalent to an isthmus (choice A). A bay (choice B) is a body of water, a strait (choice C) is a channel of water connecting two pieces of land, and a pass (choice D) is a narrow piece of land between mountains.
29. **The correct answer is D.** Here, you are asked to **Analyze an Argument** by answering an **Evaluation** question. "Ethnologists use evidence such as shared religions, similar houses and tools, and unique methods of cleaning and preserving food to show the link between the people of coastal Siberia and the people of coastal Alaska." That supports assertion I. "There was a bridge connecting the British Isles to the European continent, and there was one between Spain and Morocco at what is now the Straits of Gibraltar. There were bridges connecting Japan to China and Korea." That supports assertion II. "It supported many large, grazing animals including reindeer, bison, and musk oxen, as well as the lions that fed on them." That supports assertion III. Because all three assertions are supported with examples, the correct response is choice D.
30. **The correct answer is A.** You must **Draw Conclusions** to answer this **Application** question. There is no evidence to support choices B, C, or D. The Bering Land Bridge disappeared when the waters came back. The waters went away in the first place because the large ice slabs formed during the Ice Age displaced

them. When that age ended, the bridge was covered over. The correct answer is choice A.

31. **The correct answer is B.** This **Application** question involves **Identifying Cause and Effect**. According to the passage, some Native Americans object to the theory because "it contradicts most native teachings on the origins of the people" and "it seems to undermine the notion that they are truly 'native' to the North American continent." In other words, it challenges their history and status.
32. **The correct answer is D.** Read this **Incorporation of Information** question carefully to **Apply New Evidence** to the author's assertions. Your challenge is to find the response that BEST supports the idea that the continents were once connected. Answer A affects only North America. Answer B affects only Siberia. Answer C is possible, but it does not provide the unambiguous evidence that answer D does.
33. **The correct answer is C.** With this **Incorporation of Information** question, you must **Modify Conclusions** based on new information. Again, you must look for the answer that BEST challenges the idea that humans first moved from Siberia to North America. Neither choice A nor choice B would prove or disprove the notion. Choice D would throw some doubt on the theory that the two continents were connected, but only choice C would indicate that humans were already in North America prior to the forming of the land bridge.

SAMPLE PASSAGE VII: HUMANITIES

Pop! goes the weasel . . .

It's a meaningless phrase from a nursery rhyme, but some students of linguistics believe that it derives from Cockney rhyming slang, a form of English slang that originated in the East End of inner London. The Cockneys, traditionally, were those working-class citizens born within earshot of the bells of St. Mary-le-Bow, Cheapside. The word itself was a slap at the ignorant townsfolk by country gentry, who likened their urban brothers and sisters to deformed eggs, known as "cokeney" or "cock's eggs."

The Cockneys developed their own vernacular over a hundred years or so, and during the early part of the 19th century, rhyming slang became an integral part of this argot. It was associated in many Londoners' minds with the underworld, because it could easily be used as a sort of code. For their own self-preservation, Scotland Yard began to publish translations of the slang in police manuals, and thus the strange colloquialisms began to cross out of the East End and into the general population.

The rules behind the rhyming slang are as simple as the result is difficult to comprehend. A speaker puts together words, the last of which rhymes with the word he or she means to denote. For example, *loaf of bread* might mean "head." The difficulty comes as the slang becomes widespread and the original rhyme is discarded as superfluous, so that *loaf* means "head" in a sentence such as "He gave his loaf a thump."

Our own phrase "Put up your dukes" may derive from Cockney rhyming slang. Originally, the theory goes, the rhyme was "Duke of York" = "fork," an old slang term meaning the hand.

But back to "Pop! goes the weasel." Supposedly, *weasel* was from *weasel and stoat*, and referred to a coat. To pop one's weasel was to pawn one's coat, a relatively common practice on the East End as one's paycheck failed to stretch from one week to the next.

Sometimes, clearly, there was a certain deliberate irony in the choices of rhymes. For example, what are we to make of the fact that *trouble*, as in *trouble and strife*, is Cockney slang meaning "wife"? Sometimes, too, there was deliberate obfuscation. Would that bobby on the corner recognize himself as a *bluebottle* (bottle and stopper = "copper")? Would he know you were talking about him if you referred to *ducks and geese* ("police")? And finally, much Cockney rhyming slang was euphemistic, with rhymes substituted for words considered obscene or impolite.

Rhyming slang has moved out of the East End and throughout the English-speaking world. The phrase *eighty-sixed* means "nixed," or "thrown out." It is strictly American rhyming slang from the time of the Great Depression. Australia, too, has its own very elaborate rhyming slang. Many elements of rhyming slang have worked their way into the everyday speech of Londoners of all classes, and often their origins have been entirely forgotten.

Recently, rhyming slang has become popular again, with modern pop culture figures working their way into the mix, from Britney Spears ("beers") to Dame Judy (Dench) ("stench"). As with Pig Latin, the fun is in confounding the listener and creating a code that only the "in" group can decipher. So wipe that puzzled look off your *boat* (boat race = "face") and try to *rabbit* (rabbit and pork = "talk") the way *saucepans* (saucepan lids = "kids") do today!

34. The central thesis of the passage is that
   - **A.** Cockney rhyming slang developed as a means of communicating among immigrant populations without a common language
   - **B.** Cockney rhyming slang has seen a comeback among the country gentry in rural England
   - **C.** Cockney rhyming slang was and continues to be a witty way to fashion an exclusive coded language
   - **D.** Cockney rhyming slang has moved from the underworld into the everyday language of pop figures

35. The discussion of Scotland Yard shows primarily that
   A. to the police, rhyming slang was a troublesome barrier
   B. most people who use rhyming slang are criminals
   C. rhyming slang moved from north to south through Britain
   D. code breaking is one critical job of the legal profession

36. The author of the passage indicates that
   A. Cockney rhyming slang is too limited to be useful
   B. certain examples of Cockney rhyming slang are ironic
   C. rhyming slang is restricted to a certain class
   D. the Cockneys of old were aptly named

37. According to the passage, why might slang-users have called a policeman a "blue-bottle"?
   A. to offend him
   B. to confuse him
   C. to irritate him
   D. to amuse him

38. The movement of rhyming slang, as described in paragraph 6, is MOST analogous to which of these culinary changes?
   A. the development of the locally grown movement
   B. the fusion of Asian and French cuisine
   C. the use of cupcake towers in place of typical wedding cakes
   D. the incorporation of Latin spices in traditional American dishes

39. The passage suggests that today's rhyming slang is
   A. less complex than in the past
   B. limited to the underworld
   C. used by entertainers
   D. popular with teenagers

40. According to the rules for forming Cockney rhyming slang, which word might be rhyming slang for *house*?
   A. *cat,* from "cat and mouse"
   B. *rat,* from "dirty rat"
   C. *home,* from "house and home"
   D. *louse,* from "dirty louse"

SAMPLE PASSAGE VII: ANSWERS AND EXPLANATIONS

34. **The correct answer is C.** The words *central thesis* tell you that this is a **Comprehension** question that tests your ability to **Find the Main Idea.** Neither choice A nor choice B has any support in the passage. Choice D is close, but the passage

suggests that pop figures are a topic of rhyming slang and not the perpetrators of it. The statement that best expresses the main idea of the passage as a whole is choice C.

35. **The correct answer is A.** This **Comprehension** question asks you to **Choose an Accurate Summary**. The word *primarily* is critical here; it indicates that you must think about the author's main reason for including a section of the passage. The discussion of Scotland Yard tells of police publishing translations of rhyming slang in their manuals. The implication is that rhyming slang was causing them problems, and they needed to understand it better to perform their jobs. Choice A is the best paraphrase of this. Criminals did use rhyming slang, but whether most people who use it are criminals (choice B) is open to debate. The word *Scotland* may fool you into selecting choice C, but Scotland Yard is in London, not in Scotland. The author has no reason to emphasize code breaking as an important part of law enforcement, so choice D is not a good answer.
36. **The correct answer is B.** This is an **Application** question involving **Drawing Conclusions**. The author makes no statement, indirect or otherwise, in support of choice A or choice D. Although choice C was once true, the final paragraph of the passage implies that rhyming slang has moved beyond a single class. The best answer is choice B; the author states, "Sometimes, clearly, there was a certain deliberate irony in the choices of rhyme."
37. **The correct answer is B.** Again, this **Application** question asks you to **Draw Conclusions** from what is stated. Skim the passage to find the reference to "bluebottle." The author says, "Sometimes, too, there was deliberate obfuscation. Would that bobby on the corner recognize himself as a *bluebottle* (bottle and stopper = 'copper')?" The mission of the rhymer was to confuse the police.
38. **The correct answer is D.** To answer this **Incorporation of Information** question that asks you to **Combine Information**, think, according to paragraph 6, what happened to rhyming slang? The answer is that it moved from its original locale and worked its way into ordinary speech. Choice D is the most analogous to this movement: Latin spices have moved from their original locale and worked their way into ordinary American food.
39. **The correct answer is D.** This kind of **Application** question requires **Making Generalizations**. There is no support for choices A or B, and choice C represents a misunderstanding of the final paragraph of the passage. The best answer is choice D, for the author ends by suggesting that the reader learn to talk the way kids do today.
40. **The correct answer is A.** This is an **Application** question that forces you to apply what you've learned to **Solve a Problem** that is outside the bounds of the passage itself. Cockney rhyming slang begins with a rhyming phrase, but often, as the author states, "the original rhyme is discarded as superfluous." In the passage, the example given is *loaf of bread* for "head" becoming simply *loaf*. The only example

from the answer choices that follows this pattern is choice A, with *and mouse* dropping off *cat and mouse* to leave simply *cat.*

SAMPLE PASSAGE VIII: HUMANITIES

"He medalled twice in the Empire State Games." "Learn to parent more effectively." "The rise in prices will impact the bottom line."

If your toes curl when you hear nouns used as verbs, as in the underlined words, you are not alone in your word-snobbishness. Nevertheless, it's worth remembering that the greatest English writer, William Shakespeare, was notorious for coining words in just this way. He changed nouns to verbs and verbs to adjectives with aplomb, and most of his conversions remain with us to this day.

Many of us are familiar with Shakespeare's clichés, those phrases that are now part of our lore of proverbs and expressions. We would not "break the ice" or "give the devil his due" if it weren't for the Bard. No one would have a "heart of gold," lie "dead as a doornail," or "come full circle."

When it comes to word coinage, it is difficult to determine which words are truly original with Shakespeare and which are simply words that first appeared in print with his works. A large percentage of Shakespearean coinages appear to be words that have familiar roots but are used as a new part of speech.

Some of the new words are nouns formed from verbs. For example, *accused* in *Richard II* is used to denote a person accused of a crime. The verb was well known, but there is no earlier example of this noun usage. *Scuffle* in *Antony and Cleopatra* denotes a fight and is taken from a verb already in existence. Shakespeare created other nouns by adding the noun-forming suffix *-ment* to a familiar verb: *amazement* and *excitement* appear for the first time in several of his plays.

More typical was the change of a noun to a verb. He used *to blanket* in *King Lear* and *to champion* in *Macbeth. To petition* shows up in *Antony and Cleopatra,* and *to humor* appears in *Love's Labour's Lost.* Other new verbs coined from existing nouns include *to lapse,* meaning "to fail"; *to cake,* meaning "to encrust"; and *to rival,* meaning "to compete with." We have no way of knowing whether these coinages provoked the same spinal shivers that good grammarians experience nowadays at the sound of *to parent.*

Many of Shakespeare's most successful coinages were descriptive in nature. He invented *raw-boned* in *I Henry VI,* and there are few words today that better describe a certain kind of man. Similar hyphenates include *bold-faced* from the same play, *cold-blooded* from *King John, hot-blooded* from *The Merry Wives of Windsor,* and *well-bred* from *II Henry IV.*

Occasionally, coinages were stolen from another language. There's *alligator* in *Romeo and Juliet* from the Spanish and *bandit* in *II Henry VI* from the Italian. There's *to negotiate* and *to denote* from the Latin.

Of course, not all of Shakespeare's coinages survived the centuries to come. We don't use the verb *to friend* anymore; nor do we call our friends *co-mates.* Something that is secured is not referred to as *virgined,* and we don't call a messy room *indigest.* Nevertheless, to study Shakespeare is to see how rapidly a language can change and grow and perhaps to recognize that to sneer at new coinages is to ignore the way English has evolved from the beginning.

41. In the context of the passage, the word *notorious* means
    - **A.** renowned
    - **B.** disreputable
    - **C.** iniquitous
    - **D.** dishonorable

42. The central thesis of the passage is that
    - **A.** Shakespeare gave us many important maxims and adages
    - **B.** coined words are often grating to the ears
    - **C.** Shakespeare teaches us a lot about how language grows
    - **D.** modern coinages are largely stolen from Shakespeare

43. Based on the information in the passage, which of these is MOST likely to happen to the coinage *to friend*?
    - **A.** It will come back into common use.
    - **B.** It will remain strictly Shakespearean.
    - **C.** It will be changed to an adjective.
    - **D.** It will be replaced with *co-mates.*

44. The author apparently believes that
    - **A.** Shakespeare took unnecessary license with the Queen's English
    - **B.** Shakespeare's coinages are far more inventive than coinages today
    - **C.** changing nouns to verbs is an appallingly lazy way of coining words
    - **D.** coined words are an important and natural evolution of language

45. Suppose scholars found a long-lost medieval manuscript that used the word *accused* as a noun. This new information would most CHALLENGE the passage's implication that
    - **A.** nouns were frequently coined from verbs
    - **B.** *Richard II* was an original drama
    - **C.** Shakespeare coined the word *accused*
    - **D.** word coinage is a relatively new pastime

SAMPLE PASSAGE VIII: ANSWERS AND EXPLANATIONS

41. **The correct answer is A.** This kind of **Comprehension** question involves **Interpreting Vocabulary**. According to the passage, "the greatest English writer, William

Shakespeare, was notorious for coining words in just this way." Although each of the answer choices is a potential synonym for *notorious,* only *renowned* fits the context.

42. **The correct answer is C.** As do many **Comprehension** questions, this one asks you to **Find the Main Idea** of the passage. The "central thesis" of a passage is not just a passing subtheme, as choice A is; nor is it a minor detail, as choice B is. The central thesis of this passage has to do with the way that coined words add to the English language, and the author uses Shakespeare as the primary example of how this works.
43. **The correct answer is B.** This is an **Application** question involving **Making Predictions**. "We don't use the verb *to friend* anymore," says the author, using this as an example of coined words that have not survived the test of time. Because it has not survived, it is unlikely to return (choice A), and there is no support for the notion that it might change form (choice C) or be replaced by another archaic word (choice D). It will probably remain strictly Shakespearean, so the answer is choice B.
44. **The correct answer is D.** In this **Application** question, you are **Drawing Conclusions** about the author's intent. As always, you must choose the best or most likely answer. The author's interest in Shakespeare's coinages makes choice A unlikely, and there is no support for choice C. Choice B is possible, but there is not enough comparison to make it the best choice. The best or most likely answer is choice D; the author certainly implies that language evolves naturally, and that coinages are an important part of that evolution.
45. **The correct answer is C.** This **Incorporation of Information** question provides new information that might require you to **Modify Conclusions**. The discovery would not challenge but might rather support the idea that nouns were frequently coined from verbs (choice A). It would prove nothing about the originality of *Richard II* (choice B), and there is nothing in the passage that indicates that word coinage is new (choice D). An earlier finding of the word's use, however, would clearly contradict the assertion that Shakespeare coined the word. Choice C is correct.

SAMPLE PASSAGE IX: SOCIAL SCIENCES

They firmly practiced celibacy, yet their original leader, "Mother Ann," was a young woman who had birthed and lost four children. They believed in severe simplicity, yet their rituals were filled with the strange, ecstatic dances that led to their name. The American Shaking Quakers, or Shakers, were a radical group whose very contradictions would both empower and destroy them.

The Quakers were well established both in England and in America when James Wardley began to lead his flock down a new path. Inspired by the millennial French

Prophets, he instilled Quaker worship with communion with the dead, visions, and shaking. Like all radicals at the time, members of the Shaking Quakers were often harassed and imprisoned for their unusual ways of worship. During one such imprisonment, a young parishioner named Ann Lee had a vision in which she determined that she embodied the Second Coming of Christ, the female version of God as Father and Mother.

Mother Ann then became the leader of the congregation, and when another vision told her that a place had been prepared for her people, she decided to take her flock to safer harbor in America. A small group came with her. They settled on a commune near Albany, New York. Despite the American Revolution roiling around them, the group remained pacifistic, which led to further ostracism and harassment from the colonists nearby.

The tiny Shaker band got a new lease on life in 1779 when Joseph Meacham and his band of followers converted to their religion. It's important to remember what a radical leap this involved. The Shakers rejected the trinity in favor of a belief in the duality of the Holy Spirit, a spirit both male and female. They believed that the new millennium was not in the future but had already begun with Mother Ann's vision. They believed in celibacy as a symbol of a return to pre-Adam purity, and this relinquishing of typical sexual roles would lead to unusual gender equality. Unity of the commune was the goal, and unity was achieved through the suppression of individuality. Shakers lived in common dormitories, shared all worldly goods, and dressed and ate simply.

Equality and community appealed to the people from other cultures who joined the Shakers. They attracted Native Americans, free blacks, and non-Christians, and all were welcomed into the commune. Under Meacham's guidance, the commune began missions to other areas, eventually establishing 17 additional communes.

Of course, a religion with celibacy at its base must rely on missionary work for its survival. A commune, no matter how isolationist, must sometimes look outward. Many years after Mother Ann's death, Shaker communities used mail-order catalogs to sell the simple, functional furniture we know them for today.

The height of the religion was in the mid-19th century. By the end of the 20th century, only one tiny Shaker commune survived. The commune, near New Gloucester, Maine, has only a handful of elderly, female members. They continue to farm the land, make baskets and woven goods, and maintain a museum and library that are open to the public.

46. The central thesis of the passage is that
   A. no religion can survive without a mission
   B. celibacy was the best and worst thing about the Shakers
   C. the Shakers were a paradoxical sect
   D. our culture owes a lot to the Shakers

47. The discussion of the trinity shows primarily that
   A. Shaker beliefs differed radically from prevailing Christian faith
   B. Quakers believed in a duality of spiritual and corporeal being
   C. the Shakers rejected the concept of the new millennium
   D. a return to pre-Adamite purity was part of the Shaker commitment

48. According to the passage, why might free blacks have joined the Shakers?
   A. because of their antiwar stance
   B. because of their free education
   C. because of their inclusiveness
   D. because of their simplicity

49. The author of the passage indicates that
   A. Shaker values are tied to the distant past
   B. the Shakers were doomed to extinction
   C. pacifism was confined to the New World
   D. Native Americans were easily converted

50. Which of these examples from later American history is MOST analogous to the description of actions involving the Shakers in paragraph 3?
   A. a failed rebellion in 1840s Rhode Island against an undemocratic government
   B. the relocation of the communal Amana Society to Iowa in 1859
   C. a bombing during a peaceful demonstration in Haymarket Square in 1886
   D. attempts to suppress antiwar protestors in the Vietnam era

51. The passage suggests that the Shakers' use of mail-order catalogs was
   A. restrictive
   B. inappropriate
   C. fruitless
   D. practical

52. Below is a favorite Shaker symbol. Based on the passage, which of these statements does the symbol MOST likely represent?

   A. Better to have your gold in the hand than in the heart.
   B. Give your hands to work and your hearts to God.
   C. Now join your hands, and with your hands your hearts.
   D. A friend reaches for your hand and touches your heart.

SAMPLE PASSAGE IX: ANSWERS AND EXPLANATIONS

46. **The correct answer is C.** Again, the term *central thesis* indicates a **Comprehension** question on **Finding the Main Idea**. The central thesis is stated clearly in paragraph 1: "The American Shaking Quakers, or Shakers, were a radical group whose very contradictions would both empower and destroy them."
47. **The correct answer is A.** This kind of **Comprehension** question asks you to **Choose an Accurate Summary**. The example of the trinity is given specifically to point out how the Shakers differed from traditional doctrine. Although choice D is true of the Shakers, it has nothing to do with their rejection of the notion of the Father, Son, and Holy Spirit.
48. **The correct answer is C.** This is a fairly simple **Application** question involving **Identifying Cause and Effect**. According to the passage, the Shakers were a remarkably inclusive sect whose belief in equality and community "attracted Native Americans, free blacks, and non-Christians." There is no support for choices A or D and no mention at all of choice B.
49. **The correct answer is B.** To answer this **Application** question, you need to **Draw Conclusions**. You must find the answer that best shows what is implied by the passage. Although the Shaker sect is old, the author never implies that their values are outmoded (choice A). There is no support for choices C or D. However, the discussion of celibacy makes it fairly clear that the Shaker sect could not go on forever. The best answer is choice B.
50. **The correct answer is D. Incorporation of Information** questions like this ask you to **Combine Information** from within and outside the passage. In paragraph 3 of the passage, the Shakers settle in a commune, where their pacifist ways at a time of war lead to ostracism and harassment. The closest parallel is to antiwar protestors in the 1960s, which is choice D.
51. **The correct answer is D.** This **Application** question asks you to **Make Generalizations.** It might have been out of character, but the author does not present it as inappropriate (choice B). Nor was it fruitless (choice C); it seems to have been a practical way for the Shakers to sell their crafts.
52. **The correct answer is B.** This is an **Application** question that asks you to **Solve a Problem** by applying what you have learned to something new. Choice B is actually a quotation from Mother Ann. The Shakers were all about work and faith, not about money (choice A) or even friendship (choices C and D).

SAMPLE PASSAGE X: SOCIAL SCIENCES

The real estate bubble, the dot-com craze—for sheer lunacy and truly disastrous consequences, few economic swings hold a candle to tulipomania.

In 1593, a botanist brought back samples of tulips to Holland from Constantinople. He planted them in a garden with the intent of studying their medicinal value. His garden was ransacked, the bulbs were stolen, and that was the beginning of the tulip trade in Holland.

Rich Dutch homeowners coveted the new, colorful plants, and soon many of the finest houses in Holland had small plots of tulips. A mosaic virus attacked the introduced species, weakening the plant stock while at the same time causing odd streaks of color upon the petals of the flowers. These rather pretty alterations made the plants even more desirable, and shortly thereafter, prices began to rise out of control. By the year 1635, buyers were speculating on tulips, purchasing promissory notes while the bulbs were still in the ground. The trade in tulip futures became frenzied, with the prices of the most popular, damaged plants doubling and tripling overnight. Buyers bought on spec, assuming that they could turn around and sell at a profit once spring came.

Tulips have a built-in rarity, in that it takes years to grow one from seed, and most bulbs produce only one or two "offsets," or bulb clones, annually. That scarcity kept the value up even when new varieties were introduced on the market.

The tulip craze soon found ordinary citizens selling everything they owned for a single bulb, some of which were valued at the equivalent of thousands of dollars in today's currency; quite literally, bulbs were worth their weight in gold. Contemporary documents show that people traded oxen, silver, land, and houses for one tulip bulb. During the winter of 1636, when the craze was at its peak, a single bulb future might change hands half a dozen times in one day. Planting bulbs and growing flowers became wholly beside the point; the object was simply to buy and sell and resell.

As wild as this market was, it was transacted entirely outside of the established Stock Exchange in Amsterdam. It was a people's exchange. Typically, sales took place at auctions, but often they were transacted at pubs or in town squares.

Like any craze in which potential profits seem too good to be true, tulipomania was fated to end badly. In February 1637, at a bulb auction in Haarlem, the bottom fell out when no one agreed to pay the inflated prices. The ensuing panic took a matter of a few weeks; prices fell, bulb dealers refused to honor existing contracts, and the government had to leap in to try to bail the country out, offering 10 cents on the dollar for bulb contracts until even that could not be sustained. Eventually, a panel of judges declared that all investment in tulips was gambling and not recoverable investment.

Holland slowly fell into an economic depression that lasted for years and eventually overflowed its borders into the rest of Europe.

53. The central thesis of the passage is that
   A. tulipomania was a localized craze with localized effects
   B. tulipomania shows the potential devastating effects of a craze
   C. the Stock Exchange cannot prevent people from unregulated trading
   D. the Stock Exchange developed as an answer to unregulated trading

54. The passage suggests that the author would MOST likely believe that
   A. trading in futures may be ill-advised
   B. trading in commodities is safer than trading stock
   C. trading stocks is relatively risk-free
   D. trading at auctions is usually unwise

55. Which of the following assertions does the author support with an example?
   I. Tulips have a built-in rarity.
   II. Sales were transacted in pubs and town squares.
   III. Holland fell into a depression.
   A. I only
   B. III only
   C. I and II only
   D. I, II, and III

56. As described in paragraph 4, investments in tulips in the 16th and 17th centuries were similar to what types of investments today?
   A. corporate real estate
   B. start-up companies
   C. corn futures
   D. rare coins

57. The author refers to the trade in tulips as a "people's exchange." This term is used to indicate
   A. fairness
   B. informality
   C. low prices
   D. efficiency

58. The 17th-century speculation on prospective tulip growth might be compared to today's
   A. fluctuation of oil and natural gas prices
   B. exchange trading of options and futures
   C. hedge funds in the foreign exchange market
   D. issuance of risk-free municipal bonds

59. Auctions in the Netherlands continue to handle between 60 and 70 percent of the world's flower production and export. What question might this information reasonably suggest about tulipomania?
   A. whether it resulted not only in a depression but also in the death of the auction system of commodity trading
   B. whether it led the Dutch government to take over substantial debt for bulb dealers and their patrons
   C. whether it changed the Dutch way of doing business to one that was more formal and controlled
   D. whether it forced the Dutch to look into new, nonagricultural products for export and import

SAMPLE PASSAGE X: ANSWERS AND EXPLANATIONS

53. **The correct answer is B.** This **Comprehension** question asks you to **Find the Main Idea** of the passage. Although choice C may be inferred from the passage, it is not the main idea. Choice A is belied by the fact that the depression in Holland ended up moving across Europe, and choice D is incorrect, because the Stock Exchange already existed at the time of tulipomania. The passage primarily shows the damaging effects of a craze (choice B).
54. **The correct answer is A.** To answer this **Application** question, you must **Make Predictions** based on what the author has said in the passage. The author implies that the "people's exchange" was less safe than the Stock Exchange, so choice B is unlikely, but there is still no indication that trading stocks is "risk-free" (choice C). There is no opinion given about the wisdom of trading at auctions (choice D); certainly it does not work well in tulipomania, but generalizing from that to the world at large is not possible. It is more viable to generalize that trading in futures may be ill-advised (choice A), especially because the answer includes the qualifying word *may*.
55. **The correct answer is A.** This **Evaluation** question involves **Analyzing an Argument**. There is no example given of sales transacted in pubs and town squares (II), nor is there an example to show how Holland fell into a depression (III). The assertion that tulips have a built-in rarity (I) is supported by two examples: "It takes years to grow one from seed, and most bulbs produce only one or two 'offsets,' or bulb clones, annually." Because only I is correct, the answer is choice A.
56. **The correct answer is D.** To answer this sort of **Incorporation of Information** question, **Combine Information** from the passage with what you know to determine the analogy. Tulipomania was about investment in futures, which might make you assume that choice C was correct, but paragraph 4 specifically explains

that tulips' value as an investment came from their built-in scarcity, making choice D a better analogy.

57. **The correct answer is B** Although this involves vocabulary, it moves beyond simple comprehension to **Application**, requiring you to **Draw Conclusions** about the author's intent. The so-called "people's exchange" was neither fair (choice A) nor efficient (choice D), and it certainly did not hold prices down (choice C). It was an informal trading structure outside the realm of the traditional Stock Exchange.
58. **The correct answer is B** This is not a simple compare-and-contrast question; it is an **Incorporation of Information** question that asks you to **Combine Information** from the passage with what you know. "Speculation on prospective tulip growth" equals trade in commodities futures, which today takes place in exchange trading on the mercantile exchange.
59. **The correct answer is C** Again, the question works outward from the specific material given in the passage, making it an **Incorporation of Information** question, this time on **Applying New Evidence**. This question gives you a fact about the present and asks you to apply it to your understanding of the past. If Holland continues to trade tulips at auction, the auction system cannot be dead (choice A), and agricultural products must still be part of the Dutch economy (choice D). Choice B in no way corresponds to the fact from today. Choice C, on the other hand, is a reasonable question. Now that Holland appears to be successful at the bulb trade, something must have happened to change the way things worked.

Critical Analysis and Reasoning Skills Minitest

30 Questions **45 Minutes**

This minitest is designed to assess your mastery of the content in Part 2 of this volume. The questions have been designed to simulate actual MCAT questions in terms of format and degree of difficulty. They test your ability to comprehend information in a reading passage, to analyze and evaluate arguments and supporting evidence, and to apply concepts and ideas to new situations. You will need to apply the scientific inquiry and reasoning skills that the test makers have identified as essential for success in medical school.

The passages in this section cover a wide range of topics in both the social sciences and the humanities. You may encounter readings in philosophy, ethics, cultural studies, and the like. All the information you need to answer questions will be provided in the passage; no outside knowledge of the topics is required.

Use this test to measure your readiness for the actual MCAT. Try to answer all of the questions within the specified time limit. If you run out of time, you will know that you need to work on improving your pacing.

Complete answer explanations are provided at the end of the minitest. Pay particular attention to the answers for questions you got wrong or skipped. If necessary, go back and review the question-answering strategies covered in the preceding pages.

Now turn the page and begin the Critical Analysis and Reasoning Skills Minitest.

Directions: *Questions 1–4 are based on the following passage.*

Passage I

Recent research indicates that our experience of happiness can be self-regulated, regardless of external circumstances. We can actively choose to be happy. It was previously thought that levels of happiness were genetically determined; people were born with a genetic predisposition to cheerfulness or pessimism. However, studies now suggest that such predispositions, while present, are not fixed. Instead, emotion, and indeed the structure of the brain, can be modified through certain practices.

These findings are indebted to the work of psychologist Gordon Watson, who in 1930 conducted a study entitled "Happiness Among Adult Students of Education." Since happiness was considered a highly desired yet elusive and mysterious emotion, Watson's serious endeavor was startling. By the 1970s, the psychological community was researching happiness on a larger scale. Today, it is estimated that over 2000 researchers in 42 countries are actively involved in happiness research.

In that crowded field, the work of a professor of psychology at the University of Wisconsin, Richard Davidson, stands out. Davidson observed patterns of brain activity as they related to a subject's mental and emotional states, using brain science's new technologies, including quantitative electrophysiology, positron emission tomography, and functional magnetic resonance imaging. He discovered what Western science once believed to be impossible: that the brain is not a static organ—it is able to change and develop over time. This capacity is known as neuroplasticity, and it has had a profound effect on the study of happiness.

Davidson's studies found that the functions of the brain's cerebral cortex are not limited to determining intelligence, interpreting sensory impulses, and controlling motor function as once believed. In fact, this area also determines personality, including emotional predispositions. Levels of activity on the right and left sides of the cerebral cortex relate to feelings of happiness and sadness. Specifically, higher levels of activity at the left frontal area of the cerebral cortex coincide with feelings of happiness, while activity on the right frontal area correspond with feelings of sadness. Therefore, activities that generate side-specific activity can enhance those feelings.

For example, meditation has been shown to generate left-brain activity, and studies show that it produces positive emotions. Davidson studied the link between meditation and happiness through a project involving Tibetan Buddhist monks. His research brings together Eastern and Western traditions, and it links together objective reality with once-thought-to-be subjective internal states of consciousness. The connection is made through observable electrical activity in the central nervous system. When the monks in the study meditated, their brain activity was recorded. Increases in left cerebral cortex activity indicate that the practice of meditation can, over time, change the structure of the brain, increasing the size and activity level of the left cerebral cortex.

Another practice that has been shown to stimulate right cerebral cortex activity, and enhance feelings of happiness, is the altering of conscious thoughts. More specifically, when a subject repeats positive affirmations—thinking optimistic thoughts—activity in the left cerebral cortex increases. As with the practice of meditation, the repetition of positive affirmations can change the structure of the brain over time, creating feelings of happiness and well-being. These findings show that the mind-body connection cannot be denied.

1. In the context of the passage, the word *elusive* means
   - **A.** prevaricating
   - **B.** deceitful
   - **C.** frank
   - **D.** evasive
2. The author's claim that Gordon Watson's scientific study of happiness was startling is supported by
   - **A.** details about Watson's background and the publicity his study received
   - **B.** the description of the study's subject
   - **C.** the assertion that happiness was, at the time, desired but thought to be elusive and mysterious
   - **D.** the fact that he conducted the study in 1930
3. According to the passage, all of these are true EXCEPT
   - **A.** the brain is able to change over time, a process known as neuroplasticity
   - **B.** science is attempting to prove there is a mind–body connection
   - **C.** Tibetan monks increase their left-side cerebral cortex activity through meditation
   - **D.** the right frontal area of the brain corresponds with feelings of sadness
4. Based on information in the passage, which of these outcomes should someone expect after silently repeating the phrase "I am successful" for 20 minutes?
   - **A.** a feeling of well-being
   - **B.** sadness
   - **C.** a creative impulse
   - **D.** fatigue

Questions 5–11 are based on the following passage.

Passage II

In sharp contrast to the modern, confessional poetry of the 20th century, the oeuvre of Henry Wadsworth Longfellow seems quaint and primly Victorian. During his lifetime, however, he was the most celebrated poet in the country. A closer look at the history of American poetry reveals that, despite his eminence, Longfellow wrote in a mold of both form and content that was already being challenged during his lifetime. But why, a century later, do the artistic works of many of his contemporaries continue to be enjoyed and studied while Longfellow languishes in the tomb of cultural artifacts?

One answer lies in the radical shift that began to take place in poetry in the mid-19th century. Longfellow's themes and steadfast rhymes (and those of John Greenleaf Whittier, Oliver Wendell Holmes, and James Russell Lowell) gave way gradually to confessional verse, whose subjects were more personal and rhymes were looser and less conventional. But to understand this shift, one must first understand the nature of Longfellow's work and his standing in the American literary scene of his time.

Longfellow took as his subject his country's historical imagination, writing on an epic scale about Paul Revere, the Indian Hiawatha, and the pilgrim Miles Standish. He bestowed a mythic dimension on these figures, giving American readers iconic images that helped form a collective consciousness in the new country (indeed, Longfellow was a part of the first generation to be born in the United States). But Longfellow's content went beyond nationalistic pride—it was highly accessible and incredibly popular. Its accessibility is explained by his obvious themes that could be easily understood and embraced by the public. Longfellow did not challenge his readers, but appealed to their desire for stories that expounded an optimistic, sentimental, and moralistic worldview. Those themes were explored in rhyme that allowed readers to commit the poems to memory, much like songs. In 1857, *The Song of Hiawatha*, arguably his best-known poem, sold 50,000 copies, an astounding number at the time. The next year, *The Courtship of Miles Standish* sold 25,000 copies in two months and in London sold 10,000 copies in one day. His success allowed him to give up a professorship at Harvard and focus full time on his writing.

Walt Whitman, Longfellow's contemporary, wrote poetry similar to that of Longfellow—Romantic and sentimental, with conventional rhyme and meter. But in the 1850s, indeed two years before *The Song of Hiawatha*, he wrote and published *Leaves of Grass*; a more radical departure from his previous work could not have been imagined. The 12 unnamed poems comprising *Leaves of Grass* are written in free verse—that is, without conventional rhyme and meter. Yet, like Longfellow, he was determined to explore the subject of America and his love for his country.

Whitman looked to the writings of Ralph Waldo Emerson for inspiration. Emerson wrote "America is a poem in our eyes; its ample geography dazzles the imagination, and it will not wait long for metres." Indeed, Whitman paraphrased Emerson in his preface to *Leaves of Grass*, "The United States themselves are essentially the greatest poem." But by that he did not mean he would explore that nation's mythic past. Instead, he took as his subjects the commonplace and the personal, finding beauty everywhere but expressing it in unique ways. He wrote of larger themes such as democracy, slavery and the Civil War, varied occupations and types of work, social change, and the American landscape and the natural world. He also explored more intimate subjects: aging, death and immortality, poverty, romantic love, and spirituality. In his "I Hear America Singing," he brings together these varied subjects to create a vision of America that is as far from Miles Standish as one can fathom. In it, he celebrates the "varied carols" sung by Americans, mechanics, carpenters, masons, boatmen, shoemakers, and mothers in long, unrhymed lines.

Whitman's ground-breaking free verse changed the trajectory of American poetry. The next generation of poets, including Ezra Pound, Hart Crane, Sherwood Anderson, and William Carlos Williams, celebrated their debt to Whitman. Decades later, the influence of Whitman's work on Allen Ginsberg and Langston Hughes, among many others, continues his legacy.

5. According to the passage, what might be the current reputation of poets such as Whittier and Holmes?
   A. They are considered integral writers in the history of American poetry.
   B. They are reviled as part of the Victorian Romantic period of American poetry.
   C. They are regarded as antiquated due to their conventional form and content.
   D. They are viewed as an influence on the Modern movement.

6. The main argument of the passage is that
   A. Whitman's free verse is superior to Longfellow's rhymes
   B. Longfellow's standing as an American poet was diminished by a rejection of quaint subjects and conventional rhyme and meter that came in the wake of poets such as Whitman
   C. Longfellow would be read and studied more today if he had retained his nationalistic subject matter but eschewed the sentimental tone and standard forms of his poems
   D. Ralph Waldo Emerson aided in the transformation of American poetry from Victorian Romanticism to Modernism

7. Which of the following statements is NOT presented as evidence that Whitman is responsible for the radical shift in American poetry that occurred in the 19th century?
   A. He used iconic American figures as his subjects.
   B. His poetry was more personal and intimate than that of his predecessors or contemporaries.
   C. He wrote about the common man and commonplace events.
   D. He began writing in free verse rather than conventional rhymes.

8. What does the author mean by "tomb of cultural artifacts"?
   A. a resting place for dead poets
   B. a kind of cemetery in which people can pay their respects to writers of the past
   C. a crypt where culturally significant items are stored
   D. a group of ideas and works of art from the past that are considered to be dead

9. The author apparently believes that
   A. poems about iconic American figures can become best-sellers
   B. Whitman's poems are more popular than Longfellow's because people prefer free verse and more personal poetry
   C. Ralph Waldo Emerson could be considered the father of Modern American poetry
   D. contemporary confessional poetry owes much to the work of Longfellow

10. One of America's most famous Modern poets, Ezra Pound, said of Walt Whitman, "As for Whitman, I read him (in many parts) with acute pain, but when I write of certain things I find myself using his rhythms." How does this quote affect the author's contention that Pound and his generation of poets celebrated their debt to Whitman?
   A. It repudiates it.
   B. It endorses it.
   C. It denies the contention by showing Pound's distaste for Whitman's work.
   D. It calls into question the author's use of the word *celebrate.*

11. Sales figures for two of Longfellow's poems are cited
   A. to reinforce the idea that Longfellow's popularity was declining
   B. to compare his sales to those of his contemporaries
   C. because they mark a milestone in American publishing
   D. as evidence of his popularity at the time

Questions 12–17 are based on the following passage.

Passage III

On what basis might it be said that animals have rights? To partisans on either side of the debate, the question itself seems absurd. Supporters of animal rights would reply that animals, as living creatures, have the same type of rights enjoyed by all living beings. Opponents of the cause would rejoin that rights are the product of rationalism and thus are the sole province of humans.

One interesting moral perspective from which to view the debate comes from the philosophy of utilitarianism. Jeremy Bentham, widely credited as the father of utilitarianism, believed that the rightness or wrongness of actions should be judged by the effect they have on all the beings affected by the action. The entire world comprised a closed system to which the actions of any member of the system either added to the sum total of pleasure in the system or to the sum total of pain. To Bentham, the interests and desires of the participants in the system were all equal; Bentham's intellectual disciple Henry Sidgwick famously said, "The good of any one individual is of no more importance, from the point of view of the Universe, than the good of any other."

Bentham himself believed that the good of animals should be taken into consideration in utilitarianism. The issue for him was not whether animals could reason (debatable) or talk (obviously not), but whether they could suffer (absolutely). An animal's capacity for suffering, argued Bentham, implied not necessarily that it should have rights equal to those of man, but that its pain should be given equal consideration when determining exactly what rights it had. It is from this perspective that animal rights can be most justified.

Obviously, it doesn't make sense to say that animals should have the right to free speech or the right to vote, because these are capacities the animal does not and cannot ever possess. But it would be sensible to say that animals have a right to be free from unnecessary pain or suffering. This view of animal rights would preclude many current practices, such as using animals to test new drugs and cosmetics and even perhaps the mass production of animals for food and clothing.

Interestingly, utilitarianism also provides opponents of animal rights with justification for their views. Since utilitarianism is based on calculations of the total good of the system, it is possible to see animal exploitation as adding to, rather than subtracting from, the sum of happiness. For instance, the death of one cow could presumably provide food and clothing for multiple people. This increase of happiness for the many at the expense of the few would satisfy the tenets of utilitarianism. Alternately, opponents could argue that since utilitarianism operates in a closed system, the negative effect of the death or suffering of one creature can be negated by the birth or pleasure of another creature. Since there are many times more animals that are born and live out their natural lives free from human-inflicted cruelty, the supposed suffering of those animals used for food, clothing, and experimentation is neutralized.

12. The word *province* as used in the passage MOST nearly means
   A. boundary
   B. subdivision
   C. responsibility
   D. domain

13. A utilitarian who supported animal rights would believe an animal had the right to all of the following EXCEPT
   A. a right to be free from cruel and unnecessary actions
   B. a right to be not used as a test subject
   C. a right to be not confined in uncomfortable positions
   D. a right to possess a secure habitat

14. The passage implies that Bentham and Sidgwick believe
   A. there is no privileged frame of reference in the world
   B. animal rights are just as important as human rights
   C. animals possess the capacity to reason
   D. animals possess the capacity to suffer

15. The author MOST likely included the parenthetical references in order to
    A. insert his or her personal beliefs into the discussion
    B. emphasize the factors Bentham thought most relevant
    C. present the viewpoint of animal rights supporters
    D. preempt possible objections to Bentham's logic

16. The passage implies that utilitarianism could be used to justify all of the following EXCEPT
    A. the use of people as means to ends rather than ends in themselves
    B. the death penalty
    C. torture of dangerous criminals
    D. indiscriminate killing

17. The primary purpose of the passage is to
    A. provide an ethical framework from which to view a controversial issue
    B. explain how utilitarianism can be used to justify animal rights
    C. argue for the end of cruelty to animals
    D. detail Bentham's and Sidgwick's views on animal rights

Questions 18–23 are based on the following passage.

Passage IV

In literature, the period typically referred to as the 20th century actually begins in the previous century. To many, Queen Victoria's Jubilee in 1887 effectively marked the end of a literary epoch. The prevailing aesthetic sensibility, art for art's sake, was dying a slow death, as the gulf between artists and writers and the rest of the public widened, resulting in the widespread idea of the artist as one alienated from the rest of society. This viewpoint was spurred on by the bohemian culture movement, which arose in France and quickly spread. At its core, the bohemian movement scoffed at the limits placed on the individual by polite society and sought to isolate the artist from society as one who both rejects and is rejected by society.

Across the channel, developments in England further accentuated the separation of the artist from society at large. The Education Act of 1870 made elementary education mandatory, creating a massive class of literate, though still mostly uneducated, consumers. In response to this new market, new forms of entertainment were created, including the cheap and sensational "yellow press," which focused on scandal, crime, and other base aspects of human nature. Furthermore, publishers now divided up the literature audience into low, high, and middle "brow" members and churned out writing to satisfy the larger proportion of low- and middle-brow consumers. Although there has always been literature directed at specific audiences, the degree and the speed at which these audiences became fragmented occurred at an unprecedented rate in the early 20th century.

The emergence and mass production of such so-called popular literature provided more fodder for the artistic elite's war on the crude and unsophisticated philistines in the public square. Perhaps this divide and the artist's growing awareness of difference led to a prevalence of pessimism and stoicism in the literature of the late Victorian period. Hardy, Housman, and Stevenson—all of these writers expressed at least some form of overweening negativity or passivity in their prose and poetry.

The end of Victoria's reign brought Edward VII to the throne, and Edwardian England seemed to articulate all those qualities the artistic elite had grown weary of. Edward VII has been described as self-indulgent, and his 10-year regime was a boon to those who had the means to enjoy a life of idle pleasures. Although in the past artists and writers enjoyed the patronage of the royal family and other notables, now they strove to keep their distance from such decadence, perhaps to avoid contaminating their art, perhaps to further their sense of alienation from society.

The Edwardian period lasted a mere decade, the prevailing cultural mentality changed by the ascendancy of George V to the throne in 1910 and thoroughly extirpated by England's entry into World War I in 1914. With the advantage of hindsight, the Georgian period seems an especially crucial one, a necessary balancing point between the gilded nature of the Edwardian age and the somewhat artificial staidness of the Victorian period. It was in this brief four-year period that English literature held its breath, and when it exhaled, at the end of the Great War, the old order in Europe was no more.

18. In the context of the passage, the word *polite* means
    A. cultured
    B. nice
    C. affable
    D. deferential

19. According to the passage, a bohemian would likely reject
    I. current fashion trends
    II. prevailing mores
    III. capitalistic thinking
    A. I only
    B. II only
    C. I and III only
    D. I, II, and III

20. The author implies that the Education Act of 1870
    A. increased the education level of the English population
    B. led to more people attending secondary school
    C. had mixed results
    D. angered the artistic elite

21. The passage indicates the 20th century differed from earlier artistic periods because
    A. artists viewed the public as crude and unsophisticated
    B. divisions in society were deeper than before
    C. the public was just as educated as the artists were
    D. artistic works were pessimistic and stoic

22. The passage implies that Hardy, Housman, and Stevenson were all
    A. popular writers of the late Victorian period
    B. influenced by the trends of their times
    C. esteemed novelists
    D. writing for low- and middle-brow audiences

23. The author's contention about the Georgian period would MOST be challenged if it were TRUE that
    A. after World War I, English literature entered a neo-Victorian phase
    B. writers in America continued to embrace French bohemianism
    C. writers and artists worked to reintegrate themselves into society
    D. the reign of George V came to an end

Questions 24–30 are based on the following passage.

Passage V

Engineers and computer scientists are intrigued by the potential power of nanocomputing. Nanocomputers will use atoms and molecules to perform their functions instead of the standard integrated circuits now employed. Theorists believe that the amount of information a nanocomputer could handle is staggering.

A professor at MIT has attempted to calculate the computational limits of a computer with a weight of 1 kilogram and a volume of 1 liter. According to the laws of physics, the potential amount of computational power is a function of the available energy. Basically, each atom and subatomic particle in the computer has an amount of energy attached to it. Furthermore, the energy of each particle or atom is increased by the frequency of its movement. Thus the power of a computer that uses nanotechnology is bounded by the energy available from its atoms.

Specifically, the relationship between the energy of an object and its computation potential is a proportionate one. As Einstein has famously calculated, the energy of an object is equal to its mass times the speed of light squared. Thus a theoretical computer weighing a mere kilogram has a huge amount of potential energy. To find the total computational power, the minimum amount of energy required to perform an operation is divided by the total amount of energy.

The absolute minimum amount of energy required to perform an operation is determined by Planck's constant, an extremely tiny number. Dividing the total amount of energy possessed by a 1-kilogram computer by Planck's constant yields a tremendously large number, roughly 5×10^{50} operations per second. Using even the most conservative estimates of the computing power of the human brain, such a computer would have the computational power of five trillion trillion human civilizations. The computer would also have a memory capacity, calculated by determining the degrees of freedom allowed by the state of all the particles comprising it, of 10^{31} bits.

These numbers are purely theoretical, however. Were the computer to convert all of its mass to energy, it would be the equivalent of a thermonuclear explosion. And it is unreasonable to expect human technology to ever achieve abilities even close to these limits. However, a project at the University of Oklahoma has succeeded in storing 50 bits of data per atom, albeit on only a limited number of atoms. Given that there are 10^{25} atoms in 1 kilogram of material, it may be possible to fit up to 10^{27} bits of information in the computer. And if scientists are able to exploit the many properties of atoms to store information, including the position, spin, and quantum state of all its particles, it may be possible to exceed even that number.

One interesting consequence of such staggering increases in computing power is that each advance could provide the basis for further evolution. Once technology can achieve, for instance, a level of computation equal to 10^{40} operations per second, it can use that massive power to help bring the theoretical limit ever closer.

24. The central thesis of the passage is
    - **A.** computing power is limited only by the laws of physics
    - **B.** new advances in computer technology allow for staggering levels of memory and computational ability
    - **C.** it may not be possible to achieve the theoretical limits of computing power
    - **D.** computers using nanotechnology have the potential to tap vast quantities of power

25. The author mentions "thermonuclear explosions" in order to
    - **A.** indicate that some of the previous discussion is not practical
    - **B.** warn of a potential consequence predicted by Einstein's equation
    - **C.** show a design flaw in the proposed computer
    - **D.** point out an absurd result of the previous discussion

26. The author of the passage indicates that
    - **A.** the theoretical computer may have even more computational power than described
    - **B.** technicians have already built computers that can store 10^{27} bits of data
    - **C.** 10^{27} bits of data is the theoretical limit of memory capacity in a computer
    - **D.** the technology exists to create a computer that can perform 10^{40} operations per second

27. According to the passage, why does the author believe that the theoretical limit of computational power may be approached?
   A. Scientists can exploit many different properties of atoms.
   B. Technological advances engender more advances.
   C. Computers only require a minimal amount of energy.
   D. Recent advances have shown the technology exists to reach the limit.

28. The ideas in this passage would MOST likely be presented in
   A. an academic journal
   B. a newspaper
   C. a tabloid
   D. a popular science magazine

29. According to the information in the passage, which of the following could increase the computational power of the theoretical computer?
   A. increasing the amount of energy it takes to perform an operation
   B. decreasing the volume of the computer
   C. decreasing the amount of energy it takes to perform an operation
   d. decreasing the mass of the computer

30. The project at the University of Oklahoma indicates
   A. current information-storing technology is still in its infancy
   B. researchers are close to achieving the predicted memory capacity
   C. scientists have learned how to use different aspects of the atom to store information
   D. work on reaching the theoretical limits of computation power is now underway

This is the end of the Critical Analysis and Reasoning Skills Minitest.

Critical Analysis and Reasoning Skills Minitest Answers and Explanations

1. **The correct answer is D.** This question has to do with interpreting vocabulary. Your first step in answering it is to scan the passage to find the word *elusive.* It appears in paragraph 2, in the context of qualities of happiness. It is not used in a negative connotation, as choices A and B (both synonyms for *lying*) would indicate. Choice C doesn't work with the other quality of happiness, which is mysterious. Something that is frank, or honest and forthright, cannot also be mysterious. Choice D is therefore the best answer.
2. **The correct answer is C.** You need to assess evidence for this question. Since authors ideally use examples to support their statements, you need to find the information that explains why Watson's study was thought to be startling. By scanning paragraph 2 for the exact reference, you will find that the second sentence contains the answer: "Since happiness was considered a highly desired yet elusive and mysterious emotion, Watson's serious endeavor was startling." This is a clear giveaway that choice C is correct.
3. **The correct answer is B.** This question asks you to locate details within the passage. If one statement stands out as false, you can eliminate all other answer choices. But often, it is easier to answer this type of question by eliminating the true statements. The last two sentences of paragraph 3 contain the information in choice A, so you can eliminate it. Paragraph 5 corresponds with choice C, and paragraph 4 corresponds with choice D. Choice B is the correct answer because the passage states that "findings show the mind–body connection cannot be denied," and not that science is attempting to prove the connection.
4. **The correct answer is A.** You are asked to identify cause and effect as it is implied in the passage for this question. Note that the example of a subject repeating the phrase, "I am successful" does not appear in the passage. However, the last paragraph notes that repetition of a positive affirmation is given in the last paragraph. "I am successful," is such an affirmation, and you could expect choice A, a feeling of well-being, to be the outcome following its repetition.
5. **The correct answer is C.** This question looks at cause and effect, not as directly presented in the essay, but rather as implied by the essay. Whittier and Holmes are mentioned once, as contemporaries of Longfellow, who also employed similar themes and rhymes. Since Longfellow's reputation is said to suffer because of these very themes and rhymes, it may be implied that the reputations of Whittier and Holmes suffer a similar fate. There is no evidence in the passage to support choice A, so it should be eliminated. Choice B is too negative; neither

Longfellow nor Whittier and Holmes are said to be held in contempt or disdain. Choice D is in opposition to the ideas found in the passage. Modern poetry is influenced by Whitman, not Longfellow, Whittier, and Holmes. Choice C works best, with "antiquated" echoing paragraph 1's "quaint and primly Victorian."

6. **The correct answer is B.** You are asked to find the main idea in this question. This type of question is passage-based, meaning you should focus on what is actually said as opposed to what may be implied or suggested. To answer it, ask "What is the author trying to say?" Typically, at least one answer choice is not found within the passage. In this case, choices C and D can be easily eliminated for that reason—neither is stated. Another type of distracter is an answer choice that is too narrow to be the main passage. Choice A is a good example; the passage encompasses much more than a simple comparison of free verse as opposed to rhymes. You are left with choice B, which is the correct answer.
7. **The correct answer is A.** This question asks you to assess evidence. To answer it, first note the hypothesis as stated in the question stem: Whitman was responsible for the radical shift in American poetry. Then determine which statements support it and which one does not. The one that does not is the correct answer. The fact that his poetry was personal and intimate (choice B) supports the hypothesis, as does his use of free verse (choice D). Choice C, choosing as his subjects the common man and commonplace events, also supports the hypothesis. Nowhere in the passage does it state that Whitman used iconic American figures as his subjects; in fact, that is what Longfellow did, and his poetry was what Whitman's shifted away from. That means choice A is correct.
8. **The correct answer is D.** To answer this question, you need to interpret vocabulary. Find the phrase in the passage and examine it in context. The sentence in paragraph 1 in which it is found reads, "Why do his contemporaries continue to be enjoyed and studied while Longfellow languishes in the tomb of cultural artifacts?" There is a dichotomy set up between continuing to be enjoyed and studied and languishing in the tomb of cultural artifacts. Being in "the tomb of cultural artifacts" is therefore the opposite of being enjoyed and studied. Only one answer choice relates to the idea of this dichotomy; if Longfellow's work is "considered to be dead," it is surely not being enjoyed and studied. Choice D is the best answer.
9. **The correct answer is B.** In this question, you are drawing conclusions about the author's intent, choosing the best or most likely answer. Sales figures for Longfellow's poems about iconic American figures are cited as facts, and not implied to be an apparent belief of the author, making choice A incorrect. While Emerson is

revealed to be an influence on Whitman, there is nothing in the passage to suggest that he could be considered by the author to be the Father of American Poetry (in fact, he is not mentioned as being a poet), making choice C incorrect. The passage clearly delineates throughout the vast differences between the work of Longfellow and confessional poetry; therefore, choice D must also be wrong. The terms the author uses to describe Whitman and his work in the last paragraph ("ground-breaking," "legacy") enforce his view that Whitman's poetry is more popular than Longfellow's (that resides in a "tomb").

10. **The correct answer is D.** This question asks you to apply new evidence to an existing argument. The new evidence is an ambivalent statement by Ezra Pound, in which he both declares his distaste for much of Whitman's work while still admiring it enough to imitate it. The author declares that Pound celebrated his debt to Whitman, which is neither repudiated nor endorsed (choices A and B) by Pound's ambivalence. Similarly, the second part of the statement (regarding imitation) does not deny the author's contention. Choice D is the correct answer because it identifies the passage's use of *celebrate* as too positive a word in light of Pound's "pain" in reading Whitman.
11. **The correct answer is D.** This kind of question asks you to choose an accurate summary. The sales figures are cited to back up the author's assertion that Longfellow's poems were "incredibly popular" (choice D). Choice C is a tricky diversion; while the author does note that sales figures for *The Song of Hiawatha* were "astounding for the time," he does not state or infer that those numbers marked a milestone.
12. **The correct answer is D.** This question asks you to interpret vocabulary. In the context of the passage, the word *province* is used to indicate something that belongs only to humans and to no other living creatures. The answer choice closest in meaning to this is choice D, "domain." Choices A and B are part of the definition of the word *province,* but they are not how the word is used in this context. The passage states that some believe rights are appropriate only for humans, but says nothing about responsibility as choice C says.
13. **The correct answer is D.** For this question, you'll have to use the information in the passage to make predictions. Based on the information in the passage, you need to predict which of the rights in the answer choices a utilitarian would not believe an animal has. The fifth paragraph states that a utilitarian would believe that animals had a right to be free from unnecessary pain and suffering, but that they may not have rights that they don't have the capacity to possess. Choices A, B, and C all indicate actions that would cause the animal pain or suffering. But an animal does not have the right to possess anything, since property is a human concept. This makes choice D the best answer.

14. **The correct answer is A.** You'll have to draw conclusions to answer this question. Look back at the passage to find what Bentham and Sidgwick believe. Bentham states that the interests and desires of the members of the system are all equal; Sidgwick states that the Universe treats all goods as equal. Thus choice A is the best answer. Choice B is unsupported because although the passage states that Bentham believes animals should have equal consideration, it is not clear that Sidgwick believes that. The passage states that Bentham is unconcerned with the issue of whether animals can reason, so his view on it is unknown, as is Sidgwick's, which eliminates choice C. And it is not clear what Sidgwick believes about choice D.
15. **The correct answer is B.** This question asks you to analyze an argument. Remember that everything an author includes in a passage is there for a reason. What role do the parenthetical inserts play in the development of the author's thesis? The discussion of Bentham indicates that Bentham is focusing not on issues of reason or speech—which are unimportant—but on the capacity to suffer, which is the key point. Choice B reflects this sentiment. There is no evidence to support choice A. The views discussed are Bentham's, not those of animal rights supporters (choice C). And the inserts serve to emphasize the important point of Bentham's argument, not to head off possible objections as in choice D.
16. **The correct answer is D.** Again, you'll have to make predictions to answer this question. Use the information the passage provides on utilitarianism to predict which situation could not be justified. Choice A is OK because the passage states that as long as the sum total of happiness increases, the action is OK. Thus in certain circumstances it may be necessary to use an individual in such a way that benefits many others. Choice B can be justified because the death penalty may increase the overall good by ridding the world of a dangerous person. Similarly, torture (choice C) may be justified if it saves the lives of other people. However, indiscriminate killing is not acceptable to a utilitarian. The killing would have to be directed to somehow increasing the good of other people.
17. **The correct answer is A.** This question asks you to find the main idea. The passage states that there is a debate about the validity of animal rights and utilitarianism and provides a framework from which both advocates and opponents of animal rights may view the situation. This is what choice A states. The passage does show how to justify animal rights, as choice B states, but it also shows how to justify not having animal rights. Choice C is wrong, because the passage presents arguments for both positions. And choice D is wrong, because although Bentham's and Sidgwick's views are mentioned, their ideas form only one part of the larger debate.

18. **The correct answer is A.** You are asked to interpret vocabulary for this question. The sentence states that the bohemian culture rejected limits placed on the society. A cultured person recognizes the standards agreed on by society for certain behaviors and so a bohemian would reject them. Although the word *polite* could be used to mean the words in choices B, C, and D, this is not how the word is used in context.
19. **The correct answer is D.** The question asks you to make generalizations. In general, the bohemian is against limits placed on the individual by society. Current fashion trends represent one way a society may limit an individual by dictating what sort of dress is acceptable. The prevailing mores of a society are the values that the society at large deems appropriate. Capitalism is also a product of the society, and a bohemian would reject thinking in the same way as the rest of the people. Thus all three statements are appropriate, and choice D is the best answer.
20. **The correct answer is C.** For this question, you must draw conclusions. The author does not directly state choice C, but implies it by saying that the Education Act led to a literate, although not necessarily educated, public. This part of the passage also makes choice A incorrect. Choice B is not supported, because the act dealt only with elementary education. Choice D cannot be inferred. It is true that the author believes the act furthered the gulf between artist and public, but it is not clear whether artists were angry about it.
21. **The correct answer is B.** This is a fairly straightforward question asking about supporting details. The answer is found at the end of paragraph 2, where the author states that the degree to which the audiences were fragmented occurred at an unprecedented rate. This supports choice B. There is no support for the other choices in the passage.
22. **The correct answer is B.** This is another question asking you to draw conclusions. The author states that the late Victorian period was marked by pessimism and stoicism and that the authors mentioned all demonstrated such sentiments. Thus it can be concluded that they were influenced by the trends of their time. It is not clear whether they were popular or esteemed, as choices A and C indicate. Nor does the passage state what audience they wrote for, which means choice D is not supported.
23. **The correct answer is A.** This is a question that asks you to modify conclusions. The author contends that after the Georgian period, the old European order was no more. However, if the literature returned to its old Victorian ways, as choice A indicates, the author's conclusion would be incorrect. The developments in America detailed in choice B would be irrelevant to the author's argument. If the artists reintegrated into society as in choice C, it would indicate a change in the

prevailing system, not a return to old ways. Choice D also is immaterial to the argument.

24. **The correct answer is C.** This question asks you to find the main idea. This passage explains that theoretically, there is a massive amount of computational power available. However, practical considerations make it unlikely that this limit would ever be reached. Thus choice C is the best answer. Choice A is a detail provided in the passage, but it is not the main idea. Choice B is incorrect, because the advances discussed are still primarily theoretical. Choice D is also only partly correct, because it doesn't deal with the practical limits mentioned in the passage.
25. **The correct answer is A.** This question asks you to analyze an argument. The author mentions thermonuclear explosions in the same sentence in which he states that the discussion of computing power is purely theoretical. Choice A best reflects this. No other answer choice is supported by the information in the passage.
26. **The correct answer is A.** You are asked to draw a conclusion in order to answer this question. The author indicates that choices B and D are still in the realm of the theoretical. The author also states that the memory limit in choice C may be "exceeded." That leaves choice A, which is supported when the author states that the calculation of the computer's power is based on "the most conservative estimates" of human computational power. Thus the proposed computers can be even more powerful then the author describes.
27. **The correct answer is B.** This question asks about supporting details and evidence. Go back to the passage and find why the author believes technology may reach the theoretical limit discussed. In the last paragraph, the author indicates that each technological advance provides the basis for further evolution, as choice B states. Choice A refers to the author's discussion of memory capacity, not computational power, and indicates a way technicians may exceed the theoretical limits described. Choice C has nothing to do with reaching the theoretical limits of computational power. The technology to reach the limits does not yet exist, as choice D seems to indicate.
28. **The correct answer is D.** This question requires you to combine information. The passage discusses computers, technology, and even physics. However, the information is presented at the level of someone with a casual, rather than expert, knowledge of these fields. Thus choice D would be the best answer. Choice A may be close, but the information in the passage is not written at the level of expertise that a reader would expect in an academic journal.
29. **The correct answer is C.** The question asks you to solve a problem. To answer it, you must first understand how computational power is calculated. The passage states that the power is found by dividing the total energy by the energy required

for an operation. Decreasing the amount of energy, as in choice C, would yield a larger quotient. Choice A would do the opposite, while choices B and D would decrease the total energy available.

30. **The correct answer is A.** This question asks you to draw a conclusion. Based on the information in the passage, choice A is the best choice. The passage indicates that thus far, researchers have only been able to store information on a few atoms. Choice B is practically the opposite of what the passage states, while the information in choice C is suggested by the author as a way to exceed the theoretical memory limit. The work at the University of Oklahoma relates to memory capacity, not computing power as choice D indicates.